WOODROW WILSON AND THE BALANCE OF POWER

EDWARD H. *Henry* BUEHRIG

Woodrow Wilson and the Balance of Power

GLOUCESTER, MASS.

PETER SMITH

1968

Grateful acknowledgment for permission to quote from the following publications is made to their publishers: *American Historical Review*, "Theodore Roosevelt and American Neutrality," by Russell Buchanan (Vol. 43, 1937–38); The Bobbs-Merrill Company, Inc., *War Memoirs of Robert Lansing*, copyright © 1935, used by special permission of the publishers; Doubleday & Company, Inc., *Life and Letters of Woodrow Wilson*, by Ray Stannard Baker, copyright 1931 by Ray Stannard Baker; Harper & Brothers, *Why We Went to War*, by Newton D. Baker, 1936; Houghton Mifflin Company, *Grey of Fallodon*, by G. M. Trevelyan, 1937, and *The Letters of Henry Adams*, edited by Worthington C. Ford, 1938, and *The Intimate Papers of Colonel House*, edited by Charles Seymour, 1926; The John Day Company, Inc., *The Bugle That Woke America*, by Hermann Hagedorn, 1940; The Johns Hopkins Press, *Germany's Drive to the West*, by Hans W. Gatzke, 1950; Princeton University Press, *Rise of American Naval Power*, by Harold and Margaret Sprout, and *Toward a New Order of Sea Power*, by Harold and Margaret Sprout, 1940; Charles Scribner's Sons, *America and the World War*, 1915, by Theodore Roosevelt, *Letters From Theodore Roosevelt to Anna Roosevelt Cowles*, 1924, and *Theodore Roosevelt and His Time*, 1920, by Joseph Bucklin Bishop; Yale University Press, *Mahan: The Life and Work of Captain Alfred Thayer Mahan*, by W. D. Puleston, 1939; and *Neutrality for the United States*, by Edwin Borchard and William P. Lage, 1940.

Reprinted, 1968 by Permission of
Indiana University Press

to the memory of

MY FATHER

Foreword

THE central theme of American foreign relations in the nineteenth century was the mutual accommodation progressively achieved between ourselves and Great Britain. The main theme in the present century is quite different, offering a melancholy contrast. At the turn of the century Germany and the United States had already emerged as great powers, and Japan was in process of attaining that status. Presently Russia took on new form and vigor, and Italy was to entertain high political ambition. Later still, India began to emerge, as did China. Coincident with this revolutionary change in the old order, the United States has come to blows twice with Germany and once each with Japan and Italy. Moreover, we have fought China and must consider the danger of war with the Soviet Union. At the halfway mark, the new century has witnessed serious conflict between ourselves and all our rising contemporaries save India.

Such a vast change of fortune suggests the presence of general causes, overshadowing the specific causes attending each of the successive crises. How shall we characterize these broad movements of history, and what is the connection between them and our involvement in the first World War?

We can see today, what was much less clearly visible at the time, that the first World War signalized the decline of Europe from its former pre-eminence in world politics. With it, indeed, the Columbian era, that brilliant period of European expansion of which we ourselves are lasting evidence, was drawing to a close. Sooner or later such a decline was bound to occur. But the manner of its occurrence is a matter of particular interest. In the actual event, Europe did not succumb to superior alien forces but to her own internecine strife. German ambition, beyond the capacity of Continental Europe to cope with, engaged the energies of Great Britain. In fact, Anglo-German rivalry became a major point of tension, and Britain was no longer able to remain detached from Continental politics. Absorbed in the compelling necessities of European politics, Britain also ceased to serve effectively as a buffer between Europe and the United States.

Had it been accustomed to acting on power considerations, the United States might have based a policy forthrightly on Germany's attempt to supplant Great Britain. But the United States was not habituated to viewing international politics in such harsh terms. Moreover, it did not desire a future different from the past, nor was it covetous of either the glory or the responsibilities of world power. There was, consequently, no head-on collision with Germany. Rather German-American relations entered a legalistic maze in the perplexing intricacies of which the two countries eventually came to blows. It seems unlikely that the lawyers, by taking paths other than those actually chosen, might have significantly altered the outcome. Nor was commercial, any more than legal policy, the truly basic factor. The United States and Germany became embroiled because of their differing attitudes toward British control of the seas. Germany felt that she must challenge that control in the interest of her own future freedom of action. The United States, for its part, regarded British power benevolently, as a factor contributing to American security.

This is the state of affairs which the probing of the submarine revealed. Unwittingly, it was the instrument which laid bare the political connection with Europe which most Americans had ceased to believe existed, and which they were disposed to act on instinctively, rather than face the full implications of what was disclosed.

It is a pleasant duty to acknowledge my indebtedness to the Institute for Advanced Study where, during my membership in 1948-49, this study took its present shape and character. I shall always be grateful for the constant encouragement of the late Professor Edward Mead Earle of the Institute, who gave time and energy with that graciousness and unselfishness so typical of him. To Professor Arthur S. Link of Northwestern University I express warm thanks for generously sharing his deep knowledge of the Wilson period. The judgments expressed in this study, however, can be attributed only to myself.

A succession of graduate assistants helped in the preparation of the manuscript in its various stages. I acknowledge with pleasant memories the assistance of Gilbert Bailey, Ian Cox, Marjorie Hunt Gordon, Peter Grosvenor, and Fred A. Sondermann. To the staff of the Manuscripts Division of the Library of Congress I express my appreciation for their courtesy and many helpful suggestions. Financial assistance was afforded by a Social Science Research Council fellowship and a grant from the Graduate School of Indiana University.

I have greatly appreciated the cooperation so freely given by the Indiana University Press and especially the patient and imaginative labors of Miss Jane Rodman.

E.H.B.

Indiana University
July, 1955

Contents

ONE

Prior to 1914: Anglo-American and German-American Relations

WRITING to an English friend on June 8, 1917, Henry Adams said that to his bewilderment he found the United States and Britain fighting side by side in a world war, and thus, he added, "I find the great object of my life . . . accomplished in the building up of the great community of Atlantic Powers which I hope will at last make a precedent that can never be forgotten. . . . Strange it is," Adams concluded, "that we should have done it by inducing those blockheads of Germans to kick us into it." [1]

For nearly a hundred years before the outbreak of the first World War Great Britain was virtually the only power with which the United States came into contact. Only Great Britain was in a position seriously to impede our international freedom of action. In the decades following the War of 1812 there was continued friction between the two countries. In the case of the West Indian trade this friction was purely economic in character, but it frequently took the form

of the most dangerous of all quarrels, involving territory and strategic advantage. In Central America
there was competition for ascendancy in the small
unstable fragments of Spain's shattered Empire. The
long anticipation of an interoceanic canal was accompanied by serious strain, not finally allayed until conclusion of the Hay-Pauncefote treaty of 1901, by
which Great Britain surrendered her right (recognized
by the United States in the Clayton-Bulwer treaty of
1850) to share control of such a waterway. Closer
home there were constant irritations along the Canadian border, and there was the large problem of
Oregon. The Texas question of the 1830's and 1840's
invited British intervention, which, however, did not
materialize. When Anglo-American relations survived
even the Civil War without a major break, differences
from that time on proved for the most part manage-
able within the confines of arbitral procedure, with a
resulting record of arbitration unique in the history
of international relations.[2]

In the course of the nineteenth century Anglo-
American relations developed progressively in the direction of accommodation and away from hostility.
This was the result of a number of factors, at least one
of which was a product of circumstance. The Revolutionary War had shown that British actions in the
New World could be frustrated—and the War of 1812
had demonstrated that they could be seriously hampered—by the importunities of European politics. This

was again the case at the end of the nineteenth
century when Great Britain accepted the views of
the United States in the Venezuelan dispute, surrendered her rights in an isthmian canal, and withdrew
her principal naval forces from the Caribbean. Confronted with European powers too strong to be ignored, Britain at this time surrendered her remaining
claims to major political influence in the Western
Hemisphere and sought to secure the United States
as an ally. The growing strength of the United States
was also an important factor in Anglo-American relations. Canada, after the Civil War and until it became
a self-governing dominion, served as a hostage to the
United States for British good behavior.

The power situation was one of the factors condi-
tioning the relations between the United States and
Great Britain, but it was by no means determining.
Governments, because of bad judgment or desperation
or recklessness, often fly in the face of adverse circumstance. Moreover, the close of the Napoleonic wars
found British naval power at a new peak, and until the
end of the nineteenth century Britain felt free to stand
somewhat apart from European politics. During most
of that century Great Britain had a surplus of power
which was not absorbed in European rivalries. The
development of an Anglo-American accommodation
in the Western Hemisphere was in accord with any
realistic estimate of the practical limits imposed by
the power situation; but this is to say merely that

neither country was foolhardy. Such an accommodation was not preordained and it stands as a tribute to wise statesmanship on both sides.

The two countries conducted with restraint their own politico-territorial rivalries in the Western Hemisphere. Neither country felt an imperious need to expand territorially in Latin America, and not only did each refrain from calling in the aid of outside powers to bolster its position against the other, but jointly they forbade entrance to third powers. The delicate balance of Anglo-American relations, as it began to appear after the War of 1812, is indicated by the circumstances surrounding enunciation of the Monroe Doctrine. The immediate stimulus was the design of the restored Bourbon Government in France, with the consent of the Holy Alliance, to join with Spain in extinguishing the newly acquired independence of the Latin American countries. Great Britain, determined that this vast area should not revert to the closed door as regards trade, and fearing lest France rebuild her power on the basis of a connection with the New World, sounded out the United States as to the possibility of joint action, but eventually moved independently and confronted France in October 1823 with a virtual ultimatum, the famous memorandum of Foreign Secretary George Canning to the French ambassador in London, Prince Jules de Polignac. The United States, for its part, completely aware of the fortunate implications of the British position, desiring to avoid any permanent political connection with Europe, and conscious that Britain herself was the greatest of all potential menaces to American freedom of action, proceeded independently in December 1823, when President Monroe set forth in his message to Congress the doctrine of hemispheric security which bears his name. American and British policies were parallel. They were also connected. For the greater part of the nineteenth century the United States omitted formulating a naval and military policy which normally would have been expected and required as the companion of the Monroe Doctrine. Instead there grew up an implicit reliance on British sea power. These are the conditions which explain the rather remarkable fact that in the course of the nineteenth century Latin America, unlike other politically weak areas such as Africa and Asia, escaped European control. The Anglo-American community of interest and policy prevented the Western Hemisphere from passing into the swift currents of international politics.

This political accommodation could hardly have been achieved if British colonial sovereignty and sea power had been used in the nineteenth century as in the eighteenth. If a policy of monopoly, excluding or severely handicapping all but British shipping and goods in Empire ports, had prevailed, there could have been no real adjustment of Anglo-American relations—nor could Great Britain have prevented her remaining North American and West Indian possessions from following the rebellious example of the Thirteen Colonies. In the Jay Treaty of 1794 direct trade between Great Britain and the United States was placed on a reciprocal, nondiscriminatory basis, and American ships were admitted to the British East Indian trade. It was in the Western Hemisphere, however, that the old colonial system was most strongly entrenched, and the customary restrictions on commerce and navigation, relaxed during the wars of the French Revolution and Napoleon, were reasserted by Britain after 1815. This recrudescence was to be short-lived, but until 1830 serious friction existed between the United States and Great Britain over the ban on American ships in British West Indian ports. In that year a reciprocity arrangement was agreed to which satisfied American interest and provided for lifting of retaliatory measures against Britain in American ports. Yet even before this, in 1822, the British Parliament had taken the first steps leading to the great revolution in its commercial and navigation policies which culminated in 1860 in virtually complete freedom of commerce and shipping in the relations of the British Empire among its parts and with the rest of the world.[3] This liberal policy pursued by the world's dominant trading nation reduced international tensions by lessening the economic significance of sovereignty. The consequences were demonstrable not only in Anglo-American relations in the Western Hemisphere, but also in the Far East. Despite the fact that

Britain assumed the chief burden of breaking down Chinese exclusion, all nations, and notably the United States, entered into the enlarged Chinese trade on a basis of equality. Not even for bargaining purposes toward other Western nations did Great Britain claim, after the Anglo-Chinese War of 1840–41, a preferred status in China's trade.

Also contributing powerfully to the decline of hostility and to the growth of friendly relations between the United States and Great Britain was the common culture of the two countries. The same language served to promote that homogeneity of values and attitudes which is basic to political confidence and stability. Moreover, the similarity of governmental and legal institutions reinforced a feeling of community.

Political accommodation, economic liberalism, and cultural affinity gave rise to another major aspect of Anglo-American relations: the insensitivity of those relations to considerations of fighting effectiveness. It was a significant fact, both as a reflection of and as an element contributing to healthy relations, that the United States and Great Britain escaped the vicious circle which the assumption of violence so frequently imposes upon nations. The policies pursued by the two countries vis-à-vis one another were to a remarkable degree unburdened by any expectation that force was a likely arbiter of their affairs. The Rush-Bagot agreement of 1817, by which naval vessels of both countries were prohibited on the Great Lakes and which has been continuously in force to the present day, was an important contribution to the demilitarization of Anglo-American relations. It was a most fruitful precedent, for Canadian-American frontier fortifications eventually fell into disuse. In 1871 the last Imperial troops were withdrawn from Canada (except for the garrison at the naval base of Halifax), and in the early years of the present century the British withdrew their West Indian naval squadron.[4]

Although the British army in the nineteenth century was of little effect in the international scales, except in time of war, the British navy—as we have mentioned —was a heavy makeweight. In the case of the United States, of course, neither the American army nor navy had international significance. Since Britain was the only major power with which the United States had substantial contact, the insensitivity of Anglo-American relations to considerations of fighting effectiveness was tantamount, on the American side, to disarmament. The United States did not feel impelled to maintain a correlation between foreign policy and military policy. This is perhaps the most distinctive feature of America's nineteenth-century experience with international politics.[5]

Such, then, was the position of the United States in world affairs in 1914. Security and freedom of action had come to be taken for granted in such degree that the conditions which accounted for the phenomenon had ceased to be an immediate object of attention.

Security was not a problem making demands on policy. These were the circumstances in which the American assumptions of abstention and impartiality as regards European politics had come to wear the aspect of permanent national policy.

II

It was inevitable in a dynamic world that the conditions permitting the relatively effortless adjustment to foreign power and policy which the United States had made in the nineteenth century would sooner or later change for the worse. It is a matter of absorbing interest to reflect on how the inevitable came to pass. It did not involve any falling out with Great Britain; nor was the United States initiated into the realm of high politics by sharp, persistent collision with any other power. It would be ingenuous, however, to suppose that the world collapsed about a wholly preoccupied America to whom the stirrings of a wider ambition and the anxieties of prestige and security were entirely unknown. Without the stimulus of frustration or international crisis an urge to look outward was already manifest in the beginnings of a modern navy in the 1880's.

Initially the American naval program signified hardly anything more than due regard for the ludicrous state of neglect into which the navy had fallen and was informed by no politico-strategic conceptions beyond the ancient one of commerce raiding and certain maladroit notions about defense of coastal cities.[6] This minimum and defensive conception of a navy's function could not have survived the construction of an isthmian canal by the United States, which would automatically impose the necessity of controlling the approaches to the canal and would entail exclusive naval domination of the Caribbean.

Change in the character of the naval program, however, did not await force of circumstance, but was fathered by the theoretical writings of an American naval officer, Alfred Thayer Mahan. The publication in 1890 of Mahan's *Influence of Sea Power on History, 1660–1783* coincided with the crucial period of transition in naval technology and with renewed stirrings of European expansion. Mahan's book was an intellectual performance which was a powerful stimulus to navalism in the world capitals and not least in Washington. Addressing the question of broad public policy and basing his analysis on the record of British imperial success in the mercantilist age, Mahan held that the key to national growth, prosperity, and security was sea power—not on a local but world scale, and not in the form merely of fighting ships. Sea power to be complete and viable must rest on a productive homeland, on an active merchant marine, and on colonies or at least overseas bases. Such a combination of factors would provide the sinews of a fighting navy and also the *raison d'être* of such a navy. It was, Mahan believed, the prescription for national great-

ness. Mahan did not fail to point out the significance
of time and place which combined to place Britain
at the commanding crossroads of the world. But he
failed to appreciate fully that geography made no
provision for and history was not likely to repeat the
necessary conditions for the appearance of a similar
center, with the same powerful leverage, at any other
time or place.

There is a spurious element in all such grand conceptions of politics, but this did not prevent Mahan's
theory of sea power from attracting disciples who accepted it with even less caution than it had been pro-
pounded by its author. It was so accepted by Theodore
Roosevelt with direct results for American foreign
policy. It also contributed to the fatal Anglo-German
naval rivalry, which made the war of 1914 a world war,
enmeshing the United States in its bitter intransi-
gence.[7] Because of the influence of Mahan's writings on Theodore Roosevelt and Henry Cabot Lodge,
the Spanish-American War, quite unexpectedly for the
country at large, resulted in the acquisition of the
Philippine Islands. The assumption of territorial responsibility in the highly unstable area of the Far
East required in turn that the United States concern
itself with the rivalries of the great powers there.
Roosevelt's mediation in the Russo-Japanese War, and
his Far Eastern policy in general, mark the first departure from the indifference toward high politics
which for so long had characterized American policy.

The Pacific rather than the Atlantic witnessed this initial abandonment of a passive attitude. Yet the future of international politics was being fashioned across the Atlantic. Not Asiatic but European politics was destined to give rise to the major challenge to American statecraft. The problems which were presently to come unsolicited issued not from the periphery but from the center of Western civilization. It is interesting to note that the first expression of American power on the world stage not only did not assist but probably hindered the United States in identifying and meeting the main challenge in 1914. The venture in Asia had a theoretical and gratuitous quality; it was further rendered suspect by the highly personal element supplied by Theodore Roosevelt as assistant secretary of the Navy and subsequently as President. The strong and indignant anti-imperialism generated in America by the untoward consequences of the Spanish-American War reinforced the already indigenous but considerably different attitude of isolationism.

The American people and government were ill-prepared by experience to meet the challenge of 1914. Nor was the form of that challenge calculated to make the American response any easier. That the first half of the twentieth century in its tragic unfolding should have cast the United States and Germany in the role of leading antagonists cannot be accounted for in any simple and direct way.

There was little in German-American relations prior

to 1914 to suggest the denouement of 1917. To be
sure, a rivalry had sprung up in the Caribbean.
Whereas Great Britain had gracefully accepted the
dominant position of the United States in the New
World, Germany displayed an eagerness here as elsewhere to respond to any opportunity. The ambitious
character of German policy in the Caribbean had for
sometime been cause of growing concern in the United
States. A still broader rivalry extending to other parts
of the world was another unpromising factor in German-American relations. The two navies eyed each
other as competitors. Certainly the armaments race in
Europe was no small factor precipitating war in 1914.
What ultimate significance was attached to the German-American counterpart of the European madness?

Naval competition between these rising new powers
was evident in various diplomatic incidents. There
had been friction over Samoa in 1889 and over the
islands in the Pacific set adrift by Spain's defeat in
1898. These were small episodes, not without a farcical
element; yet they left a residue of irritation. Of more
consequence were the incidents arising out of the
German quest for footholds in the Caribbean. But, in
comparison with the grim and implacable Anglo-German naval rivalry, that between Germany and the
United States had about it an academic quality.

As if in response to Mahan's teaching that national
policy reached its apex in sea power, the two navies
became keen competitors, adding another facet to the

navalism which so suddenly and ominously overtook world politics at the turn of the century. Alfred Vagts, the leading student of German-American relations of this period, remarked that "Wherever comparison of any kind, however far fetched, seemed possible . . . it was drawn by the offices and officers of the two navies." [8] Each establishment used the other as example and justification for its own appeals for public approval and legislative support. With evangelistic fervor, shared by the civilians in the respective navy leagues, professional interest was unqualifiedly identified with national need.[9]

Hardly anyone, least of all the navalists, foresaw the actual circumstances which would cause the two nations to clash. The prediction on both sides was of a German expedition against North America. In the actual event, of course, it was to be an American expedition that embarked overseas; yet as late as 1916 Admiral von Capelle, German minister of the Navy, thought that the danger of America's sending troops to Europe was "zero, zero, zero." [10] And on the very eve of our entry into the war the best-informed opinion in the United States anticipated no more than the possibility of sending volunteers for the land fighting.

Almost wilfully, it would seem, Britain's crucial role in German-American relations was ignored. Great Britain, possessed of vast interests in the New World, was the third element in a triangular situation, and events were to show that the Anglo-German naval rivalry was of more consequence for the United States than the German-American. So long as Britain's position in the Atlantic world remained intact and vigorous, the United States and Germany could not have become serious antagonists. Any misfortune befalling Great Britain, however, would have confronted us anew with the problem of stabilizing our transatlantic relations.

All else remaining equal, it would have required an uncommon display of irresponsibility and the worst of luck to have precipitated bilateral hostilities between ourselves and Germany. There was no legacy of old scores to be settled, nor was there intense struggle for immediate gain one over the other. Neither the past nor the present, but the future, was uppermost. And the future could not be judged except in relation to Britain's power on and across the seas. Germany viewed it as an obstacle to the fulfillment of her destiny. The United States, on the other hand, viewed it not only with complacency but satisfaction. The first World War threw these differing attitudes into sharp relief and induced a mounting tension in German-American relations which finally reached the breaking point.

TWO

The Submarine: Point of Departure
for American Policy

THE SUBMARINE was a novel weapon in
1914 whose potentiality as a destroyer of
commerce was unappreciated even by the Germans. It
was destined, however, to play a singular and wholly
impromptu role in the unfolding of history; and it was
instrumental in leading the United States to establish
once again—after an interval of a hundred years—a
political connection with Europe.

The extraordinary role in which the submarine was
cast becomes apparent if we ask what America's relation to the war would have been had technology
required a few years more in which to perfect the
new weapon. Britain's peril, restricted in that event to
the threat of German mastery over Belgium, would
have been less apparent—and less real. There would,
moreover, have been no maritime atrocities to arouse
indignation against Germany. By the same token, Anglo-American relations would have been subject to
greater strain, for in the absence of the submarine

the freedom of the seas issue would have arisen in its old familiar form, requiring of the British utmost caution in interfering with American trade.

Though a potent destroyer of Allied commerce, the submarine proved in the end less a military asset to Germany than a political liability. Whether it was occasion or cause of American entry into the war, we need not now decide. It is enough for the present to give an account of how the submarine provided the point of departure of American policy.

I

It was on February 4, 1915 that the German Admiralty gave notice that, beginning on the eighteenth, the waters surrounding Great Britain and Ireland would be a war area in which enemy merchant ships were subject to destruction without passengers and crew being accorded the safety required by international law. Because of the contingencies of naval warfare, and misuse by the British of neutral flags, neutrals were warned of the danger to which their vessels were exposed in the zone, where they might unavoidably become victims of torpedoes directed against enemy ships.[1] The German Foreign Office in an explanatory memorandum undertook to justify this infringement of neutral rights. A previous designation by Great Britain of the area between Scotland and Norway as an area of war, Britain's extended contraband list, and her seizure of noncontraband German property on neutral vessels were illegal acts, the memorandum asserted, which warranted retaliatory measures. It was further contended that the neutrals had made only "theoretical protest" against these British practices, in justification for which Great Britain had pleaded her vital interests. Consequently "Germany must now appeal to these same vital interests." [2]

In his historic reply of February 10, President Woodrow Wilson declared that should Germany "destroy any merchant vessel of the United States or cause the death of American citizens," the United States would view the act as an "indefensible violation of neutral rights," would hold the German Government to "strict accountability," and would take any steps necessary to "safeguard American lives and property and to secure to American citizens the full enjoyment of their acknowledged rights on the high seas." [3]

In this exchange of notes an issue was drawn which two years later led to deadlock and war. The fateful German declaration of unrestricted submarine warfare, dated February 1, 1917, differed, however, in one important respect from the declaration of February 4, 1915. In 1915 the German Government acknowledged that the submarine was under instruction "to avoid violence to neutral ships in so far as they are recognizable," whereas in 1917 all shipping, enemy and neutral alike, was subject to deliberate destruction.

It is noteworthy that at no time between February 1915 and February 1917 was the sinking of American

ships and the loss of lives on such ships a matter of
major controversy between the United States and Germany. During this two-year period eleven American
ships were attacked by German submarines or raiders;
six were sunk, one surrendered, and four damaged,
with a total loss of three lives—all on the *Gulflight,*
May 1, 1915.[4] Although questions of fact and the mode
of determining the amount of compensation were matters of diplomatic exchange, Germany in no case denied
responsibility in principle.[5]

The adoption in 1917, however, of a policy of indiscriminate torpedoing of neutral and enemy vessels
introduced an issue which Germany had skirted in
1915 and avoided so far as it concerned relations with
the United States. That the experience of other neutrals before February 1, 1917 was decidedly less favorable than that of the United States, is indicative of
the strong restraint which the sharp response and
potential power of the United States exercised over
Germany's actions. American shipping was safe from
the submarine in greater degree and for a longer period than that of any other neutral.[6]

The friction between Germany and the United States
during 1915–17 arose not over loss of life on American
vessels but on Allied vessels. Up to February 1917
ten belligerent vessels (eight British and two Italian)
had been attacked by the Germans with loss of American life; total American losses were 176, of which 128
perished in the *Lusitania* disaster.[7] Wilson's decision

for war in April 1917 was precipitated by the deliberate sinking of American ships. Nonetheless, it is useful to examine at length the controversy over Germany's actions toward enemy merchantmen. Such an
examination will suggest the underlying motives of
American policy, and will help to decide whether,
as some students have contended, this policy was responsible for Germany's ultimate resort to unrestricted
submarine warfare.

The first incident in which an American citizen was
killed while traveling on an Allied ship occurred when
the British ship *Falaba* was sunk in the Irish Sea on
March 28, 1915 by a German submarine. There was a
large loss of life including that of one American, Leon
C. Thrasher. The incident foreshadowed the major
crises which arose in the next twelve months with
German attacks on the Allied vessels, *Lusitania, Arabic,* and *Sussex*. The essential question presented by
Thrasher's death was whether the formula of "strict
accountability," set forth by Wilson six weeks earlier,
applied to the loss of American life on belligerent as
well as American vessels.

When the *Lusitania* went down on May 7 a note had
not yet been sent to the German Government in the
Thrasher case—by then several weeks old. There had
been much inconclusive discussion, with Wilson and
the counselor of the State Department, Robert Lansing, tending to a position which would virtually outlaw the submarine in relation to enemy commerce,

and with Secretary of State William Jennings Bryan and a legal adviser, Chandler P. Anderson, tending to a view considerably less extreme.

Lansing advised Bryan that an American citizen traveling on a belligerent ship was entitled to full protection of the rules of maritime warfare. Such a position, Lansing was aware, would be tantamount to prescribing for Germany the methods of warfare which that country could and could not employ in the struggle with Great Britain.[8] Lansing prepared and sent to Bryan a draft note. He admitted that its language was harsh and unconciliatory, and confessed that he felt the "gravest anxiety" as to the results if the note were sent. It did not mean war, but it meant "intense hostility and the charge of open support of the enemies of Germany." This risk "after mature consideration" he was prepared to take.[9] In another communication to Bryan on April 7 Lansing recognized that expediency would favor warning Americans not to take passage on belligerent merchantmen; but he contended that the "dignity of the Government and its duty to its citizens" demanded a policy in harmony with strict accountability. He raised the question of what would be done if a "*neutral* vessel with Americans on board should be torpedoed and the Americans drowned," and concluded that for the "sake of the future, we cannot afford to allow expediency or avoidance of the issue to control our action in the Thrasher case."[10]

As early as February 15 Lansing had prepared a
memorandum arguing that from Germany's standpoint
the advantages of war with the United States would
appear to outweigh the disadvantages, since Germany
would gain a free hand to interrupt American trade
with the Allies and in other respects there would be
no material change in the military and naval situation.[11] On the occasion of the torpedoing of the *Falaba*
at the end of March 1915 he invited the attention of
his chief, Bryan, to this memorandum, adding that
since writing it he had been "informed through different channels that German public opinion takes a very
similar view of the situation." President Wilson's own
comment on the memorandum was that he appreciated
its force to the full—"But it ought not to alter our
course so long as we think ourselves on the firm ground
of right"; with specific reference to the Thrasher case,
the President added that "we must compound policy
with legal right in wise proportions, no doubt." [12] Yet
the proportion allotted by Wilson to "policy" would
undoubtedly have been greater had the permanent interests of the United States been regarded as coincid-
ing with the German cause.

Chandler P. Anderson took a different view of the
Thrasher case. In his diary he set down that Lansing
was "unwilling to disregard the law" since "the American people would be dissatisfied with any weak or
half-way measures in dealing with a case involving

the loss of an American life." [13] Anderson then gave his own views:

I do not agree with him about this, and have already heard one of the most intelligent people I know say that if the American people are willing to put up with what has happened in Mexico, they will stand anything.[14] Furthermore, the case as reported does not involve an affront to the United States, as Thrasher's death was not the specific purpose of the attack by the submarine, being merely incidental to the destruction of the ship. The attack on the ship of course was unlawful in the opinion of the United States, but inasmuch as we came in contact with the case only through one of its indirect results, it seems to me that we might place the matter on the plane of a claim for pecuniary damages resulting from an unlawful act. Germany would of course deny that the act was unlawful, and this would raise a question of a legal nature.

Anderson prepared a memorandum along these lines which was sent to the President. Incorporated in his diary is a copy of the memorandum, attached to which is a transmittal slip addressed to Lansing: "Dear Bert: This is a solution of the Thrasher case which will keep us out of trouble. C.P.A." [15]

The practical consequence of Anderson's view (which, to be entirely workable, required a prohibition of Americans traveling on belligerent vessels) would have been refusal by the United States to quarrel with Germany over methods of warfare employed against Great Britain; the American Government would have confined itself to claiming damages in event of harm to an American citizen. Lansing replied to Anderson that the fundamental difficulty with such a position was the "necessity of admitting that the illegality of the method employed by . . . [Germany] is open to question." Lansing thought that "we go as far as we ought when we leave open for discussion the legal right to sink a merchant vessel on the high seas after the persons on board have been given time to reach a safe distance from the vessel." It was not permissible, he said, to debate the legality of killing nonbelligerents. "We must start out our consideration of the course to be taken in this case on the proposition that the act of the commander of the submarine was illegal, inhuman, and indefensible." [16]

Writing to Wilson, Secretary Bryan perceived that "We can hardly insist that the presence of an American on a British ship shall operate to prevent attack unless we are prepared to condemn the methods employed as improper in warfare." He was unwilling to take such a forward position and suggested that "the doctrine of contributory negligence has some bearing on this case —that is, the American who takes passage upon a British vessel knowing that this method of warfare will be employed, stands in a different position from that occupied by one who suffers without any fault of his own." Bryan would not only avoid contending with Germany over her methods of warfare against Allied merchantmen; he was also dubious about even demanding an indemnity.[17]

Wilson quickly inclined, however, to Lansing's view. He replied to Secretary Bryan that he did not like the Thrasher case: "It is full of disturbing possibilities." But, he added, it was clear to him that Thrasher "came to his death by reason of acts . . . which were in unquestionable violation of the just rules of international law with regard to unarmed vessels at sea." He thought therefore that "it is probably our duty to . . . insist that the lives of our citizens shall not be put in danger" by such acts. This judgment was based on the explicit assumption that the British merchant ship on which Thrasher had been traveling was unarmed. Accordingly on April 6 Wilson raised the complicated question of the armed merchantman. Information had reached the American Government that British merchantmen, a few of which were known to be armed, were under orders to attack submarines by gunfire or ramming. Wilson asked Bryan whether the German commander who, he hypothesized, might have found it "impracticable . . . to ascertain whether the *Falaba* was armed," would be justified in "acting upon the theory that the British authorization [to attack] had in effect transformed all vessels and made them liable to attack as such." This aspect of the *Falaba* case had also occurred to Bryan, who replied to Wilson that it was as yet unknown whether the *Falaba* was armed, or if not armed, whether the fact that the vessel was unarmed was known to the commander of the submarine.[18] Nonetheless, after further investigation, no evidence was adduced showing that the *Falaba* was armed, and this possibly troublesome aspect of the case was put aside.[19]

On April 22, 1915 the President seemed finally to have decided on a policy. "Although I have been silent for a long time about the case," he wrote Bryan, "I have had it much in my mind . . . to work out some practicable course of action." He outlined a strong note to the German Government, which followed Lansing's recommendations. He suggested that Germany be told that the American Government took it for granted that "Germany had no idea of changing the rules (or, rather, the essential principle) of international law with regard to the safety of noncombatants and of the citizens of neutral countries at sea, however radical the present change in practical conditions of warfare." He would then raise the whole question of the use of submarines against merchant vessels, "calling attention circumstantially to the impossibility of observing the safeguards and precautions so long and so clearly recognized as imperative in such matters." The German action was to be protested "as contrary to laws based, not on mere interest or convenience, but on humanity, fair play, and a necessary respect for the rights of neutrals." [20] Yet this decision failed to stick, for Wilson confessed to Bryan almost a week later that he was "not at all confident that we are on the right track in considering such a note as I outlined for Mr. Lansing to work on." "Perhaps," he added, "it is not necessary to make formal representations in the matter at all." [21] Having at first veered toward the strong views of Lansing, Wilson later changed his mind, tending toward the more cautious position of Bryan.

II

Events now overtook the Thrasher case. On April 28 and May 1, 1915 the American vessels *Cushing* and *Gulflight* were attacked by the Germans. On the *Gulflight* there was a loss of three lives. Lansing felt that these incidents, clearly covered by the Wilsonian formula of strict accountability, called for prompt protest and unequivocal demand for damages. Yet some disposition had to be made of the Thrasher case, to clear the way. To this end Lansing was ready to view that case less uncompromisingly than heretofore. He now suggested to Bryan that the Thrasher case, if compared with the recent attacks on the two American vessels, left "room for argument." He thought that "discussion of the use of submarines would be appropriate" in the Thrasher case; it was, moreover, "open to question" whether the American note of February 10 applied. He advised that a separate note be sent immediately in the Thrasher case, "so that a more moderate and less rigid representation may be made before action is taken in the other cases." [22]

Yet once again events intervened. On May 7 the

British liner *Lusitania* was sunk without warning by a German submarine. The loss of life was appalling. Of the passengers and crew numbering nearly 2,000, there perished 1,198, including 128 Americans.[23] This was the first dramatic demonstration of the indiscriminate destruction of life in twentieth-century warfare. Although we have subsequently become inured to total war, the effect of the *Lusitania* disaster on contemporary opinion was electric. The American public was horrified.

While Germany attempted to defend her act by reference to the accepted categories of international law, her strongest argument related to a circumstance unknown to international law—the employment of the submarine as a commerce raider, and its vulnerability to ramming and small-caliber cannon fire.[24] The *Lusitania* itself was unarmed, but the British had begun even before the war (for reasons unconnected with the submarine) the practice of arming their merchantmen. Moreover, in February 1915, following the German declaration of a war zone around the British Isles, confidential orders of the British Admiralty had instructed masters of merchantmen to flee from or, if circumstances permitted, fire on or ram submarines.[25] The German Government in its first *Lusitania* note stated that it was therefore "unable to consider English merchant vessels any longer as 'undefended territory,'" and that "German commanders are consequently no longer in a position to observe the rules of capture otherwise usual and with which they invariably complied before this."

Whereas in the *Falaba* case the death of one American, Leon C. Thrasher, had resulted in an inconclusive discussion of what position the American Government should take, the wholesale death of Americans on the *Lusitania* quickly brought a policy. In its first *Lusitania* note of May 13, 1915, the American Government pointed out the "practical impossibility of employing submarines in the destruction of commerce without disregarding those rules of fairness, reason, justice, and humanity, which all modern opinion regards as imperative." The incompatibility of submarine warfare with the accepted rules was dwelt upon in detail; the note reiterated that "manifestly submarines cannot be used against merchantmen, as the last few weeks have shown, without an inevitable violation of many sacred principles of justice and humanity." [26] There was a firm conclusion:

. . . the Government of the United States cannot believe that the commanders of the vessels which committed these acts of lawlessness did so except under a misapprehension of the orders issued by the Imperial German naval authorities. It takes it for granted that, at least within the practical possibilities of every such case, the commanders even of submarines were expected to do nothing that would involve the lives of non-combatants or the safety of neutral ships, even at the cost of failing of their object of capture or destruction. It confidently expects, therefore, that the Imperial

German Government will disavow the acts of which the
Government of the United States complains, that they will
make reparation so far as reparation is possible for injuries
which are without measure, and that they will take immediate steps to prevent the recurrence of anything so obviously subversive of the principles of warfare.[27]

This was strong language, but it was not an ultimatum.
Moreover, when speaking in Philadelphia three days
after the sinking of the *Lusitania,* the President had
made a most pacifistic declaration: "There is such a
thing as a nation being so right that it does not need
to convince others by force that it is right."

Secretary Bryan worked hard to prevent a break.
From May 7 to June 8—the day he resigned—Bryan
reiterated his argument of contributory negligence,
calling Wilson's attention to the fact that the *Lusitania*
carried ammunition; he urged that passenger ships be
prohibited from carrying such cargo, that American
citizens be warned against taking passage on belligerent vessels, that a strong counterbalancing note be sent
to Great Britain, and that there be employed a policy
of delay and investigation.[28] Public opinion, moreover,
evidently was adverse to a break with Germany. The
Administration was in the difficult position of having to
contend with what Wilson called "inconsistent" demands. On the one hand "our people want this thing
handled in a way that will bring about a definite settlement without endless correspondence," while on the
other they "also expect us not to hasten an issue or so

conduct the correspondence as to make an unfriendly issue inevitable." [29] Lansing, who became secretary of state in place of Bryan, was conscious of the same dilemma. Writing to Wilson he said that "the vast majority of the people" did not want war, but "at the same time they want the government not to recede a step from its position but to compel Germany to submit to our demands." To carry out both ideas, he concluded, was "well nigh impossible." [30]

Then, as the American public began to forget the *Lusitania,* the Germans on August 19, 1915 sank the British liner *Arabic,* with loss of two American lives. German-American relations once again came close to rupture. The time for debating the question had passed, Lansing told the German ambassador, Count Johann von Bernstorff. Unless Germany now declared that there would be no more surprise attacks on passenger vessels, and lived up to that declaration, the United States "would certainly declare war." [31] The efforts of Bernstorff and the civilians in the government in Berlin, in strenuous opposition to the views of Admiral Alfred von Tirpitz, finally brought a German declaration of disavowal. "The attack . . . was undertaken against the instructions issued to the commander," said the German note of October 5, 1915. "The Imperial Government regrets and disavows this act." Further, Germany was ready to pay an indemnity for the American lives which, "to its deep regret," had been lost on the *Arabic.* As to the future, the note declared that orders to commanders of submarines "have been made so stringent that the recurrence of incidents similar to the Arabic case is considered out of the question." [32] This confirmed a previous conciliatory communication by Bernstorff to the Department of State which he had made on September 1 without specific authorization from his government. He had then disclosed the decision of the German Navy to restrict the submarine as follows: "Liners will not be sunk by our submarines without warning and without safety of the lives of noncombatants, provided the liners do not try to escape or offer resistance." [33] This still left open the question of the Allied freighter; moreover, it did not preclude the sinking of liners—if safety of noncombatants were assured. The American Government, in accepting the note of October 5, indicated its willingness to close the matter on that basis.

The dispute with Germany rested uneasily in this posture during the winter months of 1915–16 while Lansing and Bernstorff worked on a formula for settling the *Lusitania* case. In November 1915 Lansing presented a memorandum indicating the position which the American Government demanded that Germany adopt: an expression of regret, a declaration that the sinking was in contravention of international law, and payment of a suitable indemnity for American lives lost. Germany balked at admitting the illegality of the act. In a memorandum of early January 1916 the German Government reiterated the argument that its submarine war was in retaliation against England's unlawful blockade. Whereas the American Government maintained that this retaliation was illegal insofar as neutral rights on the high seas were affected, Germany asserted that incidental injury to the neutral could not in the circumstances be a basis for protest. 'The neutrals, by allowing the crippling of their commerce with Germany contrary to international law . . . cannot object to the retaliatory steps of Germany for reasons of neutrality." Nevertheless the German Government was prepared to express its "deep regret at the death of American citizens caused by the sinking of the *Lusitania* and, in order to settle this question amicably, declares its readiness to pay indemnity for the losses inflicted." But Wilson rejected settlement on this basis. He wrote to Lansing that "It is a concession of grace, and not at all of right."

And so once more, for the second time since the beginning of submarine warfare, Lansing spoke bluntly to Bernstorff of the possibility of war. Negotiations were kept going at this time only through the German ambassador's own persistence in urging his government to make maximum concessions. Finally on February 16, 1916 Bernstorff transmitted a note containing the following statement:

Germany has notwithstanding [the British illegalities] limited her submarine warfare, because of her long-standing friendship with the United States and because by the sinking of the *Lusitania,* which caused the death of citizens of the United States, the German retaliation affected neutrals which was not the intention, as retaliation should be confined to enemy subjects.

The Imperial Government having subsequent to the sinking of the *Lusitania* issued to its naval officers the new instructions which are now prevailing, expresses profound regret that citizens of the United States suffered by that event and, recognizing its liability therefor, stands ready to make reparation for the life of the citizens of the United States who were lost, by the payment of a suitable indemnity.

Although the note sedulously avoided using the word "illegal" in characterizing Germany's action, Wilson thought that in the circumstances it would have to be considered satisfactory.[34] Lansing told Bernstorff next day that the note was not satisfactory, but that "in the circumstances" it was acceptable.[35] By then, however, new circumstances were arising, and the *Lusitania* negotiations came to nought.

III

A new factor had appeared on February 8. The German Government on that date had announced that "enemy merchantmen armed with guns no longer have any right to be considered as peaceable vessels of commerce. Therefore, the German naval forces will receive orders, within a short period, paying consideration to the interests of neutrals, to treat such vessels as belligerents."[36]

This declaration, a compromise between military and civilian points of view within the German Government as to the requirements of expediency in the conduct of submarine warfare, took advantage of and further intensified an already existing crisis in Washington, where the question of the armed merchantman had become acute both in the Administration's relations with the Allies and with Congress. From the standpoint of the equanimity of the American Government, the announcement could not have come at a more inopportune time. The dilemma with which the United States was now confronted was a poignant demonstration of the insecure footing of a foreign policy based on the rules of maritime warfare. An important sequel to this crisis, and to that of the *Sussex* which soon followed, was Wilson's endeavor to find a more suitable point of departure for American policy, involving an important shift of emphasis which we will examine later.

The question of the armed merchantman was not new. The State Department shortly after outbreak of the war had declared that a belligerent merchantman might carry armament for the sole purpose of defense without acquiring the character of a public war vessel. Nonetheless, as a result of an informal understanding with the British Admiralty, guns had been kept off British merchant vessels entering American ports.[37] The American Government had incidentally considered the question of armed merchantmen in connection with the *Falaba* case and also in the first *Lusitania*

note, which declared that "the lives of non-combatants
. . . can not lawfully or rightfully be put in jeopardy
by the capture or destruction of an *unarmed* merchantman." A different statement of the matter, more in
harmony with the traditional international practice
concerning armed merchantmen, subsequently appeared in the second *Lusitania* note, which argued that
it was the duty of the American Government merely
"to see to it that the *Lusitania* was not armed for offensive action." [38] The arrival of the armed British merchant vessel *Waimana* in the port of Newport News in
September 1915 prompted Lansing to point out that
the position on the armed merchantman in September
1914 was taken at a time when the submarine was still
unknown as a commerce raider. He expressed the opinion that changed conditions "require a new declaration
because an armament, which under previous conditions
was clearly defensive, may now be employed for offensive operations against so small and unarmored a craft
as a submarine." [39] Wilson suggested temporizing in
the case of the *Waimana*, but favored preparation of a
new regulation for future use.[40] The question continued under advisement during the remainder of the
year and came to the fore again with the torpedoing
of the armed British liner *Persia* on December 30, and
with the appearance shortly thereafter of an armed
Italian liner in the port of New York.

Classification of armed merchantmen as public war
vessels would, of course, have had two important conse-

quences: such vessels would have been prevented from entering American ports for purposes of trade; and they would have ceased, in the eyes of the American Government, to have immunity from sudden attack. It is therefore understandable that the British Government was concerned over the misgivings in Washington with respect to the armed merchantman. Even before the war the Admiralty had accepted the arming of merchantmen as a necessary response to the position taken by some governments at the Second Hague Conference of 1907 and at the London Conference of 1909—a position which reserved the right to convert merchantmen into cruisers. Accordingly a program had been instituted of preparing a number of British liners for self-defense. After describing these countermeasures in a statement in the House of Commons in early 1913, the First Lord of the Admiralty, Winston Churchill, made this melancholy comment: "No one can pretend to view these measures without regret, or without hoping that the period of retrogression all over the world which has rendered them necessary, may be succeeded by days of broader international confidence and agreement than those through which we are now passing." [41] In effect a form of privateering was threatening to reenter naval warfare.

Following the initial German declaration of February 4, 1915, the British Admiralty, as we have seen, issued confidential instructions directing British merchant vessels not to surrender "tamely" to a submarine.

If flight was impracticable, ramming was the recommended alternative. A subsequent order addressed to "vessels carrying a defensive armament" contained the instruction that if a submarine were in pursuit and displayed "hostile intentions," the merchantman "should open fire in self-defence, notwithstanding the submarine may not have committed a definite hostile act." [42] Experience confirmed the judgment of the Admiralty that armed vessels had a much improved position in relation to the submarine. During 1916 over three hundred armed British vessels were attacked, of which about four-fifths escaped. In the same period a similar number of unarmed vessels were attacked, of which only 67 escaped. [43]

The American Government found itself in a most perplexing situation. In the *Sussex* affair (March, 1916) it was to fall back on the assertion that the respect accorded by one belligerent to the rights of American citizens on the high seas was in no way contingent upon the conduct of any other government. But the dilemma could not be resolved on a bilateral basis. In reality, the United States was an important factor in a highly complex equation. This was recognized in a proposal of January 1916 addressed to the Allied governments. Lansing suggested "a reasonable and reciprocally just arrangement" whereby the opposing belligerents would agree

that submarines should . . . adhere strictly to the rules of international law in . . . stopping and searching merchant vessels, determining their belligerent nationality, and removing the crews and passengers to places of safety before sinking the vessels as prizes of war, and that merchant vessels of belligerent nationality should be prohibited and prevented from carrying any armament whatsoever.

Moreover, the Allies were told that the American Government "is impressed with the reasonableness of the argument that a merchant vessel carrying an armament of any sort . . . should be held to be an auxiliary cruiser and so treated by a neutral as well as by a belligerent government, and is seriously considering instructing its officials accordingly." [44] If under this threat the Allies should agree to the *modus vivendi* he had proposed, Lansing intended to approach the Central Powers in the matter.[45]

Lansing took as his point of departure "the humane purpose of saving the lives of innocent people." Yet from the standpoint of the belligerents this concern could only be secondary. Great Britain would have gained from a *modus vivendi* such as Lansing proposed, if at the same time she could have maintained her blockade of Germany in its then stringent and unlawful form. But that Germany in that case would have agreed to keep the submarine within the strict confines of cruiser warfare was inconceivable. The proposal therefore never reached the stage of negotiation. Within a week the American ambassador in London, Walter Hines Page, reported that the British foreign secretary, Sir Edward Grey, saw Lansing's proposition as "wholly in favor of the Germans theoretically and practically [and] wholly against the Allies." Grey "spoke as one speaks of a great calamity . . . his surprise and dismay are overwhelming." [46]

It was clear that Britain would refuse to cooperate. Lansing commented to the President that evidently the British expected the American Government to deny absolutely "the right to use submarines in attacking commercial vessels," and that Grey was disappointed that "we have failed to be the instrument to save British commerce from attack by Germany." Lansing thought that consideration would now have to be given to "what course we are going to take in regard to Americans traveling on vessels carrying arms. . . . I doubt whether we can insist that vessels so armed can be considered other than as auxiliary cruisers of the respective navies of the Allies." [47]

The sequel to the final threatening paragraph of Lansing's identic note of January 18, in which he had made his proposal to the Allies, and to the reiteration of that position in his later letter to the President, was paradoxically a hasty and complete retreat. On February 15, 1916 Lansing held a press conference in which he announced that if the Entente powers should reject the proposal of January 18—according to which submarines would have had to follow strictly the time-honored rules of visit and search, and the Allies in turn refrain from arming their merchantmen—then the American Government would "feel compelled to cease its efforts to have the *modus vivendi* accepted and will rely upon the present established rule of international law that merchant ships are entitled to armament for defensive purposes only." Moreover, there was "no present intention to warn Americans to refrain from travelling on belligerent merchantmen armed with guns solely for the purpose of defense," and "if Americans should lose their lives in attack by submarines without warning upon merchantmen so armed, it will be necessary to regard the offense as a breach of international law and the formal assurances given by the German Government." [48] It is probable that Allied rejection of Lansing's proposal would in itself have signaled retreat, for in addition to the usual reluctance to come to a showdown with Great Britain there had been an urgent plea from Wilson's trusted adviser, Colonel Edward M. House, in London, who feared the upset of his simultaneous negotiations with Grey concerning American mediation and possible intervention.[49] Still another consideration was Germany's announcement in early February 1916 of intensified submarine warfare, for although this German declaration—according to which submarines would attack armed merchantmen—was not inconsistent with the view then seemingly held by the American Government that the armed merchantman was a vessel of war, it became suddenly clear that the sea war was in imminent danger of degenerating into unrestrained destruction, thus stultifying American policy as regards the very point on which it had been most insistent.

On February 28 the American Government was apprised of certain slight modifications in the German declaration of the eighth.[50] But it had not been in anticipation of any concessions from Germany, small or great, that the Administration had taken the position announced by Lansing on February 15, which had been adopted with full awareness that war could result at any moment. Wilson was prepared to accept this consequence of his position on the armed merchantman. Congress, however, was less resigned. A storm in that quarter had been threatening with respect to this issue since December; and it now broke, very nearly capsizing Wilson's diplomacy. The speaker of the House, Bennett Champ Clark of Missouri; the majority leader in the House, Claude Kitchin of North Carolina; the chairman of the House foreign affairs committee, Henry D. Flood of Virginia; and the chairman of the Senate foreign relations committee, William J. Stone of Missouri, conveyed to the President their personal fears regarding his policy, and warned him further that sentiment in Congress was overwhelmingly opposed (in the House two to one at a conservative estimate, and perhaps three to one, Clark said) to a war over American citizens traveling on armed merchantmen. To this end Representative Jeff McLemore had introduced in the House a resolution which would warn American citizens not to take passage on armed belligerent merchantmen, while Senator Thomas P. Gore shortly thereafter introduced in the Senate a stronger resolution which would have prohibited passports for travel on such vessels.

A report of one of the many conferences held between the President and congressional leaders during this period is in a letter of Senator Stone of February 24. To reiterate his own misgivings and also to preclude any possibility of misunderstanding Wilson's position, Stone had written the President recapitulating an exchange of views which had occurred a few days before. Confessing that he was "more troubled than I have been for many a day," and that he was besieged by "inquiries from my colleagues," who were "deeply concerned and disturbed," he set forth this understanding of the President's position:

if Great Britain . . . insisted upon arming her merchantships she would be within her rights under international law, [and therefore] you were not favorably disposed to the idea of this Government taking any definite steps toward preventing American citizens from embarking upon armed merchant vessels. Furthermore, that you would consider it your duty, if a German war vessel should fire upon an armed merchant vessel of the enemy upon which American citizens were passengers, to hold Germany to strict account.[51]

The President replied confirming Stone's impression of his views, and explaining the basis of his willingness to accept war with Germany over the rules of maritime warfare. Through many anxious months, Wilson said, he had striven to keep the United States out of war. He did not doubt that he would continue to succeed in that aim. The "apparent meaning" of the declaration made by the Central Powers on February 8 "is so manifestly inconsistent with explicit assurances recently given us . . . that I must believe that explanations will presently ensue which will put a different aspect upon it. . . . But in any event," he continued, "our duty is clear."

I cannot consent to any abridgment of the rights of American citizens in any respect. The honor and self-respect of the nation is involved. . . . To forbid our people to exercise their rights for fear we might be called upon to vindicate them would be a deep humiliation indeed. . . . It would be a deliberate abdication of our hitherto proud position as spokesmen even amidst the turmoil of war for the law and the right.[52]

The President referred to all aspects of the submarine controversy, but in the circumstances of the moment the letter was a justification for war with Germany over the issue of the armed merchantman. The extraordinary legalism of the letter went in the face of Wilson's acknowledged doubts as to the workability of traditional rules of maritime warfare, and it defied the deep anxiety of leaders of his own party. It reflected the pro-Ally bias always present in Wilson's policy. More than that, however, Wilson at this time hoped that House in London would be able to persuade the Allies to get peace talks underway; and had the United States persisted in a policy which would have subjected Allied shipping to greatly increased hazards from the submarine, it might have wrecked House's efforts to mediate between the Allies and the Central Powers.

Wilson took direct measures against the Gore-McLemore resolutions. In a bold and unprecedented letter to Representative Edward W. Pou, chairman of the House rules committee, the President demanded a showdown on the question of American rights on armed belligerent merchantmen. The McLemore Resolution was tabled on March 7 by a vote of 276 to 142. Meanwhile in the Senate the Gore Resolution, confusingly amended, had also been tabled.

By demanding a vote of confidence, and aided by the recognized prerogatives of the executive in the field of foreign affairs, Wilson remained in command of American diplomacy. Nonetheless the episode made clear, in the words of a contemporary appraisal by the journalist David Lawrence, that Congress would "not sanction war between the United States and the Central Powers because of the loss hereafter of any American lives on belligerent ships." This, Lawrence wrote, was "the unwritten and unmistakable mandate of both Houses." He even went further. "The outstanding fact is that . . . Congress will not vote for war, however insistent the executive may be upon it." [53]

IV

On March 24, 1916, there occurred a maritime event
of signal consequences. On that date a German submarine torpedoed without warning the French channel
steamer *Sussex*. Eighty persons were killed and
wounded, and several Americans were included among
the injured. This new crisis found German-American relations at the point where another round of inconclusive note writing would be disastrous to the prestige of
the American Government. Even so, Wilson yielded
with the greatest reluctance to the logic of the situation and to the promptings of Secretary Lansing and
Colonel House. Yet his quandary might have been
greater. The *Sussex* was unarmed. Thus he was spared
a showdown with Germany on the issue of the armed
merchantman.

Throughout the crisis Lansing favored a break with
Germany. He advised Wilson without delay that "the
time for writing notes . . . has passed. Whatever
we determine to do must be in the line of action."
Lansing recommended immediate recall of Count von
Bernstorff, although he granted that such action "might
be made conditional upon the German Government
unequivocally admitting the illegality of submarine
warfare in general . . . and guaranteeing that the
present method of warfare will cease." Germany in
response to a breaking off of diplomatic relations
"might possibly go so far as to declare war against the

United States," but Lansing could see "no other course open to us." [54]

Wilson was hopeful that a torpedo had not caused the disaster. And even had it been a torpedo, there were "many particulars to be considered about the course we should pursue as well as the principle of it." The President believed, somewhat ambiguously, that "the steps we take and the way we take them will . . . be of the essence of the matter if we are to keep clearly and indisputably within the lines we have already set ourselves." [55] Wilson was in a different frame of mind from that in which he had met Congress head-on over the question of the armed merchantman; he was becoming dissatisfied with the erratic course of a policy dependent on the tactics of the German submarine.

Wilson's reaction disappointed Lansing, who continued to advocate an uncompromising position. When all the reports of the *Sussex* were in, making clear Germany's culpability, the secretary of state drafted a note which would announce to the German Government that the United States "is compelled to sever diplomatic relations . . . until such time as that Government shall . . . discontinue the employment of submarines against commercial vessels of belligerent as well as neutral nationality." [56] Considering this draft "too severe and uncompromising," Wilson revised the note substantially, making the severance of relations conditional: "Unless the Imperial Government should now immediately declare its intention to abandon its present practices of submarine warfare and return to a scrupulous observance of the practices clearly prescribed by the law of nations," the American Government would have "no choice" but to sever relations.[57] Lansing, of course, did not like this language, and he tried to convince Wilson of the need for stronger phrasing: "The phrase—'return to a scrupulous observance of the principles clearly prescribed by the law of nations'—offers an opportunity to raise the question as to what are the clearly prescribed principles." These, he said, "are not very well defined except as to visit and search." He also feared that "the whole question of the treatment of armed and unarmed merchantmen will be raised." He suggested that these difficulties might be minimized if the note were to end: "Unless the Imperial Government immediately declares that it abandons its present method of warfare against passenger and freight-carrying vessels, the Government of the United States can have no choice but to sever diplomatic relations with the German Empire."[58] Wilson accepted this revision; with certain alterations the sentence appeared in a note sent to Germany on April 18, toned down slightly by the concluding observation that the American Government contemplated this action "with the greatest reluctance." The *Sussex* note returned to the position of wholesale condemnation of the submarine taken in the first *Lusitania* note; even Lansing recognized that in its final form the note was "in the nature of an ultimatum," although he regretted that "it lacked the force of the one contained in the note which I had originally drafted." [59]

House's reaction to the *Sussex* crisis was more complicated than that of the secretary of state. Before and following his conversations in London, which culminated in the famous House-Grey memorandum of 1916, House hoped that the submarine would not force the United States into a war over freedom of the seas. He had said repeatedly to the President that the American Government as a neutral was more effectively situated to bring the war to an end, on the basis of mediation, than it would be as a belligerent. Until the attack on the *Sussex* he had continued to hold this view, and was hopeful that both sides would respond to an American call—which awaited only the propitious moment—for a peace conference.

But the *Sussex* affair brought House to the conclusion that "further parley" was impossible, and that there was no alternative to breaking relations. Predicting that Wilson would be inclined to "delay and write further notes," House, having earlier returned from London, proceeded to Washington to confer with the President and try to "make him see that we would lose the respect of the world unless he lived up to the demands he has made of Germany regarding her underseas warfare." Failure to act, House said, would result in losing the confidence of the American people, but it was loss of Allied respect and the consequent jeopardy to American influence at the peace conference which he really emphasized. Wilson "was afraid if we broke off relations, the war would go on indefinitely and there would be no one to lead the way out." House confessed to some embarrassment at this, for Wilson "was repeating the argument I have been giving him for the last six months." The colonel contended that the United States could still "lead them [the belligerents] out even though we were in." He suggested that, having sent Bernstorff home, the President should make "a dispassionate statement of the cause of the war and what the Allies are fighting for," striking "at the system which had caused this world tragedy," and stating that when that system "was righted the quarrel with Germany, as far as we were concerned, would be ended." Then, House suggested, "at the right time— which would perhaps be by midsummer— I could go to Holland and, after a conference with the Allies and with their consent, I could open negotiations directly with Berlin, telling them upon what terms we were ready to end the war." [60] This statement of the case based American policy on a different premise from that of rules of maritime warfare. If the threat of a victorious German autocracy was the real issue, the taking of those rules as the basis of American policy gave a false emphasis; in such a perspective they were not a primary consideration, but incidental. Wilson, who felt keenly his responsibility to public opinion, was more sensitive than House to the awkwardness of a shift from the rules of maritime warfare; at the same time he was experiencing increasing discomfort over the way in which his policy had formed around the question of German methods of warfare against enemy merchantmen. The President was sympathetic to House's point of view; and the procedure outlined by House, although lacking cogency even in terms of its own assumptions, probably assisted in reconciling Wilson to strong language in his *Sussex* note.[61]

The Administration regarded war as a probable sequel to the note of April 18, 1916. Indeed the German state secretary for foreign affairs, Gottlieb E. G. von Jagow, told the American ambassador in Berlin, James W. Gerard, that he thought it meant a break; and on April 25 Ambassador Page in London was instructed to inquire at the Foreign Office the wishes of the British as to representation of their interests in Berlin in event of severance of relations between the United States and Germany.[62] But after another bitter struggle between the civilians and the military, the German Government, replying on May 4, 1916, yielded—grudgingly and belligerently—to the American demands. With strong irony, the note referred to the freedom of the seas as a "principle upon which the German Government believes, now as before, to be in agreement with the Government of the United States," and continued:

The German Government, guided by this idea, notifies the Government of the United States that the German naval forces have received the following orders: In accordance with the general principles of visit and search and destruction of merchant vessels recognized by international law, such vessels, both within and without the area declared as naval war zone, shall not be sunk without warning and without saving human lives, unless these ships attempt to escape or offer resistance. . . .

The German Government is confident that . . . the Government of the United States will now demand and insist that the British Government shall forthwith observe the rules of international law universally recognized before the war. . . . Should the steps taken by the Government of the United States not attain the object it desires, to have the laws of humanity followed by all belligerent nations, the German Government would then be facing a new situation in which it must reserve itself complete liberty of decision.[63]

The important qualification contained in the last sentence of this note prompted a reply from the American Government which ruled out any possibility of future compromise:

In order . . . to avoid any possible misunderstanding, the Government of the United States notifies the Imperial Government that it cannot for a moment entertain, much less discuss, a suggestion that respect by German naval authorities for the rights of citizens of the United States upon the high seas should in any way or in the slightest degree be made contingent upon the conduct of any other government affecting the rights of neutrals and non-combatants. Responsibility in such matters is single, not joint; absolute, not relative.[64]

In the final event the break with Germany did not turn on the narrow question of submarine attacks against Allied merchantmen—the issue on which German-American relations had hung in tremulous balance for so many months. The German declaration of unrestricted submarine warfare, which took effect on February 1, 1917, subjected all merchantmen—armed and unarmed, enemy and neutral—to attack without warning.[65] Thus at its climax Germany's submarine warfare confronted the United States with a new issue—one less controversial than that involving the safety of Americans on Allied merchantmen.

Even had the intensification of submarine warfare stopped short of neutral shipping, the position previously taken by Wilson in the *Sussex* affair very nearly precluded any response except breaking diplomatic relations, with its sequel of war. But we must note here, what will be emphasized in subsequent chapters, that Wilson during the course of 1916 had become increasingly reluctant to accept Germany's manner of attacking Allied shipping as the point of departure of American policy. Although German submarines soon failed to conduct themselves in accordance with the *Sussex* pledge, Wilson refrained from making vigorous protest. A new rash of sinkings occurred late in 1916; in two instances, that of the British *Marina* and the Italian *Palermo*, American lives were lost. Moreover, in a large number of torpedoings of Allied and neutral merchantmen, notably in the case of the British liner

Arabia, American lives were endangered, although not lost.[66] The German Government attributed the sinking of the *Marina* and *Arabia*, the only cases in which diplomatic exchanges passed beyond the preliminary stage, to "mistakes," and declared a readiness to accept liability.[67] Lansing advised the President that the American Government could not accept this defense "without receding from our position that there can be no such things as mistakes when American lives are lost or put in jeopardy. . . . If . . . we live up to our *Sussex* declaration, as I feel we are honorably bound to do, what course remains other than to reject the explanations offered and announce that we have no alternative but to break off diplomatic relations?" [68]

Provocation was not lacking, but Wilson, preoccupied with his endeavor in late 1916 to achieve a negotiated peace, chose to ignore the incidents. On December 18 he launched his appeal for a peace conference and continued to be absorbed in this endeavor until the German declaration of unrestricted submarine warfare. Yet the peace offensive was not the sole reason for Wilson's failure to react to the constant sinkings. House recorded in a significant diary entry of January 4, 1917, that Lansing "desires the President to press the submarine issue and to send Bernstorff home." But Lansing did not expect that Wilson would do so, because "the President told him the other day that he did not believe the people of the United States were willing to go to war because a few Americans had been killed." [69]

If the rules of maritime warfare encompassed all of American national interest that was at stake in the European war, then, as Wilson seemed to imply, it was a very narrow interest indeed, hardly justifying the vigor of the American reaction to the submarine. Actually, however, as early as the autumn of 1914 another current of policy, reflecting a very different understanding of the national interest, had been set in motion. In the peace note of December 18, 1916 and in Wilson's address to the Senate on January 22, 1917, it had come to a climax simultaneously with the submarine issue. There was only a fortuitous connection and no inherent relationship between these two elements in American policy. But before considering the second and broader aspect of Wilson's policy, we must examine further the intricacies of submarine warfare and neutral rights.

THREE

The Submarine in German Policy

FROM THE outset, a strong bias of the American Government against Germany was evident in the manner of applying the rules of maritime warfare. Yet if the United States had been moved by true impartiality, would those rules have been workable? Would the submarine have stayed within the tolerable limits of international law? Was it American policy which eventually drove the Germans to adopt measures of desperation? Such an inquiry is the more inviting inasmuch as the long evolution of rules designed to regulate belligerent interference with neutral commerce had only shortly before the war reached a culmination in the Hague Convention of 1908 and the Declaration of London of 1909.

Yet to scrutinize from the lawyer's point of view the three-sided controversy of Germany, Great Britain, and the United States over use of the Atlantic seaways would be singularly unrewarding. For the truth of the matter is that the formula of freedom of the seas was incapable of resolving the conflicting demands. Although the nineteenth century, by fostering a distinction between private and public affairs, had lent itself to the laudable attempt of international law to minimize the destructiveness of warfare, it is clear in retrospect that total rather than circumscribed warfare was bound to emerge. The French Revolution having already demonstrated the aggravating effect of nationalism on warfare, it remained only for science and the industrial revolution to work their transformation in the material realm. The present century soon witnessed the consequences for the laws of war: the blurring, and indeed virtual obliteration, of distinctions between private and public property, combatant and noncombatant, belligerent and neutral. The traditional rules of maritime warfare were destined in the event to suffer eclipse from natural causes; for that reason alone, if for no other, a legal critique of American neutrality would be barren of useful conclusions.

This judgment is reinforced if we examine the considerations which led the German Government to adopt ruthless submarine warfare. Such a decision could not have been forestalled by the United States short of extreme measures outside the compass of international law—on the one hand virtual collaboration with Germany, or on the other defiance backed by force coupled with unmistakable intention to employ it to the full.

I

Early in 1916 the question of using unlimited submarine warfare was being fully discussed within the German Government. In January and February of that year
the chief of the admiralty staff, Admiral Franz von
Holtzendorff, the secretary of state for the Navy, Admiral Alfred von Tirpitz, and the chief of the imperial
general staff, General Erich von Falkenhayn, all wrote
Chancellor Theobald von Bethmann-Hollweg in favor
of unlimited submarine warfare. Their main point was
that decisive defeat of Great Britain was necessary for
victory and Germany's future security. None believed
that the intervention of the United States would have
adverse consequences of major character.

Holtzendorff argued that the war had

now come to the point where the question as to how a
favorable outcome can be brought about has attained a
singular urgency. . . . Once . . . the possibility of a victory in the war on land against Russia and France is eliminated, there remains the war on the ocean against England, the third of our enemies and, in her position as the
soul of the entire opposition, our most dangerous one. . . .
The opinion of the Government and public opinion in England is openly attributable, of late at least, to the idea that
even a defeat of the French would not bring about a decisive result, but would simply make it necessary for England to take up the admittedly uncomfortable task of
blockading the French coast as well; but that no victory
on land could do Germany any good as long as it was cut

off from intercourse by water and that, under all circumstances, England would be able to guarantee this. . . . The last means left at our disposal is the U-boat war against commerce, which England believes to have brought to an end with the assistance of the United States.

The war "in increasing measure manifests a tendency toward exhaustion," Holtzendorff stated; nonetheless his memorandum did not raise the question of a negotiated peace. He assumed that the submarine, if its potentialities were fully exploited, could bring a German victory by the fall of 1916, which would offer "the chance of concluding a peace which will for the next decades guarantee to Germany a politically assured existence containing the germs of economic recrudescence and development." Britain, Holtzendorff believed, would fight to the last to prevent Germany from imposing upon her even such minimum demands as an indemnity and a new status for Belgium, which, he acknowledged, would constitute "a terrible blow delivered against the faith of the colonial populations in the unshakable permanence of the British rule" and "would make it necessary for England to develop new channels for the maintenance of her existence as a State in the face of extraordinary difficulties." Holtzendorff anticipated that in event of Germany's defeat the consequences would be no less severe on the German side; he called upon Bethmann-Hollweg to realize that "the war of commerce which has been announced by our foes," and which would be continued after conclusion of peace by means of a calculated isolation of Germany, "can only be organized by England." But he believed that this "dangerous menace" could be avoided by "concluding a treaty of peace and commerce with England, which can only be done in case of a victorious peace."

Confident that within six months, "at the most," the submarine would bring Great Britain to her knees, Holtzendorff strongly discounted the practical effects of American entry into the war. He hoped that the difficulties with the United States "might reach a stage of negotiation," contending in this connection that Germany "thus far has given sufficient indications of its readiness to do full justice" to the maritime standards prescribed by the United States, whereas on the British side "a barbarous method of conducting the war is actually taking root," and Britain "has proceeded more and more toward the viewpoint that these methods are founded on purely military necessities." But in any event the probable intervention of the United States "may be weighed against the advantages to be gotten from the one surviving means of bringing the war to a successful issue within a measurable time. In my opinion, it must be admitted that the scale would tip on the side of the advantages in question." [1]

Memorializing the chancellor on February 13, Admiral von Tirpitz stated his belief that "we shall not be able to defeat England by a war on land alone."

The most important and surest means which can be adopted to bring England to her knees is the use of our U-boats at the present time. . . . England will be cut to the heart by the destruction by U-boats of every ship which approaches the English coast. . . . The more the losses take place with merciless regularity at the very gates of the island kingdom, the more powerful will be the material and moral effect on the English people. . . . A timely U-boat war is . . . , if vigorously carried on, the form of warfare which will unconditionally decide the war to England's disadvantage.

Tirpitz then set forth his conception of the "correct view of America's attitude in the U-boat question." While recognizing that from the beginning the attitude of the United States had not been a friendly one, he believed that there was, "at least so far as the government was concerned, a certain objection against openly taking sides with either party," and that if in February 1915 "we could have afforded to pay no attention at all to the objections urged by the United States against the U-boat war, the unrestricted conduct of this war would not . . . have led to a break with the United States." The "enormous" deliveries of ammunition and war materials, however, made possible by "the restrictions imposed upon the conduct of the U-boat war," had connected American economic interest with the British cause "in a manner quite different from that existing at the beginning of the war." As a consequence, "America is directly interested in the fate of England's economic existence and . . . in England's intention to crush Germany." Tirpitz was also of the opinion that the United States was becoming convinced "of the growing dangers involved in Japan's hostile attitude" and that understandings "unquestionably exist . . . whose purpose is to give Japan a very definite setback . . . after the war." This would be possible, he said, "only if England can be absolutely secured against any danger emanating from Europe, that is, if Germany is overpowered." This rather too elaborate explanation of American policy, which suggested that the United States "whether they desire to be so or not . . . have become a direct enemy of Germany," reinforced Tirpitz in his argument for throwing off all restraint and seeking total victory. He concluded that if the United States should push the economic and political aspects of its position to the "logical conclusion and let matters come to a break with us, the resulting circumstances would suffer no material change, provided this break were limited to a refusal to maintain diplomatic relations." Even if the United States should declare war, he was of the opinion that the bottleneck of tonnage would render the American action relatively harmless. "The entrance of America into the list of our opponents would be of no definite assistance to England." [2]

On February 13 General von Falkenhayn submitted his opinion to the chancellor on the Belgian and submarine questions, which he considered to be closely related.

Regarding the future of Belgium, no doubt can be entertained on the point that the country must remain at our disposal both as a place of assembly for the troops required for the protection of the most important German industrial regions, and as a hinterland for the base on the coast of Flanders which is absolutely indispensable for the purposes of our fleet. . . . Without this condition, Germany's war in the west is lost.

The importance of permanent German control over Belgium, and certain knowledge that England would resist such control "to the bitter end," settled the submarine question in Falkenhayn's mind. With or without unlimited submarine warfare, Great Britain, no less than Germany, was committed, Falkenhayn believed, to fighting the war out to a clear combat decision. As a matter of "duty and conscience" he considered it necessary to urge unrestricted use of the submarine. Thereby "England would undoubtedly be cut straight to the heart; I assume that the efficiency of the means must be admitted, in accordance with the official opinion of the Chief of the Admiralty Staff." As for the reaction of neutrals, the "advantage which the *certainty* of overcoming England would bring us can not be outweighed by the disadvantage of the *possibility* of complications with neutrals." [3]

These arguments, however, failed to convince the

civil branch of the German Government of the ability of the submarine to strangle Great Britain. In a long memorandum of February 29, Bethmann-Hollweg argued forcefully that "an absolute cutting off of England is out of the question. Whether with or without convoy, England will always be able to get a certain number of ships through the wide meshes of our U-boat net, and through our mine fields." Moreover, he predicted that Great Britain "would sacrifice the last man and the last penny" before she would acknowledge that her "supremacy at sea had been destroyed by Germany's sea power."

The chancellor was doubly sure of the folly of the proposed submarine policy because of the great material and moral importance which he attached to the entrance of the United States into the war. For Germany to bring down on herself the whole weight of American power would be playing "a win-all lose-all game in which our existence as a . . . nation would be at stake." The question whether Germany was in such a desperate situation as to take this chance was to be answered "unqualifiedly in the negative." Bethmann was not prepared to accept the assumption that "a termination of the war is . . . only possible after England or we ourselves have been crushed to the ground."

No human being can state with absolute certainty that this point of view is erroneous. As a matter of fact it is sustained by the assertions of Mr. Asquith and of Mr. Sazonoff.[4] But just as impossible is it for us to deny . . . the possibility of ending the war even without the application of the unrestricted U-boat warfare in the course of the year 1916. It is certainly reasonable to argue that our military successes in the west, the failure of the great and long heralded enemy offensives in the spring, the increasing financial straits of the Entente, and the absence of all prospects of starving us out in the current year, will so increase the general recognition of the fact in England that the prolongation of the war is a bad business, even from the standpoint of British interests, as to make England desist from attempting to carry on the war to the point of our exhaustion.

Wishing to avoid a situation in which there was "no alternative but to fight the war through to the bitter end, come what may," the chancellor maintained that the submarine war must be carried on "in such a way as to make it possible to avoid the break with the United States. In this case, we shall be able to list as pure profit all the injuries which we inflict upon England."

Seeking to confine himself to the limitations imposed by the American attitude, the chancellor outlined those conditions for the conduct of the submarine war which would, he believed, bring optimum results. A conventional war on commerce against enemy and neutral ships on all the seas, as well as mine warfare along the enemy coasts, was still open to the submarine, he said. Moreover, unrestricted use of the submarine against unarmed enemy freighters in the war zone surrounding Great Britain and Ireland, which had been in force since February 1915, was justifiable retaliation against England's "policy of starvation." The chancellor took the position that such employment of the submarine was not precluded by the guarantees subsequently given the American Government, which, he remarked, applied only to passenger ships without the United States having demanded similar guarantees for freighters. He recognized the possibility of complications with the United States over American sailors employed on Allied freighters and over American goods shipped on such vessels, but pointed out that American crewmen "occupy such a peculiar relation of dependence to the State whose flag is flown, that they must share the fate of the ship in the capacity of enemy crews." He similarly discounted any legal ground for serious trouble over the loss of American goods on enemy vessels.

As for armed—rather than unarmed—enemy merchantmen, Bethmann-Hollweg reiterated the position which the Foreign Office had announced a few weeks previously, that such vessels automatically acquired a belligerent status and might be sunk on sight, even when they were outside the war zone. There was nothing in international law nor in the pledges given to Washington, he maintained, which obliged Germany to except the armed passenger vessel. As a practical matter, however, he emphasized that "it is essential that *Lusitania* cases, even if an armed liner is involved, be not repeated. A new *Lusitania* case would, under any and all conditions, bring about a break with the United States. A strict order that liners are not to be sunk, even if they are armed, is therefore absolutely essential to an understanding with the United States." [5]

If, despite all precautions, the German-American differences over the armed merchantmen should lead to a break, the chancellor was prepared to accept the outcome as a "working out of destiny from which we cannot escape."

For we can not avoid treating as ships of war enemy merchant ships which are provided with orders to attack, and with arms as well, because of the caprice of President Wilson. To give in on this point would not be consonant with our dignity, and would amount to a practical renunciation of the U-boat weapon. If the break should follow, then the unrestricted U-boat war against England and America would result. . . . Our position with the rest of the Allies would be a more favorable one, coming as the result of a break brought about by the United States, than if the break had been brought about by us through our adoption of the new unrestricted U-boat warfare, which would be looked upon by all those neutrals who should suffer from its severity, in the light of a challenge issued to all alike.[6]

The great controversy was settled momentarily in early March 1916. The Kaiser, torn between his civilian and military advisers, decided in favor of the more moderate submarine warfare advocated by the chancellor, and instructions were so issued to submarine commanders.[7]

The inevitable incident which would put Bethmann's prescription for a *modus vivendi* with the United States to the test occurred with the torpedoing of the French channel steamer *Sussex* on March 24. The German Government not only was forced by this incident to withdraw from its previously announced position on armed merchantmen, but also to abandon the war zone around Great Britain and Ireland. The distinctions which German diplomacy had endeavored to build up and which Bethmann-Hollweg was hopeful of maintaining—between the war zone and the high seas, between armed and unarmed vessels, between freighters and liners—were all wiped out by the strong American protest, the *Sussex* ultimatum of April 18. Germany's retreat was conditional, however; complete freedom of action was reserved in event that the American Government failed to force Britain to observe "the rules of international law universally recognized before the war."

How shall we interpret this yielding of the German Government? The simple fact was that the skepticism of the civilians over the efficacy of unrestricted submarine warfare had been reinforced by the small number of submarines on hand. This was a temporary situation. The pace of the submarine building program was being rapidly increased. Whereas on April 1, 1916, there were available 36 submarines of all types, there were 54 on

July 1 and 85 on December 20 of that year.[8] An additional consideration which for a time helped to bolster
Bethmann and the Foreign Office was the opportunity
which a delay gave for obtaining a negotiated settlement favorable to Germany. To this end the German
ambassador in Washington, Count von Bernstorff, was
instructed to urge Wilson to take the initiative in proposing peace negotiations; and ultimately on December 12, 1916, the German Government itself proposed
peace talks.

Meanwhile, the summer did not pass without the
naval high command again opening the question of
unrestricted submarine warfare. The whole matter was
reconsidered at a meeting at Pless, the headquarters of
the Supreme High Command of the Army, on August
31. On this occasion the Army came to the support of
Bethmann-Hollweg, but for none of the reasons which
the latter had so often reiterated. Field Marshal Paul
von Hindenburg declared that "We would shout with
joy if we could begin the U-boat war immediately."
But because of the entrance of Rumania into the war
on August 27, the Army's manpower at the moment was
fully committed. Unrestricted submarine warfare would
involve "the possibility of new declarations of war and
of landings in Holland and Denmark," and Hindenburg concluded that the decision would have to be
postponed until the Rumanian situation had been
brought under control. The Army could then spare
the divisions which would be required on the Dutch

and Danish borders to restrain those countries from declaring war and inviting Allied landings.

Bethmann summed up the consensus of the conference by saying that "in view of the present war situation, we have decided that the decision must be put off until later, since Field Marshal von Hindenburg has stated that he will have to await the development of the Roumanian campaign before a definite policy can be adopted with regard to the question." [9] Weakening before the relentless pressure to which he was subjected, Bethmann was conceding that the decision would ultimately turn on military rather than political considerations. This marked the beginning of his capitulation.

The German Navy was no more content to accept postponement for the military reasons advanced by Hindenburg and General Erich Ludendorff than for the political reasons advanced earlier by Bethmann-Hollweg. After the August conference, the Navy felt that in the end the chancellor would have to give in to the field marshal if the latter took a firm stand, and so concentrated its fire on the Army. Captain von Bülow, a naval representative at Army General Headquarters, sought to persuade Ludendorff early in September that danger from Holland and Denmark was a "phantom." Ludendorff did not agree. The submarine war, he said, should not begin before the army, after settling the Rumanian problem, was "firmly on its feet." But except for this reservation he assured Bülow that the Navy could consider it as "settled" that the Supreme High Command of the Army was in favor of the U-boat war. Ludendorff disclosed that he had been uneasy in the spring over the small number of submarines then available; now, however, he felt assured on this point and "believed in success." For the moment Ludendorff could do nothing more than hope that the military situation might be in hand by the beginning of October—although he thought this unlikely because the Austrians were "like a sieve" ("whatever you poured in from above ran out again from below").[10]

By December the Rumanian Army was in rout. Bucharest fell on December 7. From the military point of view the way was now open for submarine warfare. The German peace note dispatched on the twelfth was a momentary cause of delay, for to proceed with ruthless U-boat war would have been awkward until the Allies had made known their response. The peace overture by Wilson on December 18 further complicated the situation. But there was no expectation in Army and Navy circles that diplomacy could produce a satisfactory result; the armed services were united in their determination to unleash the submarine, which the Navy predicted would force surrender of England by July 1, 1917.

Ludendorff, pointing out that the British Prime Minister, David Lloyd George, had rejected the German peace proposal, pressed the chancellor on December 20: "the U-boat war should now be launched with the greatest vigor." [11] In conversation with a representative of the Foreign Office at Pless on December 22, Ludendorff announced that Field Marshal von Hindenburg "would no longer be able to shoulder the responsibility of the campaign" should the government not agree to a ruthless submarine campaign.[12] On the twenty-third Hindenburg himself wired the chancellor.

England will not be overthrown by the mere fact of torpedoing armed enemy merchant ships. More severe measures must be attempted in order to break England's will. . . . Whether America is entitled to certain considerations, must be made a matter of proof. The efficiency of the U-boat war must not be permitted to be interfered with to any definite extent by reason of this. I emphatically reserve my position with regard to this matter.[13]

Finally on January 8, 1917, Hindenburg sent a virtual ultimatum to Bethmann. The military situation, he declared, was such that unrestricted U-boat warfare could begin on the first of February and for that very reason should so begin. The decision was taken at Pless on the following day. Bethmann, concurring, remarked that "of course, if success beckons, we must follow." [14]

During this final phase Bethmann-Hollweg had fought a delaying action. The one step which he was freely disposed to take, namely, to declare the armed merchantman subject to unannounced attack, was not open to him until his and the President's peace notes had run their course. On January 10 Bernstorff, in accordance with instructions, transmitted to the American Department of State a note plainly intimating that the German Government would soon act on the assumption of the offensive intention of the armed merchantman. But by then the decision in favor of unrestricted submarine warfare had already been taken, and actually there was no longer room for German diplomacy to maneuver.

II

An interesting question to which the foregoing account gives rise is whether unrestricted submarine warfare could have been forestalled by a different and conceivably more "correct" application of the rules of neutrality by the United States. Was there a point at which the controversy over use of the Atlantic seaways could have been stabilized within the frame of the accepted rules of maritime warfare?

The American position was open to serious question both in regard to the United States Government's failure to prohibit American citizens from traveling on belligerent merchantmen, and its refusal to classify the armed merchantman as a vessel of war. Despite the fact that in early 1916 President Wilson had rigidly insisted on what he deemed the letter of the law on these matters, he was not wholly convinced of the correctness of his policy. By January 1917 his doubts had mounted. We have seen in the preceding chapter his refusal to respond to Lansing's urgings that diplo-

matic relations be broken off over the recurrent sinkings; Wilson was reported to have said that he "did not
believe the people of the United States were willing
to go to war because a few Americans had been
killed." He wavered also at this time in regard to the
American position on the armed merchantman.

The German note of January 10, 1917, presented in
strong terms the legal case against the armed merchantman, and heightened the expectation in Washington that German submarines soon would treat such
vessels as warships.[15] There was further confirmation
in a cable of the twenty-first from Ambassador Gerard
in Berlin, which stated that in spite of assurances from
members of the German Government he believed Germany would "resume reckless submarine warfare by
way of attacks without notice on armed merchant
vessels." Gerard thought that the German Government
was endeavoring to force the United States to consent,
tacitly or openly, to such a policy.[16]

This cable prompted Wilson to inquire of Lansing
whether the latter had "come to any fixed conclusions
. . . as to whether the recent practices of the British
in regard to the arming of their merchantmen force
upon us an alteration of our own position in that
matter." [17] Lansing had been pondering the perplexi-
ties of the problem and had already stated to the
President on January 17 that the United States could
delay no longer in "determining upon a very definite
policy." The difficulty, he declared, was that there were

"reasonable arguments on both sides of the question which lead to conclusions utterly irreconcilable." He was unable to find any "common ground for compromise," even though he was "taking up the question from the politic as well as the legal point of view." [18]

The matter was still hanging fire on the thirty-first when Wilson raised it again with Lansing, saying that it was "quite the most puzzling and difficult question we have had to deal with." He believed that the British were "going beyond the spirit, at any rate, of the principles hitherto settled in regard to this matter and that the method in which their ship captains are instructed to use their guns has in many instances gone beyond what could legitimately be called defense." Wilson was dissatisfied with the technical tests of offensive armament. He said it was not so much a question of the caliber of the guns and their location on the vessel as "whether their guns have been *used* only for defense." Lansing in reply transmitted to the President a memorandum clearly the product of the "politic" considerations of which he had spoken earlier. Lansing did not modify in any essential respect the highly legalistic position to which he had reverted after his abortive note of January 18, 1916. Handing the memorandum back to Lansing, the President indicated that he doubted its soundness.[19] But by this time, the evening of January 31, Bernstorff had brought the news of unrestricted submarine warfare. The issue of the armed merchantman had become academic; beginning on February 1, 1917, not only unarmed but even neutral vessels, found in English waters, were to be subject to unannounced attack.

Wilson's long vacillation over the question of the armed merchantman invites speculation as to whether American entry into the war would have followed had the German Government departed from its promise of satisfactory behavior—the so-called *Sussex* pledge of May 4, 1916—only to the extent of attacking armed merchantmen. But to speculate on this point would be to little avail. The American ultimatum at the time of the *Sussex* affair left Berlin no choice but to believe that American action, regardless of the degree of intensified submarine warfare, would be to break diplomatic relations; to this Wilson was publicly committed.

It is relevant, however, to inquire whether an opportunity had existed in the spring of 1916, before the freezing effect of the *Sussex* notes, for American policy to avert excesses by the submarine.[20] Could an American policy, cut to the pattern suggested by Bethmann-Hollweg in his memorandum of February 29, have enabled the German chancellor to win a permanent victory over his Army and Navy? This is, of course, one of the imponderables of German-American relations in the first World War, but there is reason for believing that the course of American policy was not the controlling factor in the chancellor's ultimate capitulation to the Supreme Command.

We have seen that Bethmann opposed the view that German policy should at any cost be aimed at total victory. Nevertheless, although entertaining the possibility of a negotiated peace, he neglected to produce war aims lending themselves to such a purpose. Whatever his private thoughts, his public utterances gave aid and comfort to the German annexationists.[21] We shall return again to Bethmann's losing battle with the extremists in Germany. It is enough at present to note the character of the war itself as it had developed by 1916. By the time of Verdun and the Somme, the war was no longer a quarrel over immediate and tangible objectives, but a gigantic struggle for power— indeed, for survival—defying any resolution short of a fight to the finish. In view of these circumstances it is difficult to see how the United States, even if American application of the rules of maritime warfare had been above legal reproach and in every respect skillful, could have deflected the eventual assault on its own commerce.

The German decision for ruthless submarine warfare sprang from both desperation and hope, and the latter ingredient is particularly striking and significant. Its presence is readily apparent in an exhaustive analysis of submarine policy prepared by the chief of the admiralty staff, von Holtzendorff, and transmitted to Hindenburg on December 22, 1916. This document argued that the limited cargo space available to Britain, together with the poor harvests in Canada and the United States in the previous summer, had placed "a very unique opportunity" in the hands of Germany, of which she dare not fail to take advantage. It was calculated that Great Britain by February 1917 would have to begin to draw on Argentina and Australia for foodstuffs and provender, which owing to the relatively greater distances would divert 720,000 tons of cargo space. If in these straitened circumstances England were to be hit by unrestricted submarine warfare, she would within a period of five months, prior to the new harvests in America, be reduced to starvation. And not only would there be a crisis in breadstuffs. The submarine would also cut off the supply of fats from Denmark and Holland, of metal from Spain, and of metal and wood from Scandinavia. Lack of wood would cause a decline of coal production, which in turn would affect production of iron, steel, and munitions. Still another consequence was mentioned, but without emphasis and only incidentally. Unrestricted submarine warfare would afford the opportunity "so long desired" to take effective steps against Britain's importation of munitions from neutrals, "and to that extent ease the burdens of the army."

These results could be accomplished only if the submarine were used without any restriction whatsoever. A limited use of the submarine, "even if all armed vessels were to be considered as open to attack," would fall short by fifty per cent of accomplishing the requisite amount of damage. On the other hand, ruth-

less submarine warfare against neutral and enemy shipping alike would in five months' time reduce British
trade by thirty-nine per cent (this calculation being
based on the assumption that 600,000 tons of shipping
per month would be destroyed outright, and that at
least two-fifths of the neutral ships would be fright-
ened away).

It was anticipated that the bottleneck of cargo space
would prevent American goods, men, and money from
affecting the actual fighting. Thus the only question
as regards America which need be considered was her
attitude toward "the question of concluding peace—
the peace for which England would be forced to sue."
Holtzendorff was of the opinion that the United States,
eager to resume normal commercial relations, would
not hinder a peace settlement.

Admiral von Holtzendorff asserted that Germany's
peace move of December 12 showed that unrestricted
submarine warfare could not fairly be interpreted "as
the preliminary step of a war of conquest." Nevertheless
it is clear that the motive behind the policy was something more than extraction of Germany from the exigencies of the immediate situation. "If it is true,"
Holtzendorff went on to say, "that England considers
the maintenance of her dominion of the seas as a condition of her existence, we cannot do otherwise than
attack this claim. To bring this about must be said to
be our first and foremost war aim. . . . Germany is not
in a position to drop the sword and still admit that Eng-

land can wield the overlordship of the sea." The policy of a first-class German Navy, initiated in 1897 by the Kaiser and Admiral von Tirpitz, "was not the expression of an arbitrary demand," but "justifiable recognition of the fact that matters were running their course according to historical precedent." Having once broken down English dominion of the seas, "we shall have fought a victorious fight. There is no middle course between this and Germany's ruin." [22]

It is worthy of note that this major effort at persuasion did not suffice to put civilian doubts at rest. The secretary of state for the interior, Karl von Helfferich, to whom Bethmann-Hollweg referred the Admiralty document for analysis, submitted an opinion that "paradoxical as it sounds, it is not altogether impossible . . . that, compared with the limited U-boat war on commerce, the unrestricted U-boat war would not in the last analysis, have a harmful effect upon the supplying of England with breadstuffs, but would rather operate in favor of such supply." Helfferich pointed out that limited submarine warfare might actually have a greater intimidating effect on neutral commerce than would unrestricted warfare, because the latter would transform the neutral into a belligerent and thus "the voyage to England would no longer mean a mere act of commerce . . . but a war move in connection with which resulting losses and deaths would play no particular part." He also suggested that once in the war America would be "just as much interested in England's being victorious as she would be in a cause exclusively her own" and would be prepared to make great sacrifices to that end, such as the restriction of "its own consumption of cereals in favor of England." [23] This remarkably far-seeing analysis reached Bethmann-Hollweg at Pless on the very day, January 9, 1917, that the chancellor finally gave in to the Army and Navy demand for unrestricted submarine warfare.

A record of less intractability on the part of the American Government would, of course, have strengthened Bethmann-Hollweg's hand. Yet it is highly doubtful whether in the end unrestricted submarine warfare could have been averted. Only if the United States, by drastic pressure on the British blockade, could have started a substantial flow of trade with Germany, would the German military and naval authorities have been disposed to neglect the opportunities which they believed the submarine afforded. The German Government would have had to consider whether it was deriving benefits equivalent to those anticipated from unrestricted submarine warfare.[24] But such a spectacular result could not have been achieved within the confines of the customary rules of maritime warfare, and indeed its accomplishment would have required nothing short of American collaboration with Germany to deprive Britain of the advantages of her sea power.

And this would have had the further effect of assisting the German Navy in its objective of permanently overthrowing Britain's historic maritime position.

The elaborate system of rules purporting to regulate maritime warfare fostered a belief that there existed a prearranged way by which the United States might trade with belligerents without undue complications. But the rules could not cancel out, indeed had never been designed to cancel out, the political impact of neutral trade; and the influence of American commerce on the course of the war was so great that no belligerent, merely in deference to law, could ignore it. "Freedom of the seas" could have served as a buffer for the United States only in a war of limited objectives, in which the belligerents sought to avoid the irreconcilable extremes of total war.

FOUR

The Defense of Trade

IT IS a relatively simple matter to understand
the purpose of Germany's submarine policy.
In part it was supplementary to the fighting on land,
designed to hamper the supply of Allied armies. It
had also a second objective: so decisive a defeat of
Great Britain as to end her traditional control of the
seas. The latter objective was uppermost in the decision for waging submarine warfare without restriction. These two aspects of German policy—one relating to land and the other to sea power—were not
inherently antagonistic. The reservations entertained
in 1916 by Bethmann-Hollweg and his civilian colleagues were based on the feeling that to challenge
British maritime supremacy attempted too much, placing Germany in danger of losing all.

The factors determining American policy in relation
to the submarine are not so clear. Obscurity arose in
part from the fact that the law of neutrality, subject
to the pressures of total war, was incapable of reconcil-

ing neutral and belligerent interests, and the fiasco in 1914–17 of the traditional rules of maritime warfare explains in some measure at least why the United States arrived at an impasse with Germany. But pressure upon American rights came from the British as well as the German side. During the two and one-half years preceding the rupture in German-American relations, Great Britain had imposed an ever-tightening control over the flow of neutral commerce. As early as March 1915 a British Order in Council not only placed trade to and from Germany under penalty of confiscation, but subjected to close supervision the trade of the outside world with neutrals bordering on Germany.[1] The American Government protested that the measure was "a practical assertion of unlimited belligerent rights over neutral commerce within the whole European area, and an almost unqualified denial of the sovereign rights of the nations now at peace."[2] Why, notwithstanding, did ominous crises in Anglo-American relations fail to develop? Or considering that both Great Britain and Germany waged war on the basis of military necessity in disregard of the rules of maritime warfare, why did not the United States retreat before a world at war? This latter query is particularly pertinent because such a withdrawal was precisely the object of the so-called neutrality legislation enacted from 1935 to 1939.

During the first World War the American bias in favor of Great Britain and against Germany was from the outset very great. The reasons for this bias were several—some of them, as we have seen, going back into the nineteenth century, a period in which American–British relations were cast in a mold of accommodation. With the beginning of the World War the Germans further prejudiced their case by use of the submarine. And meanwhile, American fortunes were being ever more strongly tied to Great Britain by a rapidly developing wartime trade. This trade quickly swelled to such proportions that American domestic prosperity virtually depended upon it. It was perhaps only to be expected, therefore, that a popular postwar explanation of American involvement in the first World War, an explanation most widely accepted during the 1930's, was that American policy toward Europe in 1914–17—friendship toward Britain, enmity toward Germany—was a direct result of the economic situation.

I

At the simplest level, publicists in the 1930's ascribed American participation in the first World War to the influence of munitions makers. Investigations in the United States and elsewhere, together with numerous books and articles, revealed questionable practices of munitions makers in conducting their business. Much evidence was adduced that these manufacturers artificially stimulated markets abroad, and within their respective countries urged armament expenditures and a belligerent foreign policy. It was an unsavory picture which lent itself to exaggerated conclusions about self-seeking munitions makers as a cause of war.

But this argument is inapplicable to American participation in the first World War. As Wilson's secretary of war, Newton D. Baker, wrote during the thirties, it was "easy to demonstrate that the condition of cotton farmers . . . was infinitely more a subject of concern and anxiety on the part of the Government . . . than the interest or welfare of the munitions makers." In 1914, moreover, "there was no munitions industry in the United States . . . and by 1917 the industry in that field which had been created here, either by or on behalf of the Allied nations, was merely a part of America's industrial plant diverted from peacetime to wartime production." The charge against munitions makers was "a singular selection of a particular group out of a much larger and quite indiscriminate mass." [3]

Rather than searching for direct influence by munitions makers on the government, it is more germane to ask whether the volume of munitions shipped by the United States to the Allies played an important role in prompting Germany to decide for unrestricted submarine warfare.

The wartime trade of the United States with England, France, Italy, Russia, and Canada represented an increase of 184 per cent, from a total of $3,445,000,000 for the period 1911–13 (these are fiscal years ending June 30) to $9,796,000,000 for the comparable three-

year period 1915–17.[4] Difficulty of definition makes it
hard to determine the proportion of this latter amount
represented by munitions. From June 30, 1914, to June
30, 1917, the United States shipped $506,674,000 worth
of gunpowder and $665,237,000 in other explosives.[5]
Firearms were sent in the amount of $113,229,000;
cartridges, $104,022,000; and barbed wire, $45,104,000.
Metals, in various states of semi-manufacture, were
shipped: zinc, $98,302,000; steel, $182,577,000; brass,
$553,625,000; and copper, $551,779,000. In all these
instances (except copper, where the increase was 277
per cent) the increase over the three-year period
1911–13 was so extreme as to indicate that before the
war the countries in question imported these com-
modities from the United States in only negligible
quantities.

The sum representing "essential war materials"
which was arrived at in connection with the Senate
investigation of the munitions industry was $2,167,-
000,000, which would be 23 per cent of the United
States's trade with the designated countries. The remainder of the trade was only indirectly related to
actual battle, but it was no less important to the
Allied war economy. Wheat was shipped in the amount
of $581,509,000, an increase of 683 per cent; wheat
flour, $112,068,000, a 205 per cent increase; sugar,
$130,533,000, 3,883 per cent; and meat, $469,863,867,
240 per cent.[6]

There was indeed bitter resentment in Germany

over the shipment of munitions by the United States to the Allies, evidence of which occurred again and again in the dispatches of the American ambassador.[7] In April 1915 Germany formally protested such shipments, alleging that "an entirely new industry" which had hardly existed in the United States before the war was being created, and that despite the theoretical willingness of this industry to supply Germany it was "actually delivering goods only to the enemies of Germany."[8] Nonetheless our examination in the foregoing chapter of Germany's decision for unrestricted submarine warfare does not suggest that this very natural resentment was the controlling factor in Germany's action; in fact, an absence of munitions in the American trade with the Allies could hardly have altered the chain of circumstances leading to the impasse over the submarine. We have seen that the British wheat supply and the tonnage available to the British trade were primary objects of German attack. Germany was striking at the whole British economy and aiming at total victory, just as Britain through the blockade was striking at the whole German economy and was likewise unreceptive to a negotiated peace. American trade was of the utmost usefulness to the Allies, but its significance did not turn solely on munitions; it attached just as much to the nonmilitary content of the trade.

Actually the portion of the hearings which the so-called Nye Committee, the Special Congressional Com-

mittee Investigating the Munitions Industry, devoted
to American entrance into the war did not, despite
the committee's appellation, pin the blame on munitions makers so much as upon bankers. Indeed, the
importance of finance in ensuring in 1914–17 the flow
of American goods to the Allies cannot be questioned,
and this aspect of America's relation to the war calls
for a close examination.

The bulk of American shipments was paid for by
the Allies through the sizable balance which the United
States owed Great Britain on the outbreak of the war;
through wartime export of goods, services, and gold to
the United States; and through sale of securities in
the American financial market. By the time the United
States entered the war, however, the British, French,
Russian, and Italian Governments owed private American investors $2,260,827,000.[9] Leaving out of account
Canadian purchases, which to April 1917 had required
for war purposes only $120,000,000 in credit, this
means that 27 per cent of the American exports to the
Allied countries was financed by publicly issued bonds
and other forms of credit in the United States.

Reliance by the belligerents on American money was
a prospect which the Wilson Administration had
frowned upon at the beginning of the war. When in
August 1914 J. P. Morgan and Company had inquired
whether the State Department would object to the
making of private loans to belligerents, the reply had
been that such loans would be "inconsistent with the

true spirit of neutrality." [10] Before stating this position
Bryan had presented the problem to Wilson, arguing
that "money is the worst form of all contrabands because it commands everything else," that expressions
of sympathy for one side or the other would be intensified "if each group was pecuniarily interested in
the success of the nation to whom its members had
loaned money," and that the "powerful financial interests . . . would be tempted to use their influence
through the newspapers to support the interests of
the government to which they had loaned because the
value of the security would be affected by the result
of the war." Yet at this stage Bryan's concluding observation was alone decisive: "The floating of these
loans would absorb the loanable funds and might
affect our ability to borrow." [11]

The Government's objection to loans was not based
on statutory authority. Nevertheless the eventual abandonment of the policy did not result from its extra-
legal character. To be viable, such a financial restriction required a willingness by the various elements
in the American economy to accept a falling off of
export business. Ultimately the restriction succumbed
to an irresistible combination of forces: commercial
need and American sympathy for the Allied cause.

The financial ban was modified as early as October
1914 when the State Department made a distinction
between loans and short-term credits, thus permitting
an extension of $10,000,000 in credit to the French

Government by the National City Bank of New York.[12]
By mid-1915 an additional $100,000,000 of private
funds had been made available in one form or another
to the French and Russian Governments.[13] The question of a large public loan, which could not be indefinitely avoided, became acute in August 1915 when
sterling exchange, which until then had been pegged
by purchases of J. P. Morgan and Company, began
to decline in value.[14] If dollars could not be borrowed,
Great Britain would have to ship gold in large quantities, a hazardous operation in wartime. A wholesale
transfer of the metal would also have had undesirable monetary repercussions both in England and the
United States. Another alternative, but one which the
British Government was understandably reluctant to
adopt, was the large-scale liquidation of British-owned
securities.

Writing to Wilson in August 1915, Secretary of the
Treasury William G. McAdoo said that it was "imperative for England to establish a large credit in
this country." In his opinion the position taken in
August 1914 was "most illogical and inconsistent. We
approve and encourage sales of supplies to England
and others but we disapprove the creation by them of
credit balances here to finance their lawful and welcome purchases. . . . To maintain our prosperity we
must finance it. Otherwise it may stop and that would
be disastrous." Contrasting the nation's credit resources
with those of a year earlier, he said that they were

"simply marvellous now. They are easily 5 to 6 billion dollars." [15] Lansing wrote to the President in similar vein on September 6. Pointing out that American exports in 1915 would exceed imports by an estimated two and a half billion dollars, he said that the European countries must find the dollars to pay for this excess of purchases or "they will have to stop buying and our present export trade will shrink proportionately. The result would be restriction of output, industrial depression, idle capital and idle labor, numerous failures, financial demoralization, and general unrest and suffering among the laboring classes." Observing that "we have more money than we can use," Lansing felt that "the practical reasons for discouraging loans have largely disappeared." Moreover, he believed that "popular sympathy has become crystallized in favor of one or another of the belligerents to such an extent that the purchase of bonds would in no way increase the bitterness of partisanship." [16] The upshot was that the earlier policy was now discarded. In October 1915 a joint Anglo-French loan of $500,000,000 was floated.

Recognizing that general commercial considerations rather than the narrow financial interests of bankers forced the change in Administration policy, one must still ask whether the loans, having been made, created a stake in Allied victory which then proceeded to determine governmental policy. That such a connection existed was widely believed by popular and congressional opinion in the thirties. A typical assertion was that of Senator Gerald Nye himself that "When Americans went into the fray they little thought that they were . . . fighting to save the skins of American bankers who had bet too boldly on the outcome of the war and had two billions of dollars of loans to the Allies in jeopardy." [17]

This assumption is actually more revealing of the postwar intellectual climate than it is of the factors leading to American entrance into war in 1917. Sympathy for the Allied cause among leading New York bankers—such as J. P. Morgan, who had long operated London and Paris offices—greatly facilitated the financial accommodation of the Allies. Rather than following as a consequence, partisanship preceded the making of the loans. Still more to the point is the fact that the diplomatic record, which made it virtually impossible for the United States to pull back in 1917, had already been substantially completed in the autumn of 1915; by that time the Wilson Administration had set its course on the question of neutral rights. The final crystallization of the American policy of neutrality in the first four months of 1916 cannot reasonably be attributed to anxiety over the safety of Allied loans, which had begun to be sizable only in the autumn of 1915.

It is also necessary to point out that the greater part of the Allied indebtedness at the time of American entry into the war was secured with American, other neutral, and British imperial (chiefly Canadian) collateral. In the instance of the three United Kingdom loans totaling $800,000,000 (negotiated between September 1916 and February 1917), the value of the collateral, duly advertised to the investing public, actually amounted to 120 per cent of the face value of the bonds.[18] Unsecured indebtedness at the time of the American declaration of war stood at $855,000,000. The Anglo-French loan of October 1915, which was publicly issued, accounted for $500,000,000 of this total; and the remainder was mainly in the form of acceptances and other bank credits.[19] Even as regards the unsecured obligations of the Allied Governments, the hypothesis that the bankers and their clients were anxious over their investments has not been supported with evidence.[20] An important negative test of the prevailing attitude in the United States is the absence of any movement to escape loss by selling Allied bonds in the market. Finally, there has been only supposition, without actual demonstration, that Administration officials and congressmen felt themselves under pressure to assure the collectibility of the loans.

II

Rejecting these explanations of American involvement which blame the cupidity or anxiety of particular interest groups, such as the bankers or munitions makers, we still must examine the proposition, which is implied generally in the economic interpretation, that the response of the American economy as a whole to the golden opportunity for trade with the Allies was the basic factor in the break with Germany.

It is obvious that the swollen trade with the Allies, representing vitally important aid purchased with cash and loans, far exceeded the normal export requirements of the American economy. The resulting prosperity was pleasing to the American Government, but the direction, content, and volume of the trade was not the result of any positive policy adopted in Washington. For all the record shows, the Administration was merely acquiescing in the operations of the free market and the profit motive. Indeed, the economic argument is essentially that a shortsighted yielding to the promptings of commercial gain resulted in the United States becoming a base of supplies for the Allies, thus compromising German-American relations. By permitting the decisions of the market place to prevail, the American Government, it is contended, allowed the nation to drift into dangerous waters.

This argument can be made still more precise. Germany was dissatisfied not only because of the large trade which the Allies enjoyed with the United States, but also because American neutrality had for Germany herself no economic value. German-American trade declined to an insignificant trickle, removing any possibility of an economic deterrent to unleashing the submarine. Trade with the Allies, the argument runs, took on such large and profitable proportions that the American defense of neutral rights against the arbitrary encroachments of the Allies became progressively weaker. Moreover, after the economy had become abnormally dependent on Allied markets, any attempt to correct the imbalance became impractical. Economic retaliation against England's flagrant violation of the rules of blockade, search and seizure, and contraband would not have been feasible; such measures would have had serious repercussions, stemming not alone from the American action, but also from retaliatory acts which Great Britain was in a position to apply with great effect.[21]

In September 1916 when resentment against the British black list of German-influenced firms and against British censorship of mail was at a high pitch, Congress at the Administration's request passed legislation giving the President discretionary power to discriminate in specified ways against belligerents who were interfering with American commerce. Exploring the practicality of employing the authorized measures, the State Department requested an opinion from the Commerce Department on what could be done "that would be effective and, at the same time, least injurious to this country." The latter department, on the basis of a closely reasoned analysis, concluded that "reprisals . . . afford no assurance of success, and threaten even the present basis of neutral commerce." It was pointed out in the supporting argument that in the belligerent countries, war for the moment is supreme; commercial considerations take a subordinate place. We can attack their commerce but our own commerce will unavoidably suffer in consequence even more than it has suffered from the restriction placed on it by the countries at war. There is little likelihood by these means of obtaining the withdrawal of the objectionable regulations. Counterreprisals would be almost inevitable. . . . At present, rubber, wool, jute, tin, plumbago, and certain other raw products essential to our industries are under export prohibition in Great Britain and in the various colonies and self-governing dominions which are the principal source of supply. Shipments of these articles have been continuously imported into the United States from British countries, however, under special agreements between the British Government and associations of leading importers of the various products. It is obvious that by a termination of these agreements, Great Britain could paralyze many of our industries.

The memorandum stated that an embargo on munitions would be the most effective measure, but that compared with the earlier period its impact would be dulled because additional factories in Britain had since been converted into munitions plants. Indeed, an embargo "might, in practice, effect the cancellation of a contract more highly regarded by the American concern than by the British Government." [22]

In short, the American Government permitted the Allies to monopolize the American market as a base of supplies. This monopoly not only invited German attack but made it difficult for the United States, whose prosperity had become in part dependent on a continuance of the Allied trade, to forestall it. This is the strongest form in which the economic argument can be put. It errs in viewing the clash between the United States and Germany as a result solely of the complications of wartime trade, but it has the merit of stating the case without resort to scapegoats. Indeed, it permits recognition of the fact that more than a purely private interest was involved in America's trade with warring Europe. A great war must inevitably affect the economy of neutral nations. The doctrine of freedom of the seas, therefore, cannot be dismissed as synonymous with the freedom of "hucksters" to make money.[23] It is related to a real national interest which a government can sacrifice but not deny. It presents a problem, moreover, which is not eliminated by the mere fact of substituting governmental authority for the private decisions of the market place.

When the hard realities of the economic problem with which the United States was confronted in the first World War are considered, the so-called neutrality legislation of the 1930's, which denied to American citizens the traditional benefits of freedom of the seas, seems unrealistic.[24] Yet if the legislation was unduly stringent in limiting the economic transactions and freedom of movement of American citizens in time of war, it erred on the right rather than the wrong side. It precluded any danger in the second World War of American policy being shaped, whether in reality or merely in appearance, by considerations of trade and travel incidental to the war itself.[25] Based on the supposition that trade was the dominant strand in our relations with Europe, the legislation, however, failed to measure up to the requirements of the time. Actually the United States could not insulate itself from European turmoil merely by foregoing commercial relations with belligerents. Within a month after outbreak of the second World War the embargo on sale of munitions to belligerents was repealed. Subsequently the ban on arming American merchantmen was lifted. Then the neutrality legislation was completely bypassed by adoption of Lend-Lease in March 1941 and the special naval measures taken that summer and autumn to protect shipments to Britain. None of these important moves by the Roosevelt Administration was made for commercial reasons.

American policy in the interwar years responded not to current events as they unfolded but to certain theories explaining our involvement in the first World War. Of course, the fact that the legislation of the thirties failed to accomplish its purpose does not argue against the interpretation of the past on which it was based. It may be assumed, however, that the first experience was sufficiently similar to the second to have consti-

tuted fair warning, and that our own perverse misread-
ing of the past assisted fate in preparing a repetition
of the ordeal.

It has been shown that wartime trade confronted the
Wilson Administration with the necessity of making
various legal and economic decisions. But a political
decision, however disguised, was also required, for
the problem of trade was basically more political than
it was legal or economic. Germany was vastly disturbed that neutral trade went not to the Central
Powers but to Great Britain and the other Allies.[26]
The various neutral governments by legal and economic measures could modify the one-sided trade
situation in its superficial aspects, but they could
accomplish no fundamental change without making a
political decision involving their relations with Britain.
British control of the seas and of the products of a
vast non-European area, colonial and otherwise—a control which had been exercised for decades and even
centuries—was at the bottom of Germany's quarrel
with Great Britain. Nothing short of virtual reversal
of the existing trade situation, which would have
denied trade to the Allies and made it available to
Germany, would have been considered by her military
and naval officials as an acceptable reason for curbing
the submarine. It was their highest objective to achieve
a disposition of sea power for the future which would
assure precisely this result, toward which German

naval policy since the turn of the century had in fact been directed.

If, by breaching the British blockade, the United States could have achieved a major shift in the direction of neutral trade, Germany would undoubtedly have abstained from ruthless assault on world shipping, for she would then have accomplished her end through virtual alliance with the United States. But, unlike Germany, the United States was not rebellious against Britain's predominant position. The argument that this showed subservience to Great Britain, so long as American prosperity was not endangered, does not cover the whole ground. It sprang mainly from the fact that the United States saw no threat to its vital interests in Britain's position and, moreover, shrank from the prospect of Germany supplanting British power. This essential difference between American and German attitudes toward Great Britain underlay the progressive estrangement and eventual rupture of German-American relations.

In an effort to adjust itself to the European war, the United States at first sought refuge behind the traditional rules of maritime warfare. But these rules, at best heavily weighted in favor of already established sea power and sorely beset by technological innovations, provided poor protection from Germany's constant probings. Thus the United States was in an exposed position, highly vulnerable to German pressure even had the American attitude toward Germany been without bias. In the actual event the pro-Allied character of American policy lent to German actions, already based on military necessity, a certain moral justification which still further facilitated German disregard for the rules.

The bias in American policy was obscured for the United States—but not for Germany—by the fact that the economic and political aspects of American policy overlapped. The situation in 1914–17 was such that the demand for wartime trade could be indulged without running counter to the Administration's underlying judgment regarding the ultimate political consequences of the war's outcome. Thus economic and political factors reinforced each other and, even in retrospect, defy separation. This particular combination of factors was, however, purely fortuitous. If because of well-established commercial contacts and the existing disposition of sea power, our trade relations had been facilitated with the side not in political favor—as subsequently happened in the case of the Sino-Japanese war in 1937 and after—the American Government would have had to separate the strands of its policy. This would have been extremely difficult in 1914–17 for there was no basic agreement of American public opinion on what the national interest required.

Had the German Government confined its use of the submarine to unannounced attack on armed enemy merchantmen, as Bethmann-Hollweg had urged, the economic and political aspects of American policy would have been forced apart, clarifying perhaps the basis on which the American Government was acting. But Germany was so intent on overwhelming the British that she failed to exploit the confusion in American policy. Judged by its immediate consequences—war with the United States—German diplomacy was ill-advised. It had a long-range consequence, too, which was unfortunate. The postwar confusion over our actions in 1917 greatly facilitated the rise of Hitler during the fateful decade of the 1930's.

FIVE

The Defense of Principle

THE American Government in its relations with the belligerents made freedom of the seas the hallmark of its policy; but this was not merely because of interest in trade. Actually, the illegality of submarine warfare offered a less controversial basis of policy than would have an expressly formulated attitude toward British sea power. And there was still another element. Wilson believed that in upholding freedom of the seas, long identified with American foreign policy, the United States was maintaining the vitality of international law. The idea that security is a function of law and morality is deeply ingrained in our internal affairs. Indeed the safety and dignity of the members of our democratic society are dependent on such an underpinning. This conviction Wilson projected from the domestic to the international area of politics.

The anxieties of human nature and the tensions of history produce the insecurity which is characteristic of all societies. The overcoming of this condition is the highest goal of politics. There must be on the one hand freedom from fear, and there must also be ability to make demands with confidence. Unfortunately these two aspects of security are not necessarily complementary, for influence, the substance of security, may be used in offense as well as defense. Thus security is a condition which, by virtue of the tension between its passive and active elements, is never completely capable of attainment. The quest for security, which is continuous and destined always to failure in some degree, goes on in a variety of ways. Moral norms appear, giving rise to security through the internal restraint of conscience. Legal norms also serve as regulators of conduct, differing from moral norms in that their creation and execution is by a formally constituted authority: the resolution of conflict comes through external institutions of society. A third regulative device is diplomacy, which consists in negotiation between mutually recognized independent entities; if conducted, as it sometimes is, without reference to legal and moral standards, relations are strictly on the basis of a material *quid pro quo*. Finally, fighting effectiveness is a form of influence; through threat or actual use of physical force one can defend what he has or obtain what he wishes. The moral pattern is most efficient in personal relations. The legal pattern is best illustrated in the national community. International society best exemplifies fighting effectiveness. All these devices, however, and particularly diplomacy, are observable at every level of social organization.

These four regulators of human action are all means to ends. But concern for security may cause any one of them (with the exception of diplomacy, which is usually too prosaic to generate an emotional attitude toward itself) to become an end in itself. In the case of international politics this is especially true of fighting effectiveness. Like material wealth, military power is a generalized form of influence which has a variety of uses, and which therefore frequently becomes itself a goal of policy. In similar fashion the search for security can take the form of solicitude for legal and moral methods of resolving conflict. This was true of American policy in the first World War. Wilson, we shall see, sought to vindicate international law. For purposes of both comparison and contrast, we shall portray Bryan's trust in morality and Lansing's reliance on democracy as guarantees of security, together with Theodore Roosevelt's emphasis on fighting effectiveness.

I

In the early period of the war Wilson found sufficient defense for the position and influence of the United States in circumspect legal and moral conduct. Appealing for neutrality in August 1914, he declared that the war's effect upon Americans was entirely within their own choice, and he urged upon his fellow citizens "the sort of speech and conduct which will best safeguard the Nation against distress and disaster." Uppermost in his mind was the fact that "the people of the United States are drawn from many nations, and chiefly from the nations now at war"; it would be easy therefore "to excite passion and difficult to allay it." Looking to the qualities of the inner man for the stuff from which to fashion security, Wilson admonished the nation to be "impartial in thought as well as in action." The United States would thus show itself

a Nation fit beyond others to exhibit the fine poise of undisturbed judgment, the dignity of self-control, the efficiency of dispassionate action; a Nation that neither sits in judgment upon others nor is disturbed in her own counsels and which keeps herself fit and free to do what is honest and disinterested and truly serviceable for the peace of the world.[1]

That this was not mere rhetoric is borne out by Wilson's address on the State of the Union in December 1914. Already demands were being made for a large increase in the army and navy. These demands Wilson deprecated, and he again announced that America's only connection with the war was that of disinterested peacemaker.

No one who speaks counsel based on fact or drawn from a just and candid interpretation of realities can say that there is reason to fear that from any quarters our independence or the integrity of our territory is threatened. Dread of the power of any other nation we are incapable of. We are not jealous of rivalry in the fields of commerce or of any other peaceful achievement. We mean to live our own lives as we will; but we mean also to let live. . . . We are the champions of peace and concord. And we should be very jealous of this distinction which we have sought to earn. Just now we should be particularly jealous of it, because it is our dearest present hope that this character and reputation may presently, in God's providence, bring us an opportunity . . . to counsel and obtain peace in the world and reconciliation and a healing settlement of many a matter that has cooled and interrupted the friendship of nations.

Accordingly Wilson opposed any departure from the traditional military policies of the nation. We must depend "in the future as in the past, not upon a standing army, nor yet upon a reserve army, but upon a citizenry trained and accustomed to arms." It was consonant with this view to develop and strengthen the National Guard

not because the time or occasion specially calls for such measures, but because it should be our constant policy to make these provisions for our national peace and safety. . . . More than this, proposed at this time, permit me to say, would mean merely that we had lost our self-possession, that we had been thrown off our balance by a war with which we have nothing to do, whose causes can not touch us, whose very existence affords us opportunities of friendship and disinterested service which should make us ashamed of any thought of hostility or fearful preparation for trouble.[2]

The strength of the nation, Wilson said in this same address, resided in self-possession, and its influence in preserving "our ancient principles of action." This confidence in the efficacy of right attitudes and correct principle, characteristic also of Bryan's view of the requirements of security, never ceased to be a strong element in Wilson's thought and policy. When three days after the sinking of the *Lusitania* in May 1915, he said at Philadelphia that there "is such a thing as a man being too proud to fight," and that a nation could be "so right that it does not need to convince others by force that it is right," Wilson was expressing a cardinal principle of his political philosophy.[3]

Nevertheless, though relying on opinion as his vehicle of influence, Wilson was a spirited contender in the political arena. His object was to overcome his opponents by legal and moral appeals. Throughout his career he held to the principle that the "dynamics of leadership lie in persuasion."[4] The exposition of this philosophy occurs at innumerable places in his public addresses, of which the following passage is illustrative:

I have neighbors whose manners and opinions I would very much like to alter, but I entertain a suspicion that they would in turn very much like to alter mine . . . ; and upon reflection as I grow older I agree to live and let live. Birrell says somewhere, "The child beats its nurse and cries for the moon; the old man sips his gruel humbly and thanks God that no one beats him." I have not yet quite reached that point of humility, and I always accept, perhaps by some impulse of my native blood, the invitation to a fight; but . . . I hope I do not traduce my antagonists. I hope that I fight them with the purpose and intention of converting them. . . . It is not a case of knock down and drag out; it is a case of putting up the best reason why your side should survive. These franknesses of controversy . . . are the necessary conditions precedent to peace. Peace does not mean inaction. There may be infinite activity; there may be almost violent activity in the midst of peace.[5]

In so speaking Wilson supposed a democratic setting. In such a setting the issue of political power is not imperiously raised, for a leader can always go on talking to an electorate and, even in the minority, if his demands are sufficiently energetic and cogent, he can exercise influence in some degree.

It was Wilson's deepest impulse to behave in international affairs as he did in domestic politics. Yet by the fall of 1915 his attitude toward national defense had undergone a change. His address on the State of the Union in December 1915, a sharp contrast to that of the previous year, was largely devoted to the problem of preparedness.[6] His proposals included establishment of a merchant marine, provision for industrial preparedness, and adequate measures against saboteurs. He deplored the "hyphenated" American. He advised good relations with Latin America. And on the principle that the standing army should be no larger than required for "uses which are as necessary in times of peace as in times of war," he asked an increase from 108,008 men and officers to 141,843. Moreover, to make the country "ready to assert some part of its real power promptly and upon a larger scale," he called for a force of 400,000 "disciplined citizens" who as volunteers would train for short periods during each of three years and be subject to call at any time throughout an additional period of three years. As for the Navy, "our first and chief line of defense," Wilson proposed a five-year program of construction providing for ten battleships, six battle cruisers, ten scout cruisers, fifty destroyers, fifteen fleet submarines, and eighty-five coast submarines. Construction of destroyers, which presently were to play a major role in warfare against the submarine, was not given priority over the other categories. Manifestly the naval program was not directed specifically toward the great war then in progress. Nor was the army program geared directly to the European war. It was partly a response to the state of affairs in Mexico, and insofar as it was designed with reference to events in Europe it was based on calculations relating solely to requirements for the defense of the continental United States against invasion.[7]

Wilson was clear and emphatic as to what preparedness did not signify. "Conquest and domination are not in our reckoning, or agreeable to our principles." Democracies, he said, "do not seek or desire war." Their thought was of "individual liberty and of the free labor that supports life and the uncensored thought that quickens it." [8] A month earlier Wilson had said that the United States would "never again take another foot of territory by conquest." [9] Wilson failed, however, to say precisely what preparedness did signify, and he offered little of a concrete nature on which to base military and naval policy. Aside from home defense, there were three possible assumptions: defense of neutral rights in the immediate circumstances of the war; precaution against a postwar situation which might contain threats to the Monroe Doctrine; and finally, the most difficult but potentially most constructive purpose, support with armaments of a diplomatic intervention designed to compromise and shorten the war. That these objectives could all be served simultaneously was perhaps one reason Wilson failed to think and speak more analytically of the problem of military policy. But it must be pointed out that Wilson was not accustomed to relating the political and military aspects of foreign policy; indeed he found it uncongenial to do so.

In a memorandum given to the President in December 1915, before his address to Congress, Wilson's private secretary, Joseph P. Tumulty, had pointed out that some newspapers were asking, "Preparedness for what?"; and proceeding to suggest an answer, Tumulty predicted that "one of the inevitable results" of the war would be "new adjustments, new alignments, possibly new efforts for colonial expansion." Such developments might "eventually threaten our own sovereignty, our own rights and our own interests in this hemisphere." Tumulty believed that "in the minds of most Americans, preparedness involves the capacity to uphold the [Monroe] Doctrine." [10] To Colonel House also dangers in new circumstances at the end of the war were of concern. In August 1914 and repeatedly thereafter House advised Wilson to build up the armed forces. Speaking of the need for strengthening the army, House told Wilson in the autumn of 1914 that if the Allies were successful there would be no need for haste; but in the event of German victory and "we then began our preparations, it would be almost equivalent of a declaration of war," for Germany would know that the preparations were directed against her. In House's judgment it was best to start building the army without delay.[11]

But it was not merely postwar contingencies that House had in view. Above all preparedness was for him a means by which American influence could be brought to bear on immediate events. When in the summer of 1915 the *Lusitania* crisis was still acute, he wrote the President that "if war comes with Germany, it will be because of our unpreparedness and her belief that we are more or less impotent to do her harm." And preparedness could do something more than restrain Germany. House believed it capable of placing the United States "in a position almost to enforce peace." [12] He was not content to stand by passively while the war destroyed the civilization of Europe. He equally opposed the United States's gambling on the success of the Allies. In late 1915 he proposed an end to the war on terms favorable to the Allies, and with Wilson's approval went to Europe to develop his plan. The result was the House-Grey memorandum, which held out the possibility of active American intervention should Germany refuse to negotiate a peace on reasonable terms.

Many imponderables surrounded this agreement, but the fact that the military power of the United States was merely potential and not actual was alone enough to cause it to fail. There was no convincing deterrent to Germany's excessive ambition. By the same token the Allies lacked strong inducement to follow the American lead and refused, in fact, to invoke the agreement despite proddings from House and Wilson. After the war it was House's opinion that the American failure to arm "to the teeth" at the beginning of the war was "the big mistake," for both the Allies and Germans would then have heeded any threat of intervention, and "we might have intervened pretty much on our own terms." Since the Allies "were getting money, foodstuffs, and arms and keeping our ships from going into neutral ports," they "probably concluded, as Germany concluded, that we were doing about as much as we would do if in the war. . . . I do not believe the Allies thought we would make any such effort as we later did, and I believe they were as much surprised as the Germans." [13]

Wilson could not have failed to appreciate the advantages of preparedness as portrayed by House and Tumulty, but he was disposed nevertheless to justify the use of force primarily as a support for the legal and moral framework within which the United States and the belligerents were presumed to function. Thus in contrast to earlier utterances, we find Wilson taking cognizance of the external world. "We live in a world which we did not make, which we can not alter, which we can not think into a different condition from that which actually exists." [14] Yet in shifting from concern for the magnanimous and dispassionate character of American motives, Wilson's approach did not lose its subjective character. The new concern was for the motives of the belligerents as judged both by legal and moral standards. American security was viewed as dependent on bringing the action of the belligerents —and particularly German use of the submarine—into conformance with these standards.

The military and naval program which Wilson was proposing at the end of 1915 was endangered by adverse public opinion, and this Wilson sought to overcome in a series of speeches delivered in the Middle West in the latter part of January and first part of

February 1916.[15] The central theme of these addresses had already been set forth in the third *Lusitania* note, in which Wilson had warned the German Government that the United States could not

abate any essential or fundamental right of its people because of a mere alteration in circumstance. The rights of neutrals in time of war are based upon principle, not upon expediency, and the principles are immutable. It is the duty and obligation of belligerents to find a way to adapt the new circumstances to them.[16]

Hence the American Government was standing for something greater than its own immediate interest. In upholding legal principle, Wilson believed, America was doing more than maintaining national sovereignty and dignity. It also was serving the international community. This was the burden of all Wilson's preparedness speeches.

The President in his addresses early in 1916 was quite explicit in explaining how the illegal practices of the submarine affected America's large and permanent interests. Speaking in Chicago, he recalled the old saying that "the laws are silent in the presence of war." "And yet," he continued, "it has been assumed throughout this struggle that the great principles of international law . . . had not been suspended, and the United States, as the greatest and most powerful of the disengaged nations, has been looked to to hold high the standards which should govern the relationship of nations to each other." Later in this same address Wilson took the true measure of the difficulty of the task when he said that the United States was expected "to assert the principles of law in a world in which the principles of law have broken down." He saw an alleviating circumstance, however, since it was not "the technical principles of law" for which the United States was contending, "but the essential principles of right dealing and humanity as between nation and nation." [17]

There were other arguments in these preparedness addresses. Particularly notable are the references to the special interest of the United States in the Western Hemisphere. "We have made ourselves the guarantors of the rights of national sovereignty . . . on this side of the water," Wilson said at Topeka. "You would be ashamed, as I would be ashamed, to withdraw one inch from that handsome guarantee." Moreover, Wilson recognized that this was a matter which did not hinge on international law. "The Monroe doctrine is not part of international law." Not having "been formally accepted by any international agreement," it "merely rests upon the statement of the United States that if certain things happen she will do certain things." [18] Here was an object worthy of attention quite apart from the methods employed by Germany against her enemies. For the most part, however, Wilson gave the impression that German-American relations turned solely on the legality of Germany's behavior.

There was still another element in these speeches. As much as the American people loved peace, Wilson said, they loved even more "the principles upon which their political life is founded." He also spoke of Americans as "free men banded together to vindicate the rights of mankind." [19] Thus he introduced democracy as one of the issues at stake. But not until the War Message did it finally emerge as the dominant theme.

Shortly after the preparedness swing through the Middle West the crisis which had been gathering over the question of the armed merchantman came to a climax. It involved not only the relations of the American Government with the belligerents but also Wilson's relations with Congress. We have taken note of Wilson's remarkable letter of February 24, 1916, to Senator Stone, the import of which was that the United States would be justified in going to war if American lives were lost as the result of unannounced German attack on Allied merchantmen, even if the ships were armed. This letter, which stated in measured language the point which Wilson was making extemporaneously on the platform three weeks earlier, contended that Germany's questionable methods of warfare involved nothing less than the security of the United States.

For my own part, I cannot consent to any abridgment of the rights of American citizens in any respect. The honor and self-respect of the nation is involved. We covet peace, and shall preserve it at any cost but the loss of honor. To forbid our people to exercise their rights for fear we might be called upon to vindicate them would be a deep humiliation indeed. It would be an implicit, all but an explicit, acquiescence in the violation of the rights of mankind everywhere and of whatever nation or allegiance. It would be a deliberate abdication of our hitherto proud position as spokesmen even amidst the turmoil of war for the law and the right. It would make everything this Government has attempted and everything that it has achieved during this terrible struggle of nations meaningless and futile.

It is important to reflect that if in this instance we allowed expediency to take the place of principle, the door would inevitably be opened to still further concessions. Once accept a single abatement of right and many other humiliations would certainly follow, and the whole fine fabric of international law might crumble under our hands piece by piece. What we are contending for in this matter is of the very essence of the things that have made America a sovereign nation. She cannot yield them without conceding her own impotency as a nation and making virtual surrender of her independent position among the nations of the world.[20]

This letter marks the high point of Wilson's policy based on freedom of the seas. As we shall see, a new phase of his policy had already emerged based not upon the rules of maritime warfare but upon the ultimate political consequences of the war.

It should be pointed out in passing that Wilson was not eccentric in the emphasis which he chose for so many months to place on legal principle. There was, on the contrary, a very general receptivity to this manner of defining the national interest. Charles Evans Hughes, the Republican nominee for president in 1916, in his acceptance speech charged Wilson with lack of diligence in upholding the law:

We have had a clear and definite mission as a great neutral nation. It was for us to maintain the integrity of international law; to vindicate our rights as neutrals; to protect the lives of our citizens, their property and trade from wrongful acts. Putting aside any question as to the highest possibilities of moral leadership in the maintenance and vindication of the law of nations in connection with the European War, at least we were entitled to the safe-guarding of American rights. . . . Had this Government . . . left no doubt that when we said "strict accountability" we meant precisely what we said, and that we should unhesitatingly vindicate that position, I am confident that there would have been no destruction of American lives by the sinking of the *Lusitania*.[21]

Still further perspective on Wilson's manner of argument is afforded by Elihu Root's views of American policy. Shortly after the sinking of the *Lusitania*, Chandler P. Anderson at Lansing's suggestion interviewed Root.[22] The latter, a loyal Republican and distinguished public servant, at first secretary of war and then secretary of state in Theodore Roosevelt's cabinet, told Anderson that "the President had unquestionably taken the right course." He felt, however, that instead of leading public opinion the President "had waited until he had been forced to action by public opinion." Moreover, Root "feared that the President was not acting from conviction, but from expediency, and if that was so, he would seek some compromise which would be in effect an abandonment of the higher ground which the United States should occupy on this question." What precisely was the "higher ground" of which Root spoke? He seemed to give it two meanings. On the one hand, there was international law. Root said, according to Anderson's account,

that as between Germany and Great Britain, and Germany and any of the other belligerents, we were not particularly concerned with their conduct of the war, but we were concerned with everything which was done by any of the belligerents which involved the sanctity of treaties to which we were parties, and the rights of neutrals; that in his opinion we should have from the beginning insisted, on behalf of all the nations at peace, that the belligerents must strictly observe their rights under treaties and international law, and that if necessary an attempt should have been made to bring together all nations at peace to protect those rights.

Here Root probably was referring to events in Belgium, as well as to freedom of the seas, but in any event his measure of American interest was international law. He then went on to state "in his opinion a duty was imposed upon the American people to insist that the principles of government and humanity and civilization upon which our government was founded must be maintained." Here he definitely referred to democracy.

Root on this latter point was emphatic. Anderson reported that

he described from a historical point of view the influence which the United States has had upon the world; the meaning of its form of government, and the political and governmental principles which it represents, and what American citizenship means, and the effect and benefit which all this has had upon other nations, and the inspiration and helpfulness which it gives to the future of the world. He brought out strongly the effect of popular government both upon the individual and upon the nation, and its antagonism to aggressive warfare as a national policy. He contrasted all this with the conditions prevailing in countries under the rule of military despotism, the influences of which were almost without exception opposed to those resulting from popular government. He said the time had come for the people of our country to test the value of their form of government, and for the people of this country to decide whether it was worth preserving because the issue to-day was distinctly between the continuance or suppression of that form of government.

Root believed that "this country had a higher mission to perform than merely to maintain neutrality on the basis of impartiality." But to counsel the taking of sides was not consistent with simultaneous espousal of freedom of the seas, for only on the basis of impartiality could freedom of the seas have been an honest and valid issue.

This merging of freedom of the seas and democracy, implicit in Root's views, was present also in Wilson's. How then did this assimilation surmount the logical objection to it? American opinion had been beset by two contradictory tendencies: on the one hand, the disposition to oppose Germany; and on the other, reluctance to become entangled in European affairs. The resulting dilemma was fortuitously resolved by the frightfulness of submarine warfare which made possible an anti-German policy in the name of the law of neutrality. Undersea warfare was viewed less as a new technological development than as a typical manifestation of autocratic power. In this way freedom of the seas was identified with humanity, civilization, and democracy.

II

Wilson's break with Bryan in 1915 was the result of disagreement over the correct American response to Germany's submarine warfare. We have seen that Bryan viewed the death of Leon C. Thrasher on the *Falaba* as incidental to an act directed against Great Britain. He argued that in the absence of a direct affront to the United States there was no real basis for opposing the methods of warfare employed by Germany against her enemies. Citing the rule of contributory negligence, Bryan was uncertain even whether monetary damages might appropriately be demanded. The President was strongly inclined to take direct issue with Germany, but Bryan shook Wilson's confidence; no action had yet been taken with respect to Thrasher's death when on May 7, 1915 more than a hundred Americans went down on the *Lusitania*. Acting in accord with his original inclination, Wilson at that point made demands which left no recourse except war, should Germany fail to keep the submarine within bounds acceptable to the United States.

Bryan had wanted to retard the course of the *Lusitania* dispute by means of investigation by an international commission. For the future he proposed warning Americans against taking passage on belligerent vessels, and suggested banning munitions from the cargo of American passenger ships. Bryan, of course, was as strongly opposed to war with Great Britain as with Germany, and in the months immediately after August 1914 he approved the measures taken by the American Government to accommodate neutral trade to British sea power. In the *Lusitania* crisis Bryan was doubly alarmed. Not only did he foresee collision with Germany, but it seemed to him that Wilson's position would make the question of war or peace for America turn on a decision in Berlin. "If the initiative were with us," he wrote the President, "I would not fear war, for I am sure you do not want it, but when the note is sent it is Germany's next move." [23]

Important temperamental and philosophical differences underlay the break between Bryan and Wilson. Whatever the merit of Bryan's arguments with respect to the submarine, the fact remains that for him neutrality was less a legal status than an attitude of mind. His confidence in neutrality could not be disturbed by difficulties over the interpretation and application of the rules of maritime warfare, which he viewed as technicalities subordinate to neutrality's essential character as a nonviolent, pacific posture in world politics. Unlike Wilson, Bryan believed that in all circumstances except actual invasion it was in the national interest to refrain from going to war.

Both Bryan and Wilson, to be sure, carried into the international realm the democratic assumptions of American domestic politics. They saw international security in terms of law and morality. But whereas Bryan was content to rely on inner restraint and purity of motive as sufficient supports for American interest and influence, Wilson was prepared to use force to uphold the law. Speaking in 1916 shortly after Germany's capitulation in the *Sussex* case, Wilson acknowledged that there were those who believed that "the present quarrel has carried those engaged in it so far that they cannot be held to ordinary standards of responsibility," and that they asked "why not let the storm pass, and then, when it is all over, have the reckonings?" But he contended that America as one of the chief nations of the world must act "more or less from the point of view of the rest of the world." Elaborating this point in a semihumorous vein, Wilson disclosed the divergence between his philosophy of politics and Bryan's:

If I cannot retain my moral influence over a man except by occasionally knocking him down, if that is the only basis upon which he will respect me, then for the sake of his soul I have got occasionally to knock him down. You know how we have read—isn't it in Ralph Connor's stories of western life in Canada?—that all his sky pilots are ready for a fracas at any time, and how the ultimate salvation of the souls of their parishioners depends upon their using their fists occasionally. If a man will not listen to you quietly in a seat, sit on his neck and make him listen; just as I have always maintained, particularly in view of certain experiences of mine, that the shortest road to a boy's moral sense is through his cuticle.[24]

Bryan's imperturbability was based on two firmly held convictions. One of these was that Christian love was more powerful than force. His strong native bent in this regard had been confirmed and greatly strengthened by Tolstoy, whom he had visited in Russia in 1902, and whose writings he had studied. Bryan told an audience in 1910 that Tolstoy was a great example of an individual who practiced as well as preached the doctrine of love. "There he stands," Bryan said,

proclaiming to the world that he believes that love is a better protection than force; that he thinks a man will suffer less by refusing to use violence than if he used it. And what is the result? He is the only man in Russia that the

Czar with all his army dare not lay his hand on. . . . The power that is above him, the power that is over him and the power that is in him is proof against violence. . . . I believe that this nation could stand before the world today and tell the world that it did not believe in war, that it did not believe that it was the right way to settle disputes, that it had no disputes that it was not willing to submit to the judgment of the world. If this nation did that it not only would not be attacked by any other nation on the earth, but it would become the supreme power in the world. I have no doubt of it and I believe that the whole tendency is toward that policy.[25]

Consistent with his idealistic tenets was Bryan's opposition to the program of the influential League to Enforce Peace, organized under the leadership of William Howard Taft. In a debate with Taft in 1917 Bryan argued that the League would substitute physical force for moral influence, which would be a "step down" from what America had always stood for in the world. "The idea," he contended, "is vital and controls destiny." A nation which relied on character and service would "command not only confidence but increasing consideration and influence." Bryan believed that "the threatenings of a League whose 'vital principle is force'" would be incompatible with the teachings of Christ. To those who suggested that "we cannot afford to adjust our governmental methods to the teachings of the New Testament until other nations are ready to do so," Bryan's rejoinder was that the basic principle of Christianity was that "its truths are to be propagated by example." [26]

The second belief of Bryan was abounding faith in the ascendancy of democracy and in America as its chief exponent. He saw history as obedient to an immanent law of progress and the United States as its instrument of fulfillment. Such a view, as we shall see in Lansing's application of similar tenets, did not necessarily imply pacifism. Its militant optimism was, moreover, inconsistent with the profound sense of tragedy and frustration out of which there arose Bryan's first tenet, the doctrine of Christian love. The discord between these two elements in Bryan's thought could be resolved theologically only on the assumption that there could be salvation in this world. Reflecting the nineteenth-century belief in the benevolence of history, Bryan combined democratic idealism with trust in the self-rewarding quality of virtue and arrived at a prescription for national policy. Bryan did not reject international politics or retreat before its importunities. Rather he would meet the world with morality and example, not law and force.

The submarine brought a crisis not only between Bryan and Wilson, but within Bryan himself. The underlying cause for the secretary's resignation in 1915 was the irreconcilability of his pacifism with war which, he reluctantly recognized, might arise from the discharge of his official responsibilities.

III

More than any other of Wilson's advisers, it was Lansing who was most prepared to accept war with Germany over the submarine. We have seen that he was so disposed in the cases of the *Lusitania, Arabic,* and *Sussex;* and again in the autumn of 1916 and in January 1917 he urged Wilson to break with Germany over the submarine attacks on Allied shipping. Yet Lansing never failed to be reconciled to delay; and it was he who strongly argued the case for revising the American position on the armed merchantman.

It is apparent that Lansing was subject to the erratic influence of the contradictory assumptions of neutrality and support for Great Britain which underlay American policy. But, unlike Wilson, he seems to have been without illusion as to the manner in which the submarine masked a pro-British policy. One does not find in the public or private records any praise by Lansing of neutrality as such, nor any strong regard for freedom of the seas as emblematic of law and humanity. On the contrary, he appreciated fully the disruptive effect of the submarine on traditional international law.

Evidence for this does not reside alone in Lansing's attitude toward the armed merchantman. Germany's declaration of February 1915 announcing intended use of the submarine in contravention of the accepted rules of international law was supplemented by a memorandum justifying this new departure as a measure of retaliation. Knowledge of this supplementary statement first came to the State Department through the press. In transmitting a press clipping to the President, Lansing said that the memorandum impressed him "as a strong presentation of the German case and removes some of the objectionable features of the declaration, if it is read without explanatory statements. In my opinion," he added, "it makes the advisability of a sharp protest, or of any protest at all, open to question." He believed that there was "ample time to consider the subject," since the provisions of the declaration "do not come into operation until the 18th instant." [27]

Wilson's reply nonetheless held Germany to "strict accountability." In applying this phrase shortly afterward in the *Falaba* case, Lansing first interpreted it as covering the death of Leon C. Thrasher on this British vessel. But the cumulative effect of Bryan's contrary view, Chandler P. Anderson's adverse legal opinion, Wilson's prolonged vacillation, and the attacks on the American vessels *Gulflight* and *Cushing*, caused Lansing eventually (if only momentarily) to hold that "strict accountability" referred only to acts affecting American shipping. Lansing, at this time counselor in the State Department, found it difficult to adjust to a policy the outlines of which had not yet fully emerged, and which as a matter of fact never ceased to be equivocal over whether it was international law or Great Britain on whose behalf Germany was being opposed.

The thoughts which Lansing committed to his diary

at this time actually suggest serious reservations about defending law and morality. "The civilized world has through centuries of effort," he wrote on April 15, 1915, "constructed an elaborate system of ethics in which altruism has become more and more pronounced. Society, both individuals and nations, has come to accept these rules." But under the impact of the war "the splendid structure of morality" was crumbling. Since the nations engaged in the war believed that their very existence was at stake, "every principle of justice and morality is submerged in the supreme effort to succeed. Public and private rights are swept from the path by military necessity." [28]

Some days later Lansing in his diary addressed himself more specifically to the question of international law. "New means of communication, new methods of locomotion, new engines of destruction untested in actual war, and the consequent changes in military and naval operations created new conditions, to which the long-established rules of war did not and could not apply," he wrote. "Willingly or by force of circumstances," the belligerents abandoned the old rules. As a consequence the "neutral nations . . . have had to meet conditions which have converted legal order into chaos. . . . The result is a jumble of contradictions." Considering the matter from the viewpoint of the belligerents, Lansing asked: "Would you do differently, if you were convinced that the future independence of your country were in peril? Would you leave a single stone unturned or relinquish a single method of attack for the sole reason that the laws of war directed you to do so?" The most sensible course for a neutral, Lansing concluded, was to "treat the warring nations as if irresponsible for their acts." Although representations were desirable as "a reservation of rights, on which to found future claims," he was sure that "they will not in the least affect the present state of affairs." [29]

The *Lusitania* disaster somewhat qualified Lansing's skeptical regard for the rules of maritime warfare. Yet he was still prepared to recognize that in the behavior of nations "honor and . . . morality are always subordinated to . . . existence and . . . independence. I do not recall a case in history in which a nation surrendered its sovereignty for the sole purpose of being right." And whereas "an individual possessing a high sense of honor might prefer to give up liberty and even life" rather than bear the condemnation for "cruel, inhuman, immoral, or lawless" acts, nations "stand on a lower plane. . . . Everything must give place to the supreme object of self-preservation." Was Germany culpable? Lansing had narrowed down German guilt to rather small dimensions:

The question of what is and what is not humane conduct would thus seem to resolve itself to this: If military success or advantage can only be gained through the perpetration of acts considered by the civilized world to be cruel, inhuman or otherwise reprehensible, a belligerent may be reasonably expected to commit the acts. Furthermore, it is a query how far acts of that character in those circumstances can justifiably be condemned. If, however, the act of a belligerent, which the world condemns generally as cruel, inhumane or reprehensible, has no material effect on the success of military operations, it is stamped with wantonness and is entitled to universal condemnation.[30]

Standing on this narrow platform, Lansing was prepared to enter the war over the question of submarine tactics.

Actually, however, this point of departure was more convenient than substantial. Lansing set forth his real considerations in a private memorandum of July 11, 1915, written shortly after he assumed the duties of secretary of state. "A triumph for German imperialism *must not be*," he wrote, and to prevent such an outcome he was ready to countenance "the actual participation of this country in the war in case it becomes evident that Germany will be the victor." Lansing believed that precautionary measures were immediately required in Latin America, and particularly Mexico, where he would straightway recognize the faction of General Carranza. He would settle Colombia's claims over the seizure of Panama. He looked upon purchase of the Danish West Indies as urgently necessary to prevent the islands from falling into German hands through conquest of Denmark by Germany. Meanwhile he would cultivate "a Pan-American doctrine with the object of alienating the American republics from European influence, especially the German influence."

But Lansing did not believe that battening down the Western Hemisphere would suffice. If in a triumphant German Empire, or one which no more than broke even in the war, "the present military oligarchy" maintained itself, it would only "with its usual vigor and thoroughness prepare to renew its attack on democracy." Such a government as that of Imperial Germany "would sow dissensions among the nations with liberal institutions and seek an alliance with other governments based to a more or less degree on the principle of absolutism." The nations which "would probably be approached . . . would be Russia and Japan, which are almost as hostile to democracy as Germany and which have similar ambitions of territorial expansion." The success of these three empires, Lansing conjectured, would "for the time being at least" mean a division of the world. "I imagine that Germany would be master of Western Europe, of Africa, and probably of the Americas; that Russia would dominate Scandinavia, and Western and Southern Asia; and Japan would control the Far East, the Pacific and possibly the West Coast of North America." "Even the most optimistic cannot deny," Lansing wrote, that such a triumph was "a reasonable expectation," should these three autocratic empires enter into partnership.[31]

This was prophetic insight into the twentieth century, when many familiar landmarks would disappear and new empires rise and fall with bewildering rapidity. But, in judging Lansing's forecast, and also his recommendations, we should consider his argument. "Only recently," he wrote in his memorandum of July 11, "has the conviction come to me that democracy throughout the world is threatened." His characterization of the war as a struggle between autocracy and democracy he would repeat again and again, and it was the premise on which he made his recommendations to the President. But did Lansing really fear for the future of democracy or was he using the ideological argument to cut through the inhibitions and controversies which beset American policy and thus bring the United States in on the right side of the war— that of the Allies? Perhaps; but as in the case of Wilson's championing of freedom of the seas out of a similar search for an argument generally acceptable to public opinion, the motive was mixed. In fact both law and democracy furnish criteria relevant to the shaping of American foreign policy—although questions of definition and tactics are bound to invite differing opinions.

In defining democracy, Wilson and Lansing were undoubtedly very close together, and both were equally devoted to its future. But the policies favored by each man were sharply at variance until, in his War Message, Wilson finally embraced the viewpoint which Lansing had so untiringly urged. Wilson saw the future best secured through a negotiated peace; this objective, more than any other of the shifting phases of American policy, elicited his unreserved support. Lansing on the other hand believed that the best guarantee for the future lay in the overwhelming defeat of German autocracy, and to this end desired that the United States join the Allies without delay. Having learned in September 1916 of House's conversations with Bernstorff and others relative to a negotiated peace, Lansing declared in his diary that there "ought not to be and there must not be any compromise peace with the Germans." The true policy, he said, was to join the Allies "as soon as possible and crush down the German Autocrats." [32] He was sure that nothing would come of the endeavor to start negotiations, and, he added, "I hope nothing will." As for his own participation, "I will act in favor of mediation though with great reluctance, but I would not do it if I thought it would amount to anything." Above all, as to the highly strained relations with the British at the time, he would "never sign an ultimatum to Great Britain." [33]

When mediation took concrete form in the following December, Wilson held out the prospect of an American-backed league of nations as an inducement for the belligerents to abandon their aim of peace with victory. Regarding such a league, Lansing did not believe that "any Government which is autocratic can be trusted" as a member.

It is too much a prey to personal ambition, to a spirit of aggression and to greed for territory and political domination, the curse of the world in the past, to be an honest partner in an organization devoted to international peace. Such a militaristic government as rules over Germany would be an undesirable member in a Peace League. . . .

The one hope of a League for Peace is in imposing as a qualification of membership that a nation shall possess democratic institutions which are real and not merely nominal. A League of Democracies would, in my opinion, insure unity of action and the faithful performance of obligations. Democracies are not treaty breakers; they possess sensitive national consciences; they are guided by principles of justice and morality in their intercourse with one another; and they are not aggressive or improperly ambitious. All peoples abhor war and desire peace. Through democratic institutions the popular will finds expression.[34]

But at no time did Lansing have any indication that the President understood that the future of democracy was deeply involved in the war, and he had little hope of persuading Wilson to his way of thinking. It was an "amazing thing" to Lansing that the President failed to see that "on no account must we range ourselves even indirectly on the side of Germany."

In fact, he does not seem to grasp the full significance of this war or the principles at issue. I have talked it over with him, but the violations of American rights by both sides seem to interest him more than the vital interests as I see them. That German imperialistic ambitions threaten free institutions everywhere apparently has not sunk very deeply into his mind. For six months I have talked about the struggle between Autocracy and Democracy, but do not see that I have made any great impression.[35]

Some two months later Lansing still was worried. He wrote in December, 1916, that the "problem with me is to get this idea [of imperiled democracy] before the President in such a way as to convince him of the soundness of the proposition." To this end he planned the submission of the text of an address on the subject for Wilson's approval.[36] Evidence in the Wilson Papers shows that Lansing actually wrote out an address. We find a manuscript entitled "Americanism," a second draft—Wilson having already read and criticized the initial draft.[37] In this document we have a considered statement of Lansing's philosophy of international relations.

Americanism, he had written, is devotion to the principle of individual liberty

in organized society—a principle which finds its expression in democratic institutions, in the assertion and protection of human rights, and in the equality of opportunity, which have been the foundation stones of our system of government and of our national greatness. . . .

Every loyal American . . . knows that in democracy founded on liberty of thought and action there is a panacea for most of the ills with which nations have been afflicted in their relations at home and abroad. A self-governing and enlightened people possesses a great national conscience, which responds to sentiments of justice and right. The greater the freedom and the more the enlightenment so much the more sensitive is that conscience, so much the more surely does it guide the government in the path of rectitude. . . .

It is but natural that the people of this Republic . . . should ardently desire the expansion of the principle [of democracy] throughout the world. . . . The people of the United States fervently hope to see Democracy become the standing policy of the civilized world in the earnest expectation that in its general adoption the national conscience of every nation may be quickened and find full expression, and that through the responsiveness of the national conscience to a high sense of justice and right universal peace may become an accomplished fact.

With Germany clearly in mind, Lansing said that with a nation "in which education is general among all classes but which retains an undemocratic system of government in spite of the fitness of the nation for the exercise of political rights, there is unavoidably a lack of sympathy on the part of states in which Democracy is the controlling principle." In such a nation the government "cannot be inspired with truly patriotic motives," nor is it "as trustworthy and just as one which springs from the will of a free people and which is influenced by the national conscience." The conclusion followed: "in international affairs there are bound to be two distinct groups of states which though not openly hostile are by no means trustful to each other."

The virtual ultimatum which Wilson had sent during the *Sussex* crisis made American prestige the most immediate and urgent issue when Germany on January 31, 1917 announced unrestricted submarine warfare, to take effect the following day. In a conference with Wilson on the evening of January 31, Lansing placed much emphasis on this consequence of the German declaration. He told the President that

the greatness of the part which a nation plays in the world depends largely upon its character and the high regard of other nations; that I felt that to permit Germany to do this abominable thing without firmly following out to the letter what we had proclaimed to the world we would do, would be to lose our character as a great power and the esteem of all nations; and that to be considered a "bluffer" was an impossible position for a nation which cherished self-respect.

Lansing recorded that the President still "showed much irritation over the British disregard for neutral rights and over the British plan . . . to furnish British ships with heavy guns." To this Lansing replied that "Germany's declaration in any event justified such a practice." But Wilson was not certain that the argument was sound, although he did not think the question worth while discussing in view of the new turn of events.[38] Lansing reports still another observation which the President made on the evening of January 31, 1917. Wilson declared that he was increasingly impressed with the idea "that 'white civilization' and its dominance over the world" required the United States to keep itself "intact" for it "would have to build up the nations ravaged by the war." As this idea grew upon him, Wilson said, his willingness had increased "to go to any lengths rather than to have the nation actually involved in the conflict." [39]

The President could not possibly, of course, have escaped breaking with Germany, for American shipping itself had been placed in jeopardy, and accordingly Bernstorff was dismissed on February 3. But the great question of actual warfare was unsettled and would remain so for several agonizing weeks. At the Cabinet meeting on February 2 Wilson was opposed to going to war. According to David F. Houston, Secretary of Agriculture, the President said that if, "in order to keep the white race or part of it strong to meet the yellow race—Japan, for instance, in alliance with Russia, dominating China—it was wise to do nothing, he would do nothing, and would submit to . . . any imputation of weakness or cowardice." [40] At the same meeting, Lansing bypassed the submarine and the tangled legal questions to which it had given rise, and reverted to the larger, and to him primary, issue of democracy. He reported that some members of the Cabinet were "deeply shocked" by the "President's comment on the remark which I made concerning the future peace of the world." The secretary of state had said that he was convinced that an essential of permanent peace was that all nations should be politically liberalized; and that the only surety of independence for small nations was that the great and powerful should have democratic institutions because democracies were never aggressive or unjust. I went on to say that it seemed to me there could be no question but that to bring to an end absolutism the Allies ought to succeed, and that it was for our interest and for the interest of the world that we should join the Allies and aid them if we went into the war at all.

Lansing quoted the President as having said in reply, "I am not so sure of that." Wilson argued "that probably greater justice would be done if the conflict ended in a draw." Lansing was sure, however, that the President only wished to draw out arguments, and stated confidently in his diary, "I know that the President agreed with me about democracy being the only firm foundation for universal peace." [41] Nevertheless, one cannot escape the conclusion that Wilson saw rather clearly the opposing argument to Lansing's position. On the previous day (February 1), Wilson had said, in response to Lansing's contention that future peace required the destruction of Prussian militarism, that "he was not sure of this as it might mean the disintegration of German power and the destruction of the German nation." [42] Wilson, in suggesting that stability be found in an equilibrium of forces, was actually giving voice to the balance of power point of view.

After severance of diplomatic relations with Germany on February 3, 1917, events moved with great rapidity. The Zimmermann note, in which the German Government foolishly had invited Mexico into alliance in anticipation of war with the United States, was given by the British (who had intercepted it) to the American Government, whereupon it was published. American merchantmen were armed. And finally, on March 18, reports came to the State Department of the sinking by torpedo of the American steamships *Vigilancia, Illinois,* and *City of Memphis,* with loss of fifteen lives on the *Vigilancia.* These were the "actual overt acts," against which Wilson had warned the German Government in announcing severance of diplomatic relations. Lansing expressed great relief at the news, which, he wrote jubilantly in his diary, "ends all doubt in my mind as to the future. . . . Things have turned out right and the days of anxiety and uncertainty are over." [43] But after seeing Wilson the next day, the secretary had the impression that the President was "resisting the irresistible logic of events and that he resented being compelled to abandon the neutral position which had been preserved with so much difficulty." He returned to the Department "depressed and anxious." [44] The President apparently had argued that breaking diplomatic relations and arming American ships satisfied the requirements of the situation.

Later the same day Lansing wrote the President that, after carefully considering the conversation of that morning, he was in "entire agreement . . . that the recent attacks by submarines on American vessels do not materially affect the international situation so far as constituting a reason for declaring that a state of war exists between this country and Germany." [45] Lansing expressed this view again on the following day (March 20, 1917) when the Cabinet met.[46] He argued that

to go to war solely because American ships had been sunk and Americans killed would cause debate, and that the sounder basis was the duty of this and every other democratic nation to suppress an autocratic government like the German because of its atrocious character and because it was a menace to the national safety of this country and of all other countries with liberal systems of government.

Nevertheless the sinkings definitely facilitated a request for a declaration of war—a step which Lansing was convinced the President could not avoid. "The time for delay and inaction . . . has passed," he declared in the Cabinet meeting. "Only a definite, vigorous and uncompromising policy will satisfy or ought to satisfy the American people. . . . I believe that the people long for a strong and sure leadership. They are ready to go through to the very end." Lansing "urged the propriety of taking . . . advantage of the aroused sentiment of the people since it would have a tremendous influence in keeping Congress in line." He was not, he said, permitting his own judgment to be swayed by this sentiment, but he urged that it ought to be used "as a matter of expediency in affecting Congressional action." [47] And in addition to the sinkings, another event also had occurred which to Lansing argued an immediate request for a declaration of war: the revolution in Russia of March 1917 "removed the one objection to affirming that the European war was a war between Democracy and Absolutism." Again Lansing equated democracy and peace, this time going so far as to assert that "no League of Peace would be necessary if all nations were democratic."

When the President in Cabinet said "that he did not see how he could speak of a war for Democracy or of Russia's revolution in addressing Congress," Lansing replied that he "did not perceive any objection but in any event [it could be done] indirectly by attacking the character of the autocratic government of Germany as manifested by its deeds of inhumanity, by its broken promises, and by its plots and conspiracies against this country." To this the President only answered, "possibly."

The Cabinet meeting left Lansing uncertain as to whether "the President was impressed with the idea of a general indictment of the German Government." The answer came on April 2 in the War Message.

The President's indictment of Germany was unqualified, leaving nothing to be desired from Lansing's point of view. Wilson heavily underscored the autocratic character of the German Government, finding therein the cause for the disturbance of American tranquility, and making it the chief target of American policy. As Wilson defined it, the object of American policy was

to vindicate the principles of peace and justice in the life of the world as against selfish and autocratic power and to set up amongst the really free and self-governed peoples of the world such a concert of purpose and of action as will henceforth insure the observance of those principles.

Only free peoples, Wilson affirmed, could "prefer the interests of mankind to any narrow interest of their own." A "concert for peace" could be maintained only "by a partnership of democratic nations. No autocratic government could be trusted to keep faith within it or observe its covenants. It must be a league of honor, a partnership of opinion." Speaking of the "wonderful and heartening things that have been happening within the last few weeks in Russia," Wilson said that here in the new Russian regime was "a fit partner for a League of Honor." It was in the War Address that Wilson declared, "The world must be made safe for democracy."

Congress having so resolved, Wilson on April 6, 1917, proclaimed war with Germany. Compared with the tribulation of the preceding two and one-half years, the state of war was like a placid harbor which would shelter American policy until, with the end of hostilities, it would again be tossed on tumultuous seas. Lansing wrote on April 7:

The decision is made. It is war. It was the only possible decision consistent with honor and reason. Even if Germany had not so flagrantly violated our rights we were bound to go to the aid of the Allies. I have trembled lest the supreme necessity . . . would not be manifest to Congress. Some of our Senators and Representatives seem to be blind to the danger to civilization even now. They only see the infringement of our rights, and compared with the great issue they seem so little. Why can they not see that we must never allow the German Emperor to become master of Europe since he could then dominate the world and this country would be the next victim of his rapacity. Some day they will see it however.[48]

The Administration saw in Germany a menace to national safety and, beyond that, a sinister threat to the universal aspirations of democracy. Congress was not indifferent to the first of these considerations, nor immune to the blandishments of the second; but it is unlikely that Congress would have voted war with any degree of unity except for the issue of neutral rights. The Administration had been caught in the unenviable position where the larger purpose depended on the smaller.

Lansing was fully aware of the difficulty, but he had no hesitation about taking advantage of the fortuitous connection between the two widely differing ideas of national interest entertained respectively in the executive and legislative branches. Wilson, in the more responsible position, hesitated to act in the predicament which had overtaken American policy. He was deeply troubled by the incongruity and danger of erecting a large superstructure on so untrustworthy a foundation as freedom of the seas. But he was confronted with the necessity for action. Since there was no public consensus on what the national interest demanded, Wilson proceeded on the basis of sentiment, representing German autocracy as the cause for America's embroilment and democracy as the guarantee of American security. That Wilson himself ultimately found this point of view persuasive merely emphasizes the extent to which American policy was conditioned by an immature and undisciplined public opinion, unaccustomed to dealing with hard problems of foreign policy.

IV

We have seen that the dominant tendency in American opinion and policy was to view the nation's security in terms of maintenance and advancement of principle. Although somewhat differing views on law, morality, and democracy produced significant and even sharp disagreements on policy, Wilson, Bryan, and Lansing were all disposed to judge America's political connection with the rest of the world in terms of legal, moral, and philosophical ideas, universal in application. This pronounced reliance on the force of ideas, which minimized the discrete and purely national elements in our policy, had invited an opposing view emphasizing national advantage, dependent for its advancement on the use of military power and diplomatic maneuver. Theodore Roosevelt was the public figure best fitted by temperament and experience to voice such a view.

As assistant secretary of the Navy in the first McKinley administration, Roosevelt was largely responsible for Dewey's exploits in the Philippines which culminated in the annexation of those islands. As President he unceremoniously seized Panama. But if Roosevelt was overly impressed with Mahan's interpretation of history and was disposed as well to dramatic action involving strong-arm methods, he was also capable, with respect to the large questions of world politics which arose during his administration, of astute diplomacy aimed at preserving peace through a world balance of power. Roosevelt's mediation in the Russo-Japanese war of 1904–5 was a case in point, as was the calling of the Algeciras Conference on Morocco in 1906. In both instances more was involved than good offices. The influence and prestige of the United States were actively engaged. Particularly with respect to Algeciras, Roosevelt has been criticized for imprudently entangling the United States in the rivalries of the Old World.[49] Yet granting the daring of these diplomatic adventures when judged against the nation's past, they appear from present-day perspective to constitute an essentially sound reaction to the vast changes which were bringing to an end the fortunate conditions of international politics in the nineteenth century. In extraordinary degree for an American of his period, Roosevelt sensed the perilously delicate balance among the powers of Europe and the world, and he was not loathe to use the growing strength of the United States to maintain peace.

The outbreak of the World War in August 1914 did not come altogether as a surprise to Roosevelt, and it found him with certain definite views which he had held consistently over a prolonged period. He had for many years entertained misgivings about German intentions in the Western Hemisphere. As early as 1897, shortly after he was appointed assistant secretary of the Navy, he wrote to his good friend Captain Alfred Thayer Mahan of his desire to dislodge Spain from the Caribbean and to acquire the Danish possessions in that region. This would serve notice, he said, that no strong nation, "and especially not Germany, should be allowed to gain a foothold in the Western Hemisphere." He did not fear England, for "Canada is a hostage for her good behavior." [50] His apprehensions mounted as German military power increased in the years before 1914 and German diplomats became more demanding of their European opposites. Accordingly Roosevelt at Algeciras threw American influence to the French side. Several years later his forebodings were unchanged: "If Germany should ever overthrow England and establish the supremacy of Europe she aims at, she will be almost certain to want to try her hand in America." [51]

Any diminution of British power, Roosevelt believed, would also be a signal for vigorous Japanese expansion in Asia and the Pacific. Here his views were as old and consistent as with respect to Germany. In September 1914 he told friends that if Germany subjugated England he would expect an alliance between Germany and Japan and an invasion of the United States within five years. Not wishing anything to occur which would hasten such an alliance, Roosevelt in successive letters to the governor of California, Hiram Johnson, urged that the people of that state treat the Japanese with consideration. He did not fear that friction between the United States and Japan would bring America into conflict with Great Britain, Japan's ally. Rather he was afraid that the vast interests of the British Empire in the Pacific would force Britain to side with the United States in any arguments involving Japan, and thus detract from Britain's exertions against Germany.[52]

With respect to British power Roosevelt was neither apprehensive nor covetous. He believed that the United States should not compete in naval matters with England, and was content throughout his career to advocate an American Navy second to Britain's in strength. That the United States was vitally interested in maintaining Britain's position in Europe was a cardinal principle in Roosevelt's idea of a correct American policy. Before the World War he told a friend in the German Foreign Service, Baron Hermann von Eckhardstein, that

as long as England succeeds in keeping up the balance of power in Europe, not in principle but in reality, well and good. Should she, however, for some reason or other fail in doing so, the United States would be obliged to step in, at least temporarily, in order to reestablish the balance of power in Europe, never mind against which country or group of countries our efforts may have to be directed. In fact we are becoming, owing to our strength and geographical situation, more and more the balance of power of the whole globe.[53]

On the other hand, as Roosevelt wrote to Hugo Münsterberg, professor at Harvard and advocate of the German cause, it would be a disaster equal to the destruction of the British Empire if Germany were reduced to a condition similar to that after the Thirty Years' War. "At the outbreak of the war," he told Münsterberg,

I happened to have visiting me a half a dozen of our young men, including, for instance, Herbert Croly. Belgium had just been invaded. We all of us sympathized with Belgium, and therefore with England and France in their attitude toward Belgium, but I was interested to find that we all of us felt that the smashing of Germany would be a world calamity, and would result in the entire western world being speedily forced into a contest with Russia.[54]

These views, far from being incompatible with neutrality, might readily recommend it as a proper policy for the United States. This seems, in fact, to have been Roosevelt's earliest judgment. His initial reaction to Germany's invasion of Belgium points to that conclusion, although he very soon reversed himself and asked the American people to consider the war on the basis of Germany's breach of legal obligation.

Roosevelt's early opinions appeared in the *Outlook* for August 22 and September 23, 1914.[55] Belgium's fate, he wrote, taught that,

as things in the world now are, we must in any great crisis trust for our national safety to our ability and willingness to defend ourselves by our own trained strength and courage. We must not wrong others; and for our own safety we must trust, not to worthless bits of paper unbacked by power . . . but to our own manliness and clearsighted willingness to face facts.

Not without considerable personal satisfaction, Roosevelt made a special application of this lesson to Bryan's "cooling off" treaties, some thirty of which had been signed with foreign governments, and which Bryan considered a great achievement. These treaties had committed the signatories to submit any disagreement incapable of resolution by normal diplomatic methods to an investigation of facts; during the investigation and for a maximum period of one year thereafter neither party was to resort to war. Unlike the arbitration agreements of the period, the treaties did not

exclude from their purview matters affecting the vital
interests, independence, or national honor of a signatory or disputes involving third parties. What, Roosevelt now asked, would be the effect of such a commitment on the Monroe Doctrine if such small states as
Denmark or the Netherlands disposed of their possessions in the Western Hemisphere "to a great military power of Europe" either by virtue "of their own
free will, or because they were forced to do so?" Or
what if Mexico "disposed of Magdalena Bay to some
great Asiatic power?" In such instances, to delay action for a year would be fatal to America's vital interests. Roosevelt contended that "it is a dishonorable
thing for the Nation to enter into treaties which it
might be disastrous, indeed impossible, to keep."

"International law is not law at all in the sense that
municipal law is law," Roosevelt declared, because it
lacked both judge and policeman. Moreover, the Monroe Doctrine, "vital to our interests," was a policy of
the United States rather than a recognized part of
international law. "It is not a doctrine that we could
expect a court of arbitration to accept." The Monroe
Doctrine appeared the touchstone by which Roosevelt
would judge America's policy in relation to the war.
He included it in that important segment of international relations which, in his opinion, was essentially
beyond the reach of legal formulation. This was, at
any rate, the existing state of affairs, which would
continue until at some future time "we put the collec-

tive armed power of civilization, behind some body
which shall with reasonable justice and equity represent the collective determination of civilization to do
what is right."

The righting of the wrong suffered by Belgium in
the German invasion of 1914 was also a matter of the
future. Roosevelt felt strongly that "a peace which
left Belgium's wrongs unredressed and which did not
provide against the recurrence of such wrongs . . .
would not be a real peace." It would therefore be
"imperative, in the interest of civilization, to create
international conditions which shall neither require
nor permit such action" as Germany had perpetrated.
For the present, however, he hoped that he had made
"it plain that I am not . . . criticising, that I am not
passing judgment one way or the other, upon Germany's action." The Belgian case showed "how complicated instead of how simple it is to decide what course
we ought to follow as regards any given action supposed to be in the interest of peace." With reference
to the deputation of Belgians which had recently arrived to invoke assistance from the United States,
Roosevelt despite the strong pull on his sympathies
felt that American interests were not directly enough
involved to warrant any modification of neutrality on
Belgium's behalf.

What action our Government can or will take I know not.
It has been announced that no action can be taken that
will interfere with our entire neutrality. It is certainly

eminently desirable that we should remain entirely neutral, and nothing but urgent need would warrant breaking our neutrality and taking sides one way or the other. Our first duty is to hold ourselves ready to do whatever the changing circumstances demand in order to protect our own interests in the present and in the future; although, for my own part, I desire to add to this statement the proviso that under no circumstances must we do anything dishonorable, especially towards unoffending weaker nations. Neutrality may be of prime necessity in order to preserve our own interests, to maintain peace in so much of the world as is not affected by the war, and to conserve our influence for helping toward the re-establishment of general peace when the time comes; for if any outside Power is able at such time to be the medium for bringing peace, it is more likely to be the United States than any other. But we pay the penalty of this action on behalf of peace for ourselves, and possibly for others in the future, by forfeiting our right to do anything on behalf of peace for the Belgians in the present. We can maintain our neutrality only by refusal to do anything to aid unoffending weak powers which are dragged into the gulf of bloodshed and misery through no fault of their own. Of course it would be folly to jump into the gulf ourselves to no good purpose; and very probably nothing that we could have done would have helped Belgium. We have not the smallest responsibility for what has befallen her, and I am sure that the sympathy of this country for the suffering of the men, women, and children of Belgium is very real. Nevertheless, this sympathy is compatible with full acknowledgment of the unwisdom of our uttering a single word of official protest unless we are prepared to make that protest effective; and only the clearest and most urgent National duty would ever justify us in deviating from our rule of neutrality and non-interference.[56]

These views were a subdued echo of those which Roosevelt had expressed in an interesting letter of August 8, 1914 to Professor Hugo Münsterberg. The melancholy feature about the war, Roosevelt had then remarked, was that the "conflict really was inevitable," and that each belligerent was, from its own viewpoint, in the right. Subordinating the question of Belgium to observations on the ineffectiveness of international law, Roosevelt said that

all talk of international law is beside the mark, because there is no real homology between international law and internal or municipal law. The technical and the actual assault may be entirely distinct, as in the case of the Boer Republics. The power sending the ultimatum and making the attack may do so merely because it is so obvious that the other side is preparing to strike first. It is the same way about the treaties guaranteeing the neutrality of Luxemburg and Belgium, which seemingly Germany has violated even before actual fighting began.

Roosevelt may have had in mind his own intervention in Panama when he added, "I am not prepared to say that in dire need the statesmen of a nation are not obliged to disregard any treaty, if keeping it may mean the most serious jeopardy to the nation." [57]

Roosevelt's acceptance of neutrality as the appropriate policy in August and September 1914 was not necessarily inconsistent with what he wrote to his friend Sir Cecil Spring-Rice on October 3, 1914. He told the British ambassador that if he had been President he would

have acted on the thirtieth or thirty-first of July, as head of a signatory power of The Hague treaties, calling attention to the guaranty of Belgium's neutrality and saying that I accepted the treaties as imposing a serious obligation which I expected not only the United States but all other neutral nations to join in enforcing. Of course I would not have made such a statement unless I was willing to back it up. I believe that if I had been President the American people would have followed me.[58]

Roosevelt undoubtedly had in mind the precedents of his own diplomacy in 1905-6 at Portsmouth and Algeciras. In writing thus to Sir Cecil, he was referring to a policy of intervention only as regards the period immediately preceding the outbreak of war, when in his judgment the United States had an opportunity to head it off.

Soon after his initially strong support of neutrality in the *Outlook*, Roosevelt chose to make the Administration's refusal to protest the invasion of Belgium a point of sustained and derisive attack. This behavior seems highly capricious, and insofar as it was prompted by partisan motives it was irresponsible. Yet Roosevelt was becoming increasingly impressed with the prudence of cultivating friends against future trouble. The Belgian question was not only the central issue of the war in the West, but the crux of America's relation to the war. Belgian neutrality had been crucial to the balance of power in Western Europe. While one deplores German lawlessness in violating the neutrality of a weak power, the more immediate cause for alarm was the deleterious effect on French land power and British sea power which would result from the permanent control over Belgium at which Germany was aiming. Just as Belgium was the issue which brought Britain into the war, so it was crucial for the United States, and for essentially the same reason—its influence upon the European, and thereby the world, balance of power. When early in 1915 J. Medill Patterson, owner and editor of the Chicago *Tribune*, asked Roosevelt "why are you so sympathetic with the Allies? You even seem to want to get us into the war on the Allied side. Is it just Belgium, or do you feel that America itself is menaced?" Roosevelt replied that Germany "would probably not attack us at once," if she won the war.

But she would begin to meddle in the Caribbean, to effect landings in Cuba, and to threaten the Panama Canal. In this way we would be thrown into hostilities with Germany sooner or later and with far less chance of success than if we joined with the powers which are now fighting her. We can be sure of this, moreover, that if Germany and the European powers which have already suffered from

Germany's aggression—which we had not helped them to check—would be—shall we say?—extremely philosophical about the evil things happening to us.[59]

This was a privately expressed opinion. Publicly Roosevelt did not specifically name Germany as a potential enemy. Although making frequent reference to the Monroe Doctrine in his addresses and writings, Roosevelt before our entry into the war did not dwell on the possibility of the war's resulting in such a radical redistribution of power in Germany's favor as to menace the Western Hemisphere, nor on the corollary that in using its power as a weight in the scales of international politics the United States would be only taking reasonable precaution. Roosevelt doubtless knew that the amorality of power considerations was unpalatable to the American people. It is even more remarkable, therefore, that he did not choose to base his case on the public's distaste for German autocracy. Speaking at Pittsburgh in July 1917 he granted that the United States was fighting for humanity, but added that "we are also, and primarily, fighting for our own vital interests. Until we make the world safe for America (and, incidentally, until we make democracy safe in America), it is empty rhetoric to talk of making the world safe for democracy."[60] Roosevelt was extremely cautious about equating democracy with peace. "It is at least possible," he had said in September 1914,

that the conflict will result in a growth of democracy in
Europe, in at least a partial substitution of the rule of
the people for the rule of those who esteem it their God-
given right to govern the people. This, in its turn, would
render it probably a little more unlikely that there would
be a repetition of such disastrous warfare. I think that in
the great countries engaged, the peoples as a whole have
been behind their sovereigns on both sides of this contest.
Certainly the action of the Socialists in Germany, France,
and Belgium, and, so far as we know, of the popular
leaders in Russia, would tend to bear out the truth of this
statement. But the growth of the power of the people,
while it would not prevent war, would at least render it
more possible than at present to make appeals which might
result in some cases in coming to an accommodation based
upon justice: for justice is what popular rule must be
permanently based upon and must permanently seek to
obtain or it will not itself be permanent.[61]

Yet restraint was not typical of Roosevelt's contribution to the great debate. On the contrary his arguments
were for the most part impassioned and grossly over-
simplified. His themes, repeated again and again with
variation only in the accompanying invective directed
at the Administration and the pacifists, were (1) preparedness, (2) the hyphenated American, and (3)
Belgium, only later supplemented by (4) the submarine. While there were in addition frequent references to the Monroe Doctrine, the ground on which
Roosevelt urged the American people to base their

attitudes toward the contestants was Germany's bru-
tality and illegality as manifested in her actions toward Belgium, together with her conduct of submarine
warfare.

Even before the submarine prompted the Administration to cast in a similar mold its opposition to Germany, Roosevelt by January 1915 was severely indict-
ing Germany for violating Belgian neutrality, and with
equal vehemence rebuking his own government for
not taking vigorous action over this violation of international right. "The time has come," he said,

when loyalty to the administration's action in foreign
affairs means disloyalty to our national self-interest and
to our obligations toward humanity at large. As regards
Belgium the administration has clearly taken the ground
that our own selfish ease forbids us to fulfill our explicit
obligations to small neutral states when they are deeply
wronged. It will never be possible in any war to commit
a clearer breach of international morality than that committed by Germany in the invasion and subjugation of
Belgium.

Granting that "every one of the nations involved in
this war, and the United States as well, have committed such outrages in the past," Roosevelt contended
that "the very purpose of the Hague conventions . . .
was to put a stop to such misconduct in the future."

Roosevelt also asserted that Germany's violation of
those provisions of the Hague Conventions proscrib-
ing, among other things, the bombing of open towns

and punitive destruction of towns warranted official condemnation by the American Government. The United States during his presidencey had agreed to these conventions, and Roosevelt now declared that he

most emphatically . . . would not have permitted such a farce to have gone through if it had entered my head that this government would not consider itself bound to do all it could to see that the regulations to which it made itself a party were actually observed when the necessity for their observance arose. I cannot imagine any sensible nation thinking it worth while to sign future Hague conventions if even such a powerful neutral as the United States does not care enough about them to protest against their open breach. Of the present neutral powers the United States of America is the most disinterested and the strongest, and should therefore bear the main burden of responsibility in this matter.[62]

Although publicly charging Germany with lawlessness, Roosevelt consistently avoided an open espousal of the Allied cause. This omission in his book, *America and the World War,* prompted some of his British correspondents to misgivings, and to Arthur Lee, a friend of long standing, Roosevelt wrote in March 1915 that the omission was deliberate; by basing his public appeal on Belgium, he could contend that he was "not advocating action to please England but . . . to do our duty to Belgium and for the sake of our own self-respect." In speaking thus, Roosevelt believed that he would incur less opposition than if he were to argue on the express assumptions of British friendship and German enmity.[63]

The sinking of the *Lusitania* was more and better grist for Roosevelt's mill. Although the Administration in this instance did not neglect to take a strong stand, Roosevelt had only disdain for Wilson's refusal to go beyond verbal protest. "We earn as a nation measureless scorn and contempt," Roosevelt declared,

if we follow the lead of those who exalt peace above righteousness, if we heed the voices of those feeble folk who bleat to high heaven that there is peace when there is no peace. For many months our government has preserved between right and wrong a neutrality which would have excited the emulous admiration of Pontius Pilate— the arch-typical neutral of all time.[64]

From this brief survey of Theodore Roosevelt's views, one must conclude that he had a genuine capacity for sober reflection on the national interest. His feeling for the workings of international politics was instinctive, and his settled opinion as to where American interests lay furnished the basis for what could have been an important contribution to the national discussion of foreign policy in the confused years from 1914 to 1917. His contribution was indeed useful in advancing the cause of preparedness, and in combating the wavering allegiance of many of the hyphenated Americans. But on the essential question of the objective toward which American policy should be directed, Roosevelt's utterances unfortunately failed to have a clarifying effect.

In comparison with Wilson's labored but conscientious endeavor to identify American security with freedom of the seas, Roosevelt's indignation over Germany's methods of war was a transparent camouflage for support of the Allies. Actually his fury and bombast mystified and alienated, rather than persuaded. This was the effect not only of the dissemblance in Roosevelt's argument but also of his partisanship. Roosevelt was still good presidential timber in 1914–17, and had he lived he doubtless would have received the Republican nomination in 1920. Political ambition militated against Roosevelt's functioning as a constructive critic of Wilson. Actually he differed from the President not in kind but in degree.

That American security should have been viewed from such widely differing standpoints as those described in this chapter is not in itself unusual. The remarkable thing is that each of the various approaches was espoused so dogmatically. To such extremes did Wilson carry law, Bryan morality, and Lansing democracy that the result was a caricature of these various aspects of security. Indeed the impression is of a nation unaccustomed to contending with problems of security. A weighing of imponderables and consideration of tactics—these are activities which one would normally expect. Yet the debate was essentially philosophical in character.

Roosevelt was perhaps most at home in the situation. Privately, at least, he saw the shifting distribution of power as the major problem. If the shift were greatly to favor Germany, he perceived that the old, comfortable adjustments with Great Britain would be outmoded. Confronted with a victorious, ambitious power, the United States would have to enter a period of radical readjustment, with attending uncertainties and dangers. But Roosevelt, choosing not to be candid with a public which he felt was uncomprehending, voiced his alarm solely in terms of Germany's violation of legal obligation. Although castigating the moralists and pacifists whose numbers led him to despair, he yielded enough to their influence to speak in their idiom. Wariness of public opinion also conditioned Wilson's views—although certainly in less degree. Only of Bryan can we confidently say that not even subconsciously were his utterances tailored to the audience to which they were addressed, for his views were already a faithful reflection of all those attitudes—complacency, simple moralism, and easy optimism—which resulted from the nation's unhindered success during the preceding one hundred years.

Wilson emerges as a most complex figure. Though in the beginning freedom of the seas was the keynote of his policy, he succeeded, in his own thinking at least, in reducing the issue to a size commensurate with the wartime interest of the neutral in trade, to which the doctrine properly refers; and he perceived, moreover, how seriously the rules of maritime warfare were compromised by new technological developments. Eventually Wilson declared that the war was a struggle between democracy and autocracy, but he came to the position only slowly and with misgivings. Indeed his remarkable exchanges with Lansing serve to indicate that the balance of power point of view was not foreign to his thinking and that he appreciated its implications for policy. In fact, as we explore still further the various facets and shifting emphases of Wilson's thought and policy, we shall see that peace without victory became his central goal, and that the maneuvers and pressures of diplomacy were the means which he adopted to that end. It was in this connection that the League of Nations emerged and that the extraordinary role of Colonel House becomes evident.

SIX

The Emergence of the League Idea

APART from the normal vicissitudes which in
wartime have always attended neutral rights,
they were subject in the first World War to extraordinary pressure owing to technological innovations
and the total character of the war. But these obstacles to freedom of the seas were not alone in render-
ing the American position untenable. This practical
difficulty was further complicated by the paradoxical
nature of American policy itself.

Conceivably, neutrality might have been adopted by
the United States as a calculated policy based on political considerations—as indeed seems to have been
Theodore Roosevelt's first impulse. Such a policy
would have been the appropriate response to a war
like those of the preceding hundred years, from 1815
to 1914, when nations fought for limited objectives
which did not threaten a revolution in the distribution
of power. Or, again, neutrality might have been embraced from hard necessity in the manner of the small

European states. Neither of these hypotheses, however, is a satisfactory explanation of American policy in the first World War. Rather neutrality with respect to European politics was a tradition. It was not a policy consciously adapted to the particular war in progress but an attitude of mind inherited from the nineteenth century. This circumstance created the illusion that in international law the United States had a ready-made foreign policy. Yet if the form of American policy remained unaltered, it nevertheless responded to the nature of the war, undergoing as a consequence a transformation in substance. This established at the heart of Wilson's position a contradiction which he was never wholly able to overcome.

In an endeavor to minimize the confusion of his policy, Wilson imputed to the law of neutrality large values such as "order," "justice," and "civilization." Though he complained in the autumn of 1915 that "neutrality is a negative word," he nevertheless declared that "America has promised the world to stand apart and maintain certain principles of action which are grounded in law and justice." He insisted that "we are not trying to keep out of trouble; we are trying to preserve the foundations upon which peace can be rebuilt." These foundations consisted of "the ancient and accepted principles of international law." [1] But the law of neutrality was actually a very weak expression of the desire for international peace. War is the sun, one author has remarked, about which the law of neutrality revolves like a planet.[2] To be sure, the law of neutrality afforded ground on which to take exception to the methods of maritime warfare employed by the belligerents; but any correspondence between such remonstrance and the permanent interests of the United States could only be inadvertent. Logic was incapable of supporting the pretentious values ascribed to neutrality. To insist on neutral rights on behalf of the future peace of the world was basing too much on so narrow a foundation.

The exchange of notes in the *Sussex* affair in 1916 had the effect of tying the question of war or peace for the United States more firmly than ever to the tactics of the submarine. In the *Sussex* note the American Government committed itself unequivocally to breaking with Germany over any deviation from the rules of cruiser warfare which injured or endangered American life, regardless of whether the merchantman involved was allied or neutral, freighter or passenger, armed or unarmed. But no sooner had this culmination been reached than Wilson's misgivings over the relevance of the submarine issue became acute. Perceiving that somehow freedom of the seas had undergone a metamorphosis whereby it was no longer the negation but actually the vehicle of a positive European policy, Wilson shrank at the prospect of going to war over the manner in which Germany chose to assault her enemies at sea. The contradictory pressures on the American Government were not only disturbing to

Wilson's peace of mind; they reduced his policy to incoherence and threatened it with ultimate stultification.

I

Wilson's dilemma was explored in a remarkable contemporary memorandum prepared by the English publicist, Norman Angell. This document appears in the Wilson Papers. Undated, it probably reached the President during or just after the period early in 1916 when the question of the armed merchantman was agitating Wilson's relations with the belligerents on the one hand and with Congress on the other. As an example of the mental effort and travail involved in shifting the basic assumptions of American policy, the Angell memorandum is of unique interest. With great skill Angell exposed the incongruities of American policy. No less impressive is the way in which he explored the possibility of directing American policy into more promising channels, underestimating in this regard neither the novelty of his proposals nor the difficulty they might encounter.

That Angell had an influence upon Wilson is difficult to determine, but an editorial of September 16, 1916 in the *New Republic* attributed to Angell's influence the statement in Wilson's acceptance speech that "no nation can any longer remain neutral as against any wilful disturbance of the peace of the world." Recalling that Angell had spent the previous winter in the

United States lecturing and writing, the *New Republic* asserted that "in the weeks preceding the last crisis with Germany over the *Sussex,* he formulated the doctrine that neutrality was obsolete. It emerged after hours of discussion on the basis of memoranda which were recast many times. The results reached the President, not only directly, but through his confidential advisers." [3] But that Angell had so decisive an effect upon Wilson is quite improbable, for we shall see on November 10, 1915 the President had indicated to Sir Edward Grey approval of the idea of a league against aggression. In fact, it must be emphasized that the initial identification of the league with American policy was owing not to the writings of publicists but to the diplomatic process itself. Angell, however, did mirror the thinking then in progress. He was closely associated with the editors of the *New Republic* who, in turn, through Colonel House and certain of their own circle were in touch with the President.

Angell pointed out in the memorandum that for the United States to join the Allies against Germany would be tantamount to accepting the Allied claims of belligerent right, which would "undermine neutral right far more seriously than would the acceptance of the German contention that merchant ships, in order to be immune from attack, should not carry guns." Thus to go to war over the latter issue—a course which Wilson had so dogmatically defended in his letter to

Senator Stone—would be "about equivalent to pulling down the walls of a house for the purpose of fixing a weathercock on the roof." Presumably the object of joining the Allies "would be to make secure American life and trade at sea in wars between other nations." Yet, even though Germany were thoroughly defeated, "America will not know . . . whether these things have been secured or not." If the object were to gain possessions of territory, America "could by her own victory take it." Actually, however, the United States would be fighting "to compel better behavior on the part of the nations in the future."

For America to "muddle along," trying somehow to maintain existing relations with Germany, was not, Angell believed, a practical expedient because her "citizens are killed, her trade affected, her resources used to influence the war's issue. . . . It is hardly indeed a question of whether she will intervene, but what manner of intervention will best subserve her chief ends." Granting that the "rights and securities" at issue with Germany "are very nebulous at best," there was "at least the risk of recurring humiliation." A situation containing that element "is likely to break down and give place . . . to a state of war" into which America "will have drifted . . . not because it offered any real solution, but merely as the result of the irritation and humiliation of the present position." Thus the country would go to war "to satisfy its . . . indignation, its temperamental need for action of some kind," even though to take such a course "may be futile and stultifying."

Believing that there was a way out of the difficulty, Angell outlined a course which he considered less barren than "inaction on the one hand, or war of unlimited liability on the other." His proposal was designed to avoid American involvement in the fighting if possible, or, failing that, to give a tangible purpose to American entrance into the war. He also hoped that the "disregard of diplomatic precedent" and the "dramatic element" contained in his suggestion might stimulate a reconsideration by the public of accepted ideas. He proposed that the American Government proceed as follows:

At the moment that the negotiations of [*sic*] Germany over the sinking of merchantmen or any other such detail, reached a deadlock the American Government, for the purpose of raising the whole matter above the plane of mere detailed interpretation of certain law (shortly, let us hope, to be changed in any case) should make to Germany and to the world a solemn declaration of America's purpose in the dispute and her real relationship to the two combatants.

Such a declaration should set forth that the nature of the American claims which have grown up out of the war is such that the satisfaction of them is dependent in a peculiar sense . . . upon re-establishing respect for international right, that both combatants have held that right lightly; that though heretofore America has, following established practice, taken no action save where her direct interest has been affected, the whole course of her own relations with the combatants and the development of the situation which faces all alike shows that only by directing efforts first to the establishment of the rights which are common to all can the particular right of each be safeguarded.

America, therefore, links her particular claims to the defense of certain general rights and abandons her position of strict diplomatic neutrality for the purpose of so doing.

American policy by the terms of this prescription would still be related to international law. But the law involved would be a new law, differing radically from the old. Angell would have had the United States seek agreement among belligerents and neutrals alike "to submit all future justiciable causes of dispute to an international court, and nonjusticiable causes to a council of inquiry." Such an agreement would provide a delay of "at least six months" before any party to a dispute might proceed to hostilities, "on pain of opposition by all other states party to the agreement." Other terms of the proposed settlement concerned the war itself, calling in particular for the evacuation of Belgium, France, and Serbia and the indemnification of Belgium. The future relations of the United States with the belligerents would be determined by their reaction to the American call for peace on these terms. Should Germany reject them, Angell suggested that the United States offer to settle its dispute with England over contraband and block-ade, but only "on the basis of making international that virtual control of the maritime trade of the world which England now exercises."

The outstanding fact about the war, according to Angell, was that it had reached a stage where each side was fighting mainly for security from future abuse of the power held by the other. Conceivably Germany would accept a reasonable territorial settle-ment if it were not that the Allies were impelled to seek something more and were fighting for "such re-duction of German military preponderance that there shall be no possibility of aggression in the future." The declared object of the Allies, to destroy Prussian militarism, "must of course seem to Germany equiv-alent to depriving her of self-defence and placing her at the mercy of such potentially powerful rivals as Russia."

The high quality of Angell's insight is demonstrated in his warning that "to join the Allies, beat Germany and then retire" would be a frustrating adventure. Without clearly defined objectives and the will to carry them through into the peace, mere victory might actu-ally "find the American people further from their ob-jective than ever. It may worsen the chaos of mankind and make that humanity and justice of which the President so often speaks as the purpose of American power more remote than ever." Angell did not under-rate the danger of fiasco; he appreciated that what he was proposing ran counter to two deeply imbedded attitudes, one of which related to international law and the other to the traditions of American foreign policy.

Traditional to international law was the understanding "that no nation has ground of action against others, until its own particular interests or rights are violated." The effect of this view was to compel every nation "to defend itself against the rest, to base its safety upon rivalry to others." Angell argued that only by "the contrary principle of combination with others for the purpose of defending the common right" could a nation effectively protect itself. If, he said, international law is something "which gives a nation no protection against the abuse of the power of others, and is, moreover, something which hampers it in meeting that power, international arrangements will never be observed." Since no nation will put international law before national preservation, the only hope "is to identify it with national security; to make it subserve that purpose of securing immunity from the abuse of the rival's power, for which the nations are now fighting. If it could serve the common end of all, it would be worth their support; not otherwise."

Angell was also fully aware of the obstacle interposed by the traditional policies of the United States. He recognized that a course such as he was proposing had no chance of gaining support from that section of American opinion which adhered to the historical injunction of no entangling alliances; nor could understanding support be expected from those Americans who were prepared to go to war to enforce American claims of maritime right. His proposal required an opinion based on expectation that entry into the war would advance the cause of a new international law designed to come to grips with the problem of insecurity.

Angell in his unpublished memorandum did not dilate on the underlying cause of Wilson's difficulties of the moment, which lay in historical circumstance. There was, however, another contemporary analysis which did. This latter essay, published anonymously in 1913, is the more interesting for having been written in anticipation of the world war. It is an extraordinary intellectual performance, and a rare instance of correct forecast in the difficult area of international politics. The author was Lewis Einstein, who at the time was an officer in the American foreign service.[4]

According to the article, the prevailing American belief was that the United States, possessing no territorial interests or ambition in Europe, "could with impunity remain indifferent" to European politics. Einstein immediately added, however, that this traditional disinterestedness had been possible only because of the European balance of power, which had been such "a permanent factor since the birth of the republic that Americans have never realized how its absence would have affected their political status."

The continuance of this historic condition, he believed, would be endangered by such a conflict as threatened momentarily to break out in Europe.

The most ominous aspect of the situation was in his opinion the Anglo-German rivalry which, despite the many efforts to bring it under control, had grown in bitterness and shown itself implacable. Should there materialize the contest which he feared, Einstein believed that the American attitude "would in the beginning be one of strict neutrality, which would be maintained as long as possible." This did not mean

that a far-sighted policy might not under certain contingencies impose a different course of action. However considerable the responsibility incurred, however great the bait offered, it would hardly be wise statesmanship to remain passive if England should by any series of disasters be crushed. Even though the immediate consequence would be to throw Canada and the British Antilles into the lap of the United States, it would leave the latter confronted by an Empire supreme on land and sea, and would force it to pursue a preparation of armaments which for its own preservation could not be inferior to what it might be called upon to face. Unperceived by many Americans, the European balance of power is a political necessity which can alone sanction in the Western Hemisphere the continuance of an economic development unhandicapped by the burden of extensive armaments.

The "disappearance or diminution" of even one state in Europe would be cause for alarm. Yet for the United

States the defeat of Great Britain would be more serious than that of Germany, because in case of German victory land and sea power would be controlled by the same power. A British victory, on the other hand, "would be the least likely to materially alter the existing status."

Since America "only at her own eventual cost" could remain indifferent to any upset of "what has for centuries been the recognized political fabric of Europe," Einstein regarded it as axiomatic that "the diplomatic role of the United States in Europe should be far more active than in the past." He doubtless had in mind the precedent of American participation in the Algeciras Conference, where he had served as secretary to the American delegation. "Properly understood and carried out by skillful agents," American diplomatic intervention in Europe would not be resented but would earn "the gratitude of all lovers of peace," for the United States would be "without selfish designs of its own" and would aim "to preserve the rights of all." Finally, Einstein declared emphatically that the United States must preserve "its strength in such a way as ever to make its counsel welcome and its action unnecessary."

Einstein's further views on American policy, made shortly after the actual outbreak of the war, likewise merit our attention. They offered a considerable contrast to Angell's suggestions of policy. Neither held neutrality to be an end in itself. The desideratum common to both was an active American diplomacy as regards European affairs. Likewise both agreed as to the undesirability of crushing Germany. Unlike Angell's proposal, however, Einstein's was not presented in terms of legal concepts and did not involve recasting international law.[5]

"With German success upon the Continent of Europe," he stated in November 1914, "we could not expect to interfere. Keen as would be our regret at the crushing of France, or the destruction of Belgian independence, we are unable to prevent either misfortune." With regard to England, however, it would be otherwise. Her defeat would be intolerable in that it would impose on the United States the need of a thorough militarization of its power. To forestall this, Einstein proposed a startlingly simple solution:

We must extend the Monroe Doctrine to England and embrace within its scope the foremost American Power after our own. It must, above all, be made plain that this is done not on grounds of common civilization or race, or tongue, but on grounds of solid interest reinforced by the weight of tradition and sentiment, but not guided thereby. . . . Such conception may astonish by its novelty. . . . The weight of our traditions would seem to conspire against it. . . . In the presence of new conditions, new ideas become necessary, and we would do well to borrow a leaf from that German realism which gauges a situation in the cold light of fact without being deviated by other considerations. We should then be able to understand the situation which a German triumph would threaten—of a nation exalted by successful war, imbued with the doctrine of force, persuaded of the destiny impelling it onward to world domination.

Inclusion of England among those nations whose integrity would be viewed by the United States as vital to its own security, while constituting a departure from the dogma of neutrality, would not, Einstein believed, necessarily entail going to war with Germany. If worst came to worst and Germany overran the Continent, a naval demonstration in British waters, he suggested, might suffice to deter Germany from proceeding further. He would prefer a diplomatic intervention designed to bring the war to an end on terms consonant with a continuing balance of power in Europe and compatible with American interests as regards any shifts in control of colonial areas. "By whatever paths the highroad of peace be approached," it could come ultimately, he believed, only through the United States.

Einstein warned that "our hopes may find themselves shattered, if they rely too exclusively on moral weight." Financial and military influence could be brought to bear with the greatest effect. He pointed out that "in our banking resources, especially at a moment like the present, we possess a reserve of strength and a diplomatic leverage of great magnitude." On the military side, Einstein would not only husband the strength of the navy, but place a quarter of a million volunteers under military instruction. This "could in no way interfere with our neutrality, but would enable our diplomacy to speak, when the moment came, with an authority which it now lacks."

In abandoning neutrality as the guideline of American policy, Wilson had considerable latitude within which to choose a new path. Einstein's views marked the conservative course, Angell's a more radical path. They both moved in the same direction since each was predicated on an active American policy vis-à-vis Europe. But, whereas the former accorded with the customary patterns of international politics, the latter would require erecting a new framework of legal assumptions and procedures.

II

Let us recall the essential difficulty of Wilson's position. In 1914–17 he was asked to adjust to a sudden and violent shift in the foundations of international politics. Admittedly a transition in American policy from indifference to active concern for European politics was in the long run inevitable. The conditions which supported the older attitude could not maintain themselves indefinitely; for history thus to have favored the United States would have constituted an altogether unwonted benevolence. Yet so strong was tradition, and so great the desire of Americans to continue their life without the harsh intervention of international politics, that the inevitability of the transition in no way lessened the painfulness of the change.

From the ideological point of view, which was that espoused by Lansing, a crushing defeat of Germany was sufficiently attractive to justify America's entering the war on that ground alone. But a crusade was unpromising from every standpoint other than the ideological. Not only did humanitarian considerations recommend a diplomacy to stop the war; this alternative was, from the balance of power standpoint, imperative. And there was a still more immediate reason for halting the war. A negotiated peace offered the only escape from the futility of the legal tangle over conduct of the war at sea which threatened constantly to precipitate the United States into the war for peripheral reasons.

A bold diplomatic intervention thus held enticing prospects. Yet its execution required the United States to be more than an amiable intermediary. American power would have to be brought into play, incurring the danger of military involvement or, though a lesser evil, loss of prestige. The risk was probably less restraint on Wilson than the fact that diplomatic action entailed departure from neutrality's injunctions of abstention and impartiality, and any action which left out of account public understanding and support ran the danger of fiasco. The Herculean task of preparing public opinion for a positive policy was undertaken by Wilson in May

1916, when he first openly championed the idea of a league of nations. The capstone of the new departure appeared when in December of that year he actively sought a negotiated peace.

Actually, considerably prior to the President's espousal of an interventionist diplomacy, Colonel House had grasped its importance. First of all, therefore, we should note those moves initiated by House which were designed to hasten the end of the war. Although failing of their immediate objective, they had consequences of singular importance.

Even before outbreak of the war, the dangerous conditions abroad were sufficiently apparent to House and Wilson to prompt the colonel's mission abroad in the summer of 1914 designed to ameliorate Anglo-German rivalry. After a not wholly unfavorable reception to his proposals in Berlin, House had moved on to London. He succeeded there in establishing some slight ground for discussion between the two governments, and was engaged in exploiting this gain when the crisis at Sarajevo overtook him. His proposal had been that the leading industrial nations, among which he numbered Japan, and, of course, the United States, should join in a common plan for development of backward areas throughout the world.

It is interesting parenthetically to note that House was not averse to giving Germany a "zone of influence" in Asia Minor and Persia, and a "freer hand" commercially in the Central and South American republics.

The colonel hoped that a cooperative attitude toward underdeveloped areas would lessen tension, permitting in due course a reduction of armaments. His proposal anticipated the mandates system. Moreover, the sudden descent of the war suggested the utility of an international organization meeting regularly in pursuance of common ends, and this he emphasized to Wilson after returning home.[6]

The war unfortunately having started, it became House's chief object to hasten its end. The fighting was but a few days old when the colonel wrote in his diary that if Germany were badly beaten, "France and Russia will want to rend her in twain." It was, he added, clearly to the interest of England and America and civilization to have German integrity preserved, "shorn, however, of her military and naval power." Writing to the President on August 22, House said that an Allied victory would mean "largely the domination of Russia on the Continent of Europe, and if Germany wins, it means the unspeakable tyranny of militarism for generations to come." As a matter of principle it was desirable that the war end without disaster to any major power; it was also urgent that steps be taken to end it soon. "For the moment," House pointed out to the President on September 18, 1914, "England dominates her allies. Later, she may not."[7]

Wilson on August 5 sent an earnest if perfunctory note to the belligerents stating that the United States Government would "welcome an opportunity to act in

the interest of European peace." House, entertaining
no illusions about the effectiveness of such a generalized and impersonal approach, meanwhile sought confidential relations with the Washington ambassadors of
the belligerent countries, hoping to stimulate their governments into negotiation. He found in the German ambassador a person who thoroughly favored a negotiated peace; Bernstorff was prepared to labor, no less
with his own government than in America, for a peace
without victory. Indeed in a conference on September
18, House found him willing to meet the British ambassador, Sir Cecil Spring-Rice.[8]

House immediately got in touch with the latter, insisting that Sir Cecil come to New York at once, which
the ambassador did on the twentieth. He demurred,
however, at conferring with Bernstorff, whom he considered "unreliable." The ambassador had the same
opinion of the German Government, the leaders of
which, he believed, "would not play fair and would
later denounce Great Britain as being treacherous to
her Allies." It would be necessary, Sir Cecil held, for
all the Allies to be approached simultaneously. This
fear of arousing suspicion among her associates in
the war; the deep distrust of Germany, which prompted
the British Government to demand a permanent reckoning; and the general attitude of Allied public opinion, which became increasingly intransigent, prevailed
in British councils throughout the war—despite the
agonized remonstrance of a small number of individ-

uals whom Sir Cecil called Copperheads.[9] In Germany, also, distrust was the overwhelmingly dominant sentiment; there, too, was the ever-recurring hope that the next throw of the dice would be more fortunate, leading to a permanent change in Germany's favor. Thus the war was to continue unabated, resulting in the end in disaster to all. The American Government, whether employing the generalized approach of Wilson's message of August 5—the repetition of which Secretary Bryan was constantly urging—or the more personal and confidential approach of House, was unable to accomplish anything through friendly exhortation. Only the impact of a strong external force, directed with consummate and indeed super-human skill, could have averted the bloody stalemate into which European statecraft presently descended.

Despite Sir Cecil's unreceptive mood, House sought to make to the ambassador the points which the colonel had already urged on Wilson: that for the time being Britain dominated her allies; and that, if Germany were thoroughly crushed, "there would be no holding Russia back." Together the two men composed a cable for Spring-Rice to send to Sir Edward Grey in which House's position was put thus: "If war continues, either G becomes supreme or R. Both alternatives would be fatal to the equilibrium of Europe. Consequently the present moment is more propitious to an agreement favorable to the principles of equilibrium." Sir Edward was also advised that "It would be dangerous for E to persist in *non possumus* attitude." [10]

Momentarily in December 1914 the prospect for peace looked promising. When House told Bernstorff that there would be no use talking to the Allies, except "upon a basis of evacuation and indemnity of Belgium and drastic disarmament which might ensure permanent peace," the ambassador replied that "there would be no obstacle in that direction." It was therefore most encouraging to House when three days later Spring-Rice informed him of word from Sir Edward Grey, who "thought it would not be a good thing for the Allies to stand out against a proposal which embraced indemnity to Belgium and a satisfactory plan for disarmament." Much to House's surprise, Sir Cecil offered the further opinion on the twenty-third "that the indemnity to Belgium could be arranged, for all the Powers might be willing to share the damages done that brave little nation." Sir Cecil saw signs of "a general funk among the European nations," most of whom feared revolution. At the same time it was disappointing for House to learn that, while Grey was personally agreeable to negotiating on the basis of evacuation of Belgium and disarmament, he had "not yet taken it up with his own Cabinet, much less with the Allies." [11]

By January 1915 knowledge of the American feelers was spreading. At Sir Cecil's insistence, House informed the Russian and French ambassadors. Jean

Adrien Jusserand violently denounced the Germans and refused to believe the German Government sincere.[12] On the fifteenth Ambassador Page in London lunched with General Sir John French, commander-in-chief of the British Expeditionary Forces, who, the ambassador reported, "told me of a peace proposal which he said the President, at Germany's request, had submitted to England." This proposal, according to French's understanding, was "to end the war on condition that Germany gives up Belgium and pays for its restoration." In the general's opinion England would have to accept such an offer "if it should be accompanied with additional offers to satisfy the other allies, such, for example, as the restoration to France of Alsace-Lorraine and the agreement that Russia shall have Constantinople." French spoke thus of additional offers which would entail a considerable departure from the *status quo ante,* despite the fact that he characterized the military situation as a stalemate. His estimate of the future course of the war was grim, but even so, as events proved, it was too sanguine. The Germans, he told Page, "cannot get to Paris or to Calais. On the other hand, it will take the Allies a year, perhaps two years, and an incalculable loss of men, to drive the Germans through Belgium. It would take perhaps four years and an unlimited number of men to invade Germany." [13]

When House and Wilson on January 12, 1915 agreed that the colonel should delay no longer his proposed second trip to Europe in behalf of peace, it was not because success had beckoned, but because House felt that he was "travelling in a circle" and that nothing more could be done with the ambassadors in Washington. It was doubtful whether Britain's allies would be willing to return to the *status quo ante,* and there was no confirmation of any kind from Berlin of Bernstorff's indications of such a willingness on Germany's part. Moreover, it disturbed House that public opinion in both Germany and Great Britain was becoming highly critical of the United States. In Germany the securing of American munitions by the Allies was deeply resented. In Great Britain, as Sir Edward Grey wrote, the public was acquiring the impression that the protests of the United States over British measures against German trade reflected the success of pro-German agitation.[14]

House sailed on January 30, and immediately on arriving in London he went into conference with Grey. The foreign secretary was interested in exploring the future of international stability. Already in communications to Spring-Rice, Grey had raised the crucial question whether the United States were disposed to assume the exacting and thankless tasks incumbent on a great power. Grey had cabled on December 22 that agreement among the great powers looking to mutual security and preservation of peace "might have stability if the United States would become a party to it and were prepared to join in repressing by force whoever broke the Treaty." Again on January 2, having gathered that House shrank from so radical a step, Grey declared to Spring-Rice that in such a case it was "difficult to see how a durable peace can be secured without complete exhaustion of one side or the other." [15]

Accordingly, when House and Grey met early in February 1915, Grey was "fairly insistent," so House reported to the President, "that we should come into some general guaranty for world-wide peace." Evading the issue, House countered that

a separate convention should be participated in by all neutrals as well as the present belligerents, which should lay down the principles upon which civilized warfare should in the future be conducted. In other words, it would merely be the assembling at The Hague and the adopting of rules governing the game.

Grey "did not accept this as our full duty," House reported to the President, and so the two men "passed on to other things." [16]

When on February 10, 1915 Grey again argued that the United States should throw its weight into the peace settlement, House told him "more directly" than before that "we could not do so; that it was not only the unwritten law of our country but also our fixed policy, not to become involved in European affairs." Ambassador Page surprised House by saying that such a policy as Sir Edward advocated "would be possible and advisable"; and in support Grey's secretary, Sir William Tyrrell, cited America's interventionist policy at Algeciras. Nevertheless, House held that

all we could do would be to join the neutrals and belligerents in a separate convention after the peace covenant was
drawn up and signed by the belligerents. I told Grey that
it would be impossible for our Government to take part
in such questions as what should become of Alsace-Lorraine and Constantinople, and that we could not be a
party to the making of the actual terms of peace, which
this first convention must necessarily cover. I felt sure,
though, that our Government would be willing to join all
nations in setting forth clearly the rights of belligerents
in the future and agreeing upon rules of warfare that
would take away much of the horror of war.

I suggested that this covenant should forbid the killing of non-combatants by aircraft, the violation of neutral
territory, and the setting forth of certain lanes of safety
at sea in order that shipping of all countries, both belligerent and neutral, would not be subject to attack when
they were in those lanes.[17]

Before 1914 there were times when war had been
mitigated by custom and convention. In the twentieth
century, however, because of a dynamic technology,
and shifts of great magnitude in the distribution of
national power, old restraints have proved ineffective.
Actually, House's solicitude for the manner of conducting warfare offered small inducement to Grey for getting on with peace negotiations. Nevertheless the British foreign secretary, going beyond the mere "lanes of
safety" which House had suggested, made an extraordinary proposal, a small and improbable beginning
of large consequences to follow.

Grey was willing to consider immunity from capture for all merchantmen, belligerent or neutral, wherever they were.[18] But what he had in mind was a far cry from traditional ideas of war and neutrality. He was assuming existence of "a great League of Peace," which would make aggression "practically impossible." And even so, Britain could agree to exempt merchant shipping from capture only if "other countries, such as the United States, would enter into an engagement that, if this immunity was violated by any Power they would go to war against that Power." This was a crude approximation to collective security, whereby freedom of the seas would paradoxically become the nexus of an Anglo-American alliance. But this much-desired union was not all Grey had in mind. He feared that "the development of the submarine will a few years hence make it impossible for us ever again to close the sea to an enemy and keep it free for ourselves." And if this prognosis were correct, it would have to be decided what "concessions, conditions or guarantees we should demand in return for our consent to the future freedom of the seas if it is proposed to us either through or by the United States."[19] Alive to the crucial importance of Anglo-American friendship, aware of the drag of tradition and public opinion on American policy, Grey tried to make the best of House's clumsy attempt to magnify freedom of the seas into a primary object of peace.[20]

When in mid-March House proceeded on to Berlin,

nothing remained of the prospect which Bernstorff had held out in the previous December. The German foreign minister, while cordially inviting House to visit Berlin, had made clear in advance that Germany military fortunes were not so low as to require an indemnity to Belgium. House had replied by waiving the question of indemnity and suggesting conversations on assumption of German willingness to evacuate Belgium and cooperate in establishing permanent peace. But on these points Zimmermann remained noncommittal, replying that "If England would consent to give up her claim to a monopoly on the seas together with her two-to-one power standard, I think it might be a good beginning." [21]

House arrived in Berlin on March 20, 1915, and after seeing Zimmermann that same day he sent a melancholy report to the President. His opinion now was that "some serious reverse will have to be encountered by one or other of the belligerents before any Government will dare propose parleys." He foresaw "troublous times ahead," declared it would be "the wonder of the ages" if all the governments came out of the war intact, and he was at a loss, he said, what to do next. Since "something is sure to crack somewhere before a great while," it looked "as if our best move just now is to wait until the fissure appears." Zimmermann stated well the dangers facing all the belligerents when he told House "that if peace parleys were begun now upon any terms that would have any chance of acceptance," it would mean the overthrow of his government and the Kaiser.[22] Obviously mass warfare, which necessarily entailed mass opinion, was not conducive to the restraint and introspection requisite to successful diplomacy.

Although House no longer believed in the possibility of immediate peace, he still continued to advocate the idea of freedom of the seas (as amended by Sir Edward Grey), hoping, as he told Chancellor Bethmann-Hollweg, that it might be the first thread across the chasm separating the Allies and the Central Powers. Needless to say, the chancellor and his foreign minister were surprised at the radical scope of House's proposal. They were also pleased because freedom of the seas to Germany meant freeing its foreign policy from the restraint of British sea power. Since to the United States it meant merely unimpeded neutral commerce in time of war, House was hardly justified in contending that Germany and America had a common interest in the matter. He did not fail, however, to recognize the political nature of Germany's interest, for he suggested to Bethmann-Hollweg that, were England to accept the proposal, the German Government "could say to the people that Belgium was no longer needed as a base for German naval activity, since England was being brought to terms." [23]

What attraction, one might well ask, would an arrangement so advantageous to the United States economically and to Germany politically have had for Great Britain? While it would prevent England's starving because of undersea attacks upon her commerce, there would always be danger of Germany breaking any pledge to observe freedom of the seas. We have seen that Sir Edward Grey had just this contingency in mind in making his acceptance of the scheme conditional on an undertaking from the United States to go to war with any country violating the pledge. After further reflection Sir Edward hastened to make perfectly clear that Britain also could not be content with a purely defensive posture, leaving Germany a free hand on the Continent. After departing from Germany, House received in Paris a letter from Grey stating that it would not be a "fair proposition" if German commerce were to go unmolested in time of war while Germany remained free to make war on other nations at will. "If on the other hand, Germany would enter after this war some League of Nations where she would give and accept the same security that other nations gave and accepted against war breaking out between them," then a reduction in armaments and "new rules to secure 'freedom of the seas'" might be made.[24]

With this letter, attentive to future actions on land as well as on sea, Sir Edward had rounded out his thought. He desired not just freedom of the seas but a guarantee against aggression. Freedom of the seas, which House had struggled to maintain as the continuing basis of American policy, would actually be reduced to an irrelevancy. Collective security, rather than the law of neutrality and the rules of maritime warfare, would become the dominant consideration. Thus, even though House had sought scrupulously to champion only what he called the rules of the game, seeking thereby to avoid any commitment of American power, he could not preserve American policy from the contamination of high politics.

But even had this proposal of early 1915 for expanding the idea of freedom of the seas formed any real basis for negotiation, it was doomed to almost immediate failure. The sinking of the *Lusitania* in early May destroyed all further hope of proceeding in that direction. Actually freedom of the seas was destined to play a role altogether different from that envisioned by House. Instead of serving as a principle of reconciliation, it was in the end given as a reason for America's entry into the war. Irony turns to paradox when we reflect that freedom of the seas was not even mentioned in the Versailles Treaty.

III

Up to the time of the *Lusitania* disaster, Colonel House had not viewed participation by the United States in the war as either probable or desirable. Although from the very beginning he constantly had urged preparedness upon Wilson, he believed less that American arms would be used in actual combat than that preparedness would strengthen American diplomacy and, above all, by discouraging flagrant disregard of American rights, reduce the danger of involvement.

The *Lusitania* incident, however, caused House to re-
sign himself to the probability of war. In fact, having
concluded that war with Germany was "inevitable," he
decided on May 30, 1915 to cut short his European
parleys and return to the United States.[25]

When on August 19, 1915 the British liner *Arabic*
was torpedoed and sunk with the loss of two American lives, House favored sending Bernstorff home, beginning vigorous preparations for war, and entering
the war should Germany commit another such offense.
Yet the colonel was reluctant to press this course on
the President, to whom he suggested alternatives:
placing responsibility for the next diplomatic step on
Congress, in a special session (which however "would
be a dangerous move because there is no telling what
Congress would do"), or else privately informing
Bernstorff that a disavowal and complete surrender by
Germany on the submarine issue could alone prevent
a rupture.[26]

Soon, however, House's attitude toward the submarine issue underwent marked change. His views did
not henceforth remain consistent, but at no time was
he disposed to accept the submarine route to war with
the same equanimity as, for example, Ambassador
Page, Secretary Lansing, or ex-President Theodore
Roosevelt. House's reasoned judgment seemed to be
that to stay out of war offered a great opportunity to
exercise constructive influence on its course, but that,
were we to go in, a *casus belli* relating to the large

problem of shaping the peace was preferable to one turning on Germany's submarine warfare.

In the somewhat relaxed period after settlement of the *Arabic* case in the fall of 1915, House concluded that opportunity to break with Germany over the submarine issue had been lost.[27] The program of action which he at this time began to propose did not depend on the submarine for fulfillment and required, in fact, that a break with Germany on that issue be avoided. Similarly the plan required that controversy with the Allies, constantly recurring over American neutral trade, be held in abeyance. House desired instead that the United States seize the initiative and take positive diplomatic action. He sought to introduce purpose, coherence, and flexibility into American policy which instead of responding spasmodically to German torpedoings would gain a rationale and direction of its own. Unfortunately the very candor of his proposal militated against its success. Unlike the outraged opinion on which resistance to the submarine rested, House proposed a course divorced from public emotions, requiring indeed a wholly sober estimate of the national interest.

The deeply divided and partisan character of American opinion was not lost on House. On returning home in June 1915 he was impressed with the painfulness of Wilson's position. In a revealing letter of August 4 to Ambassador Page in London, he wrote that the President "sees the situation just as you see it and as

I do, but he must necessarily heed the rocks." While the American people desired a firm policy toward Germany, House said ninety per cent did not want the President to go to such lengths that war would follow. "If the President had followed any course other than the one he has, his influence would have been broken and he would not be able to steer the nation, as he now is, in the way which in the end will be best for all." Meanwhile House attributed the derision to which Wilson was subjected in England to the fact that the war had been going badly for the Allies, and likened it to the frequently captious criticism against the English on the part of their French ally. "A year ago the Allies would have been content beyond measure if they could have been assured that munitions of war would go to them from here in such unrestricted volume." They would also have found it hard to believe that the President would "demand of Germany a cessation of her submarine policy in regard to the sinking of merchantmen without warning, to the extent of a threat of war. What neutral nation has done so much? The shipping of Holland, Sweden, Norway, Denmark, and Spain has been sunk without warning and innumerable lives lost. Each of those nations, I take it, had passengers upon the *Lusitania,* and yet not one has raised a voice in protest and no criticism has come from the Allies." With respect to American opinion House noted an underlying complacency. "It is not altogether clear to Americans that we could not well take care of ourselves if needs be. Our hopes, our aspirations, and our sympathies are closely woven with the democracies of France and England, and it is this that causes our hearts and powerful economic help to go out to them, and not the fear of what may follow for us in their defeat." [28]

Nevertheless, judging by the optimism with which he entered on his new course for a negotiated peace, House did not appreciate the full implications for national policy of American public opinion. Not only was there disinclination to view the war as a threat to the traditional power relations in the world, but no single dominating interpretation of the meaning of the war for the United States had emerged in any form whatsoever. Meritorious as House's plan was in itself, it is doubtful whether Congress would have acquiesced in the employment of American force which the plan envisioned as a possibility. House could not have been without misgivings on this score, but rather than retreat before the submarine or merely drift— neither of which alternatives was without grave objection—he followed his chosen course.[29] He was profoundly worried in the autumn of 1915 over the prospect of German victory; and whether it was achieved with or without submarine frightfulness, he felt that the United States, in the interest of national security, must forestall a defeat of the Allies.[30]

Whereas Wilson's policy was strongly inclined to the side of keeping the United States out of war, House

would shift the emphasis, making the objective to
end hostilities as soon as possible on terms acceptable
to the Allies and the United States. Recognizing the
risk of involvement which such a policy entailed,
House pointed out to the President that it looked as
if Germany "had a better chance than ever of winning,
and if she did win our turn would come next; and we
were not only unprepared, but there would be no one
to help us stand the first shock." [31] House repeated the
same argument to the counselor of the Department of
State, Frank Polk. "It will not do," he told Polk, "for
the United States to let the Allies go down and leave
Germany the dominant military factor in the world.
We would certainly be the next object of attack, and
the Monroe Doctrine would be less indeed than 'a
scrap of paper.'" Polk approved House's idea enthusi-
astically, and "hoped the President would finally put
it through." Secretary Lansing, also, was "willing to
advise a strong course." [32]

A German victory, House believed, could be forestalled through a compromise peace or, failing that,
by the United States actively joining the Allies. The
former was preferable, but at what point could pressure be exerted to effect it? Unlike Wilson's peace
move of December 1916, House's plan did not call
for appeal to public opinion over the heads of belligerent governments. Nor did House evince willingness,
such as Wilson subsequently showed, to bring economic pressure on the Allies. He planned that the

United States would issue a call for a peace conference when the Allies themselves had indicated that the time was ripe. Should Germany refuse, or, having entered a conference, prove intransigent, the United States would join the Allies. German policy thus would be under constraint of American military intervention. The Allies, however, would be under no comparable inducement. Apart from a prudent desire to keep on the good side of American opinion, the Allies, House believed, would be influenced by the prospect of a postwar security based on general disarmament.

House counted at least on Britain's support of a broadly international as opposed to a narrowly national viewpoint. Like the United States, Britain was notably content with the *status quo*. Both nations, moreover, had been deeply stirred by the great humanitarian impulses of the nineteenth century. An Anglo-American attempt at meliorating the ambitions of others would, therefore, seem to be an undertaking in accord with historical circumstance.

After House's return to the United States in June 1915, a brisk correspondence set in between him and Sir Edward Grey. That the key to future peace lay in a league against aggression was Grey's constantly reiterated thought. Repeating what he had often told House, that the "refusal of a Conference was the fatal step that decided peace or war last year," Grey drew the moral that "the pearl of great price . . . would be some League of Nations that could be relied on to insist that disputes between any two nations must be settled." The powers, he said, must bind themselves to international law, and give it a sanction. Referring obliquely to House's earlier endeavor to confine American interest to the "rules of the game," Grey said that if an international legal order could be secured, then freedom of the seas and "many other things" would become easy. He made again the now familiar point that "it is not a fair proposition that there should be a guaranty of the freedom of the seas while Germany claims to recognize no law but her own on land." Another letter followed a few weeks later. In America, Grey believed, there was "a great body of reflecting public opinion so disposed that it can give a great impulse and guidance" to the idea of an international system for preventing future wars.[33]

The climax came on September 22, 1915. Writing that the great object was to get future security against aggression, Grey asked bluntly,

How much are the United States prepared to do in this direction? Would the President propose that there should be a League of Nations binding themselves to side against any Power which broke a treaty; which broke certain rules of warfare on sea or land (such rules would, of course, have to be drawn up after this war); or which refused, in case of dispute, to adopt some other method of settlement than that of war?

Only in some such agreement could Grey see "a prospect of diminishing militarism and navalism." He could not say which governments would be prepared to accept such a proposal, but he was sure that "the Government of the United States is the only Government that could make it with effect."[34]

Occupied with what he deemed the probability of mediation along the lines which House had earlier adumbrated, Grey must have read with some astonishment House's reply of October 17. Up to this point there had been no indication of American willingness to join the Allies, except as this might occur indirectly through the independent quarrel with Germany over the submarine. House now stated that the United States was prepared to intervene militarily if Germany refused a peace settlement "along the lines you and I have so often discussed." When Sir Edward considered that the time was propitious, House, having first conferred with the British Government, would "proceed to Berlin and tell them that it was the President's purpose to intervene and stop this destructive war, provided the weight of the United States thrown on the side that accepted our proposal could do it." House would not let the Germans know of any understanding with the Allies, "but would rather lead them to think our proposal would be rejected by the Allies. This might induce Berlin to accept." If Germany declined, or, having accepted, was obdurate in negotiations, "it would [probably] be necessary for us to join the Allies and force the issue."[35]

The word "probably" was added to House's draft by Wilson.[36]

Sir Edward cannot have failed to be impressed with this qualification. Moreover, when House said that the United States would "demand that peace parleys begin upon the broad basis of elimination of militarism and navalism," Grey could not be sure that he had won his point about the necessity for an American guarantee against future aggression. With reference to this latter ambiguity, he cabled on November 9: "What is the proposal of the elimination of militarism and navalism that you contemplate?" Was it, he asked, a league of nations?[37] House sent Grey's inquiry to Wilson, arguing that the influence of the United States should be put behind a league for upholding international obligations and maintaining the peace, "not only for the sake of civilization, but for our own welfare—for who may say when we may be involved in such a holocaust as is now devastating Europe?" He then circumspectly reverted, however, to the safer confines of neutral rights. "Must we not," he asked Wilson, "be a party to the making of new and more humane rules of warfare, and must we not lend our influence towards the freedom of both the land and sea?" Someone trained in the precise language of diplomacy would hardly have cast so wide a net. The colonel's suggested reply to Grey, that "the proposal contemplated is broadly speaking along the lines mentioned" in Grey's letter of September 22, also fell short of a model of clarity. Troubled by the double qualification, Wilson eliminated the phrase "broadly speaking" from the reply which on November 10, 1915 was actually sent.[38]

But, however gingerly, American policy had entered upon a new era, and it was to the President's liking. In a letter of November 11, he told House that Grey's idea about a league of nations "contains the *necessary* programme." [39]

In the autumn of 1915 the war was over a year old, and up to this point the British had been primarily responsible for advancing the idea of a league. Prime Minister Herbert Asquith had foreshadowed the idea early in the war, but it entered the actual diplomacy of the war as a result of House's endeavor to find a basis for mediation.[40] Grey desired that such an intervention, if it were to materialize, be pitched at the highest political level; he was seeking to avert the embarrassment to British naval warfare of an American diplomacy whose horizon was confined to traditional freedom of the seas; he aimed also at converting House's advocacy of disarmament into a positive commitment of power. This does not mean that Grey was insincere. He valued the idea of a league for its own sake, and realized clearly that the United States was essential to its fulfillment. We shall see, however, that Grey subsequently refused to capitalize on the historic shift away from isolationist traditions which he had induced in American policy.

SEVEN

The House-Grey Memorandum

WRITING to Colonel House in July 1915, Sir Edward Grey expressed an interesting judgment. The American reaction to the *Lusitania* disaster, he wrote, showed that it would "take very great provocation to force your people into war." Yet for this very reason he was doubtful "whether anything short of being actually involved in the war" would stir the public sufficiently to enable the President to exercise "all the influence that is possible" on the terms of peace.[1] Grey accordingly was persuaded that American influence could more effectively be brought to bear through military rather than diplomatic intervention —and was duly appreciative of the sporting chance that the submarine might at any time catapult the United States into the war.

Unless far more pressure were exerted on the British than House seemed willing to contemplate, the foreign secretary would choose to view the league as the capstone of victory rather than as an inducement to parley with the Germans. House's cable of November 10 announcing Wilson's acceptance of the league idea was of course the prelude to a new endeavor to get negotiations started. Anticipating just that, Grey wrote House November 11 that "the situation at the moment and the feelings here and among the Allies, and in Germany so far as I know, do not justify me in urging you to come on the ground that your presence would have any practical result." Nor did he see how the Allies "could commit themselves in advance to any proposition, without knowing exactly what it was, and knowing that the United States of America were prepared to intervene and make it good if they accepted it." [2]

I

American diplomacy now entered upon its most confused period. On December 28, 1915, House, still bent on furthering his plan for mediation, proceeded to Europe. This was the second of his wartime missions. The unresponsiveness of Grey's letter of November 11 could perhaps be overcome through personal contact, and House hoped, moreover, that the message approving the league idea might have made an impression on which he could capitalize. Yet the fact remained that House and Lansing and Wilson still lacked a common understanding as to the direction in which American policy should move. Each of the three men was strongly pro-Ally, and apprehensive over the consequences of a German victory, but this did not insure a coherent American policy.

From Hot Springs, Virginia, Wilson wrote House on the eve of the latter's departure for England. Had Grey seen this instruction, he would have felt that his misgivings were confirmed, for it contained some of the earlier hesitancies and ambiguities of which he had complained to House. Wilson stated that the United States could not be concerned with "territorial questions, indemnities, and the like," but only with the guarantees to be given for the future peace of the world: "(a) military and naval disarmament and (b) a league of nations to secure each nation against aggression and maintain the absolute freedom of the seas." If either party in the war agreed to discuss peace on these terms, "it will clearly be our duty," Wilson said, "to use our utmost moral force to oblige the other to parley, and I do not see how they could stand in the opinion of the world if they refused." [3] Wilson failed to make the slightest reference to that aspect of House's plan which contemplated entering the war against Germany as a possible contingency.

Uppermost in Wilson's mind was the situation developing in Congress where his diplomatic leadership was under fire. The need for House's errand, he continued, was the more pressing because of "the demand in the Senate for further, immediate, and imperative pressure on England and her allies." But mediation would have to come quickly if the impending crisis were to be forestalled. Wilson again pressed House on January 11, cabling that "it now looks as if our several difficulties with Germany would be presently adjusted. So soon as they are the demand here especially from the Senate will be imperative that we force England to make at least equal concessions to our unanswerable claims of rights. This is just at hand." [4] The negotiations between the secretary of state and Ambassador Bernstorff over the *Lusitania* seemed on the verge of success, and this would result in the pressure for neutral rights shifting from Germany to Great Britain.

But not only did exasperation in the United States over the British blockade impinge on House's mission. The question of the armed merchantman also became critical at this time. With respect to this perplexing and increasingly urgent problem, Secretary Lansing approached the Allies on January 18 with a proposal containing a threat of excluding the Allies from American ports unless they divested their merchantmen of armament.[5] House, endeavoring to persuade the British of American awareness of a common cause, was dismayed at this development. But the irony of the situation had still another, and even more arresting, side. An entry in Lansing's diary of January 9, 1916, reveals that Lansing, had he felt free from the importunities of public opinion, would have taken quite a different position on the armed merchantman. He reiterated in this entry his basic and unchanging belief that the German military oligarchy was "a bitter enemy to democracy in every form" and that it would turn on the United States "as its next obstacle to imperial rule over the world" were it to triumph over Great Britain and France. It was therefore "safer and surer and wiser . . . to be one of many enemies than to be in the future alone against a victorious Germany." But public opinion, he wrote, "is not yet ready to accept this point of view." Even renewal of ruthless submarine warfare would be insufficient to dispose Congress to "drastic action"; moreover Congress "would be resentful if the President should act without their authorization." Lansing therefore resigned himself to the necessity of preventing a situation "which will force this government into open hostility to the German Government. The time for that has not come." [6] Thus House, whose plan contained the possibility of open hostility, and Lansing differed radically in their ideas of what was practical.

To the chronic strain which the blockade imposed on Anglo-American relations was added this new dispute over the armed merchantman. A coordinated strategy might have used British alarm over American policy, particularly regarding the armed merchantman, to force a cooperative attitude toward House's efforts at mediation. An institutionalized procedure for deliberating on policy questions (such as today's National Security Council) would conceivably have led to exploring a connection between these seemingly discordant aspects of the situation. Actually, however, Wilson's individualistic bent discouraged such a procedure; more-over, traditions and machinery were lacking for that kind of approach.

Certainly the situation as House saw it in January 1916 had no mitigating element. He was confronted with a British attitude which, already skeptical of the firmness of any American commitment, chose to view the continuing complaints over infraction of neutral rights as another instance of American vagary. Re-plying to the President's cable of January 11, House assured Wilson that he had impressed on "nearly every member of the Cabinet" the state of public opinion in America. "They know your position now as well as I know it, and they appreciate it." Nonetheless the minister of blockade, Lord Robert Cecil, had told House that if he acceded to the President's urging "his resignation would be demanded at once." Cecil even went "so far as to suggest that it might come to the complete abandonment of the blockade, in which case Germany would perhaps win." There could be no halfway measures, Cecil asserted. The measures taken by Britain had "to be rigid, or not at all."

Three days later House wrote the President that it "would be a calamity if anything should happen to prevent Sir Edward's continuance in the Government until peace is made." Yet Grey, too, was likely to go, "if we push them too hard upon the question of neu-tral trade." The opinion was fixed, he reported, "that America will do nothing, and that England must fight the battle alone, with the only weapon that had so far proved effective." House was still confident that his plan could straighten things out and he assured the President that "the criticism, both in Europe and America, comes from ignorance and from partisan feeling, and can be swept aside by your final action." Meanwhile it was imperative that "our policy should be to have no serious break with the Allies over the blockade." House also added that diplomatic relations with Germany should be maintained if at all possible.[7]

The colonel's views prevailed. He had the satisfaction of being informed by the President that "We are trying to be guided by what you think and shall await your full report upon your return home before taking any steps that might alter our opportunity, providing the sea operations of the Central Powers make it possible for us to maintain the status quo." House on February 14 ventured a direct cable to Lansing concerning the armed merchantman: "There are so many other issues involved in the controversy concerning armed merchantmen that I sincerely hope you will be able to hold it in abeyance until I return. I cannot emphasize too strongly the importance of this." [8] Accordingly, Lansing at a press conference on the sixteenth did an about-face, reverting to the orthodox position on arming merchantmen. In consequence Wilson proceeded to ride out the storm in Congress on an issue which could not have been more unpropitious—the right of Americans to travel on armed belligerent merchantmen.

The lack of consistent policy in Washington was not all that House had to contend with. The British, he found, were still not disposed to agree to his plan. We have noted the continuing skepticism which he encountered as to the ability of the American Government to commit its power. No sooner had House arrived in London than he cabled the President asking a renewed expression of "willingness to cooperate in a policy seeking to bring about and maintain permanent peace." Repeating what had already been said in the message of the preceding November, Wilson replied that he would be "willing and glad" to cooperate in the furtherance of such an objective. With respect, however, to the more immediate and difficult question of what the United States would do if Germany blocked mediation, there was no reinforcement from Washington of House's promise of military intervention.[9]

Still another consideration was bound to give the British pause. Upon them would fall the chief responsibility of selling the mediation plan to the other Allies, and of determining when it should be invoked. This would be awkward at best, for it entailed risk of undermining the confidence of Britain's allies.

But, whatever the obstacles in London, House's position vis-à-vis the British was strengthened by an even stronger opposition to American mediation on the part of the Germans. The German attitude was so negative that, even were the British to accede to the House plan, they ran no appreciable risk of having to negotiate seriously with Germany. During his four-day visit in Berlin (January 26–30, 1916), House confirmed his already strong suspicion that Germany would insist on nothing less than complete victory. "Time and again" he was obliged to point out to Bethmann-Hollweg that the latter's expression of a desire for peace "meant a victorious peace and one which included indemnity from his antagonists." [10] Yet even Germany's foregoing reparations would have constituted only a small step in the direction of what House considered a reasonable peace. According to the House-Grey Memorandum of February 1916, House favored as a minimum the restoration of Belgium, transfer of Alsace-Lorraine to France, acquisition by Russia of an outlet to the sea, and compensation for Germany outside Europe. Such terms were not those of Allied victory but, as Grey pointed out later in his autobiography, "for Germany they were the terms of positive defeat." To Grey it was "inconceivable that Prussian militarism could look at such terms, while it was still undefeated and hoping for victory." [11]

Whatever the appearance, then, the American offer of mediation promised in fact to constitute the prelude to intervention on the Allied side. Yet although entry of the United States into the war was much desired by the British leaders, the situation had still another aspect requiring consideration. American military intervention might perhaps be accomplished with less bother and more certainty if it were permitted to result from submarine warfare. Thus on the one hand the determination of the Germans to achieve victory on their own terms had the effect of making House's plan more palatable to the British. By the very same token, however, the probability of intensified submarine warfare was greatly increased—thereby subtracting from House's bargaining power.

House struggled to prevent the submarine controversy from wrecking his attempt at mediation. While in Berlin he was fully apprised of the bitter struggle between the German civilians and the military over submarine policy, and appreciated the circumstances which favored eventual triumph of the military. Yet he persisted in avoiding this easy road to American intervention in the war. House cabled the President a vivid account of the tense situation he had found, and urged that final action in the still unresolved *Lusitania* case not be taken until he had an opportunity of talking with Wilson. The German Navy, he said, believed "that Great Britain can be effectively blockaded, provided Germany can use their new and powerful submarines indiscriminately." German naval leaders also believed that the failure of the Imperial Government to adopt this policy "resulted from our interference and Germany's endeavor to conform to our demands." Finally, the German military believed that war with the United States "would not be so disastrous as Great Britain's blockade." Since the civil government felt that if the blockade continued, they could no longer stand against the military, they were unwilling to admit the illegality of undersea warfare. If that point were insisted upon in the *Lusitania* negotiations, House predicted war would follow.[12]

House told Jules Cambon of the French Foreign Office that to break with Germany over the *Lusitania* was in any case not feasible because "it would place the United States at a disadvantage to go to war over an incident ten months old." Germany, he had added, "would give us another opportunity if we desired one, as the pinch of the blockade would cause her to revert to her original undersea warfare."[13] But for the time being, at least, House was resisting use of the submarine issue in any form as a *casus belli*. Again, as at the outbreak of war, he was seeking to avoid a crushing defeat for either side. Once in the war, he wrote the President February 9, the United States would lose its leverage on the belligerents and "the war would have to go to a finish with all its appalling consequences." House informed Wilson that he had told the British and French Governments and had "intimated" as much to the Germans that it was better for them, "as indeed it is better for us," to hold aloof. Any "unprejudiced person," he said, could see that it would be unwise "for America to take part in this war unless it comes about by intervention based upon the highest human motives." A policy which took its cue from the submarine did not give this assurance; his plan, House

believed, was free of that disadvantage. The way out
was clear, and he added "when I can lay the facts before you, I believe it will be clear to you also." [14]

II

Considering the obstacles that House encountered
because of both the confusion in Washington and the
unyielding situation in Europe, it is surprising that
his mission should have been productive of anything
whatsoever. Yet not long after his return to London
from the Continent, he and Grey prepared their famous memorandum setting forth House's plan for a
negotiated peace.

On the morning of February 10, House held a long
conversation with Grey, and came away very much
encouraged. True, Grey had once more expressed misgivings over the prospect of the American Government's relegating the submarine issue to a secondary
position, but "in ten minutes," so House informed the
President, "I had brought him round." The principal
argument employed by House, now as in his previous
conversations in January, was that Britain faced a
danger of standing alone against Germany. Russia,
House believed, would probably be obliged to make
a separate peace. He predicted that Italy would succumb to German blandishments, and so would France.
This was the risk which, House maintained, Britain
would be taking if she insisted on fighting the war
to a military conclusion. House also took care to in-

form Grey that he had revealed the purpose of his mission to the French. Finally, House declared, social and economic conditions in Germany were still such as to enable Germany to hold the Western Front. No revolution, he said, would disturb Germany until after the war.

These arguments, which are telling even in retrospect, evidently were not lost on Grey. House was able to report to the President that Grey was prepared to agree "that it would be best for you to demand that the belligerents permit you to call a conference for the discussion of peace terms. We concluded this would be better than intervention [on the submarine issue], and it was understood, though not definitely agreed upon, that you might do this within a very short time —perhaps soon after I returned." He added that if Germany should refuse to agree to a conference, "I have promised for you that we will throw in all our weight in order to bring her to terms." [15]

House proceeded to confer with other key members of the British Government. With Grey as host he lunched with Prime Minister Herbert Asquith, and the first lord of the Admiralty, Arthur Balfour. House warned that should Germany soon appear to be winning, the British "need not expect action from us, for it would be foolhardy for the United States to enter at so late a day in the hope of changing the result in their favor." In such circumstances, he said, the United States "would probably create a large army and navy, and retire entirely from European affairs and depend upon themselves." [16]

That evening House dined with Lloyd George, minister of munitions, and the lord chief justice, Lord Reading.[17] The climax came three days later on February 14 when with Reading as host House met with Asquith, Grey, Balfour, and Lloyd George. Whatever reservations the British leaders may have had were, for the time being, overcome by House's persuasiveness. When he presented the question as to when the United States could properly demand that the war cease and a conference be held, they agreed that such a move would be desirable. The question of timing, however, was one on which they felt unable to make a definite commitment. The matter was discussed in its many ramifications, House proposing that the psychological moment would be immediately after the Allies had achieved some important military success against the Germans. With this proposal there seemed to be general agreement, although the danger was recognized that if success were too great Allied opinion would be heartened and the demand for victory heightened. "While the conference was not conclusive," House recorded in his diary, "there was at least a common agreement reached in regard to the essential feature; that is, the President should at some time, to be later agreed upon, call a halt and demand a conference. I did not expect to go beyond that, and I was quite content." [18]

Although it is relevant to suggest that the British were prone to nurse the susceptibilities of a strong neutral, it is nevertheless clear that House had struck a responsive chord and that his patience had been in a measure rewarded. The next day Grey spoke with emotion of the prospect of ending further bloodshed and havoc.[19] Lord Reading complimented House on having succeeded in committing such rivals as Lloyd George, Balfour, and Asquith in the presence of each other, and said that Asquith privately had spoken much more strongly in favor of the scheme than he had at the conference. The intention was, Reading told House, to make a push on the Western Front at the earliest possible date.[20]

Meanwhile on February 17 House and Grey had incorporated the general and tentative agreement of the government leaders in a memorandum. Shown to Asquith, Balfour, and Lloyd George for their approval, a copy dated February 22 was initialed by Grey alone and given to House to convey to the President. Although many times reproduced, the text of this document is here given in full:

Colonel House told me that President Wilson was ready, on hearing from France and England that the moment was opportune, to propose that a Conference should be summoned to put an end to the war. Should the Allies accept this proposal, and should Germany refuse it, the United States would probably enter the war against Germany.

Colonel House expressed the opinion that, if such a Conference met, it would secure peace on terms not unfavourable to the Allies; and, if it failed to secure peace, the United States would [probably] leave the Conference as a belligerent on the side of the Allies, if Germany was unreasonable. Colonel House expressed an opinion decidedly favourable to the restoration of Belgium, the transfer of Alsace and Lorraine to France, and the acquisition by Russia of an outlet to the sea, though he thought that the loss of territory incurred by Germany in one place would have to be compensated to her by concessions to her in other places outside Europe. If the Allies delayed accepting the offer of President Wilson, and if, later on, the course of the war was so unfavourable to them that the intervention of the United States would not be effective, the United States would probably disinterest themselves in Europe and look to their own protection in their own way.

I said that I felt the statement, coming from the President of the United States, to be a matter of such importance that I must inform the Prime Minister and my colleagues; but that I could say nothing until it had received their consideration. The British Government could, under no circumstances, accept or make any proposal except in consultation and agreement with the Allies. I thought that the Cabinet would probably feel that the present situation would not justify them in approaching their Allies on this subject at the present moment; but, as Colonel House had had an intimate conversation with M. Briand and M. Jules Cambon in Paris, I should think it right to tell M. Briand privately, through the French Ambassador in London, what Colonel House had said to us; and I should, of course, whenever there was an opportunity, be ready to talk the matter over with M. Briand, if he desired it.

(Intd.) E.G.

FOREIGN OFFICE
22 *February* 1916 [21]

House on March 6 was back in Washington reporting to the President, who approved the memorandum with one alteration—insertion of the word "probably" (which appears in brackets in the foregoing text). In so doing, there is nothing to suggest that the President believed he was altering the force of the agreement. The qualification, which already appeared twice in the text, notably in the first paragraph, was in keeping with the well-known limitations on the President's constitutional powers. Moreover, the President's expression of gratitude to House was heartfelt.[22] On the following day the President himself composed the reply, which was cabled to Grey on the eighth over House's signature:

I reported to the President the general conclusions of our conference of the 14th of February, and in the light of those conclusions he authorizes me to say that, so far as he can speak for the future action of the United States, he agrees to the memorandum with which you furnished me, with only this correction: that the word "probably" be added after the word "would" and before the word "leave" in line number nine.

Please acknowledge receipt of this cable.[23]

Although, as we shall see, Wilson subsequently prodded Grey to give the signal for the United States to call for peace negotiations, we are unable to say precisely what circumstances would have been regarded by Wilson as obliging him to call upon Congress for a declaration of war. How prominently that ultimate step figured in his thinking cannot be determined. One can definitely assert, however, that he had high hopes that once in conference the warring nations would find it impossible to resume hostilities.

In a letter of March 10 to Grey, House interpreted Wilson's successful struggle with Congress over the question of American travel on armed belligerent merchantmen as indicative of the President's strength to back up the mediation plan: "If the situation continues as now, and if Congress does not restrict him, everything will go through as planned. His recent victory in Congress was complete and indicates that the matter is entirely in his hands." Explaining that the President himself had written the cable of the eighth, which constituted "complete approval" of the London memorandum, House continued that "It is now squarely up to you to make the next move, and a cable from you at any time will be sufficient." [24]

EIGHT

Wilson's Efforts Toward Peace

PRESIDENT WILSON'S reluctance to break
with Germany over the torpedoing of the *Sussex* has been noted. Losing confidence in the adequacy
of maritime rights as a guide to action, he was
beginning to judge his policy in terms of the outcome
of the war and the ultimate peace settlement. From
that point of view he saw certain advantages to choosing his own occasion and conditions for intervening,
and he preferred that intervention be diplomatic, not
military. House had for a number of months advocated
such an approach, but he urged Wilson to break with
Germany over the *Sussex* without parley. The turn of
events was not what House might have wished, but he
felt that for Wilson to maintain any standing before
the American people and the Allies, to the end of
safeguarding American influence at the peace conference, the President must live up to his past pronounce-
ments on the submarine.[1] Narrow considerations of
maritime right and broad considerations of political

purpose were thus becoming badly entangled, making more difficult Wilson's task of constructing a policy.

I

The President and House discussed at length on March 30, 1916 the proper course in the *Sussex* case. House asserted that for the United States to become a belligerent over the submarine issue "would not be without its advantages." "We could still," he insisted, "be the force to stop the war when the proper time came," and Wilson's influence at the peace conference would be "enormously enhanced instead of lessened." There was, however, an alternative course. Grey could be asked "whether or not it would be wise to intervene now rather than permit the break to come." [2] When on April 6 House again saw Wilson, the two men discussed giving the Allies a last chance to accept the American offer of mediation. House was not certain that it would be a wise thing to do, and the President wished to avoid the impression that the United States desired the Allies to act "in order to save us." In the end Wilson decided to cable Grey, because the British should know that "in our opinion the war would last longer with us as a belligerent than as a neutral." Accordingly, the following cable, prepared by Wilson, was sent to Grey over House's signature:

Since it seems probable that this country must break with Germany on the submarine question unless the unexpected happens, and since, if this country should once become a belligerent, the war would undoubtedly be prolonged, I beg to suggest that if you had any thought of acting at an early date on the plan we agreed upon, you might wish now to consult with your allies with a view to acting immediately.[3]

But far from spurring the British to take the initiative, the *Sussex* incident had the opposite effect. By admission of the cable itself, the *Sussex* was leading to an almost certain break with Germany.

Grey had already informed House in a letter of March 24 that the British cabinet had decided the time had not yet come to ask France to consider a conference. Grey felt that he could do nothing more than inform Premier Briand of Wilson's approval of the House-Grey Memorandum, after which it would be up to the French to make the next move. Grey believed, moreover, that the French would not be disposed to any diplomatic decisions until the fighting at Verdun had reached an issue.[4] This gigantic battle, unprecedented in violence, had begun with a German attack on February 21, 1916 and was to continue unabated until the end of June.

On April 7 Grey reported that he had carried out his intention of informing the French, but that during his and Asquith's visit to Paris neither Briand, nor Cambon of the French Foreign Office, had mentioned the subject. As for Great Britain, everybody, Grey wrote, "feels there must be more German failure and some Allied success before anything but an inconclusive peace could be obtained." Grey did not believe that American entry into the war would prolong it but rather that the war would be shortened. Moreover, while acknowledging House's preference for not coming into the war on the submarine issue, he saw a difficulty in the renewed activity of the submarine:

If the United States Government takes a strong line about these acts, it must, I suppose, become more difficult for it to propose a conference to Germany; if on the other hand, it passes them over, the Allies will not believe that the United States Government will at the conference take a line strong enough to ensure more than a patched up and insecure peace.[5]

The cabled appeal of April 6 was, then, of no effect, and on the nineteenth the *Sussex* note, a virtual ultimatum, was sent to Germany.

Contrary to expectations in Washington and London, Germany yielded. Once again picking up the thread of mediation, Wilson through House pointed out to Grey in a cable of May 10 that with cessation of Germany's unlawful submarine activities the feeling would increase in the United States "that the Allies are more determined upon the punishment of Germany than upon exacting terms that neutral opinion would consider just." Now was the psychological time for the President "publicly to commit the United States to joining with the other Powers in a convention looking to the maintenance of peace after the war." The parties to such a convention would "pledge themselves to side against any Power breaking a treaty" or "refusing in case of dispute to adopt some other method of settlement than that of war." There is nothing here of the ambiguity and caution which characterized the earlier references to a league of nations—although distinct echoes of the earlier position were still evident in the suggestion that the projected convention should "formulate rules for the purpose of limiting armaments both on land and sea and for the purpose of making warfare more humane." Grey was asked his opinion "as to the advisability of such a move." If not taken immediately, it was feared that "the opportunity may be forever lost." [6]

Grey's answering cable of May 12 was a great disappointment. He might have chosen to inquire whether the emphasis on a league as the keystone of the peace meant neglect of the specific territorial settlements referred to in the House-Grey Memorandum. Neither in this nor in any other respect, however, did he show interest in the plan of February 22. A conference would be premature, Grey said, for it would play into Germany's hand; there was "a belief, widespread through perhaps over confidence, that Germany is in grave difficulties which may lead to her collapse, especially if failure to take Verdun becomes final." Grey declared his sympathy for Wilson's aspirations and felt that the President's proposal of a league of nations "may be of the greatest service to humanity." But clearly it did not constitute sufficient inducement to make peace talks acceptable before Germany had been defeated and humbled.[7]

House and Wilson reacted sharply to this rebuff. "For two years," House reflected, Grey had been telling him "that the solution of the problem of international well-being depended upon the United States being willing to take her part in world affairs." House was not only "distinctly disappointed" but foresaw trouble with the Allies. "An international situation can change as quickly as relationships between individuals; that is, over-night. A situation may arise, if the Allies defeat Germany, where they may attempt to be dictatorial in Europe and elsewhere." He could well imagine that the Allies "might change their views on militarism and navalism. It depends entirely upon what nation uses it, whether it is considered good or bad." [8]

Wilson's reaction was expressed in a letter of May 16 to House. The United States had, the President said, reached a turning point in its relations with Great Britain and it was now necessary to get down to "hard pan." The situation that had existed at the time of House's conversations in London and Paris was altered altogether, for the "at least temporary removal of the acute German question" had the effect of concentrating attention on Britain's "indefensible" blockade practices, her interception of neutral mails on the high seas, and the strong measures which she had recently taken against the Irish rebels. In other words, House's plan was itself not wholly free from dependence for fulfillment on the indiscretions of the submarine.

Wilson wrote that the United States must either make a decided move for peace "upon some basis that promises to be permanent" or insist "to the limit" that the British observe American rights of trade. "Which does Great Britain prefer? She cannot escape both. To do nothing is now, for us, impossible." But the British continued to be uncooperative regarding Wilson's desire to start negotiations and, owing also to the ever-tightening control which the British exerted over neutral commerce, Anglo-American relations became seriously inflamed. Nevertheless Wilson did not push Britain "to the limit." Increasingly reluctant to accept freedom of the seas as the decisive criterion of German-American relations, Wilson was actually even less ready to accept it as the test of Anglo-American relations.

In fact, Wilson was determined to try for peace, and he proceeded to define his new point of departure.

If we move for peace, it will be along these lines 1) Such a settlement with regard to their own immediate interests as the belligerents may be able to agree upon. We have nothing material of any kind to ask for ourselves and are quite aware that we are in no sense parties to the quarrel. Our interest is only in peace and its guarantees; 2) a universal alliance to maintain freedom of the seas and to prevent any war begun either a) contrary to treaty covenants or b) without warning and full inquiry,—a virtual guarantee of territorial integrity and political independence.[9]

In all but two respects, this statement forecast the course of Wilson's policy from that time onward. The exceptions, however, were of major importance.

The feasibility of standing aloof from questions of territorial settlement was at best questionable. In the actual event the desire was wholly incapable of fulfillment. Her quarrels still irreconcilable after fighting the war almost to exhaustion, Europe would remain a disturbing influence in the world. At the peace conference, where the United States became fully engaged in territorial questions, it would be apparent that the general could not be divorced from the specific and that the American hope of only limited involvement in world politics—however much indulged in the interwar period—was in fact illusory.

And then there was always freedom of the seas. To include this as an object of a universal alliance whose purpose was also "to prevent any war begun either a) contrary to treaty covenants or b) without warning and full inquiry," was illogical. Policy addressed to the inconvenience and tragedy of war itself was not necessarily in keeping with policy looking to the long future. Without radical redefinition of freedom of the seas, the association was incongruous.

Wilson concluded his letter of May 16 by directing House to endeavor once more to persuade Grey that the Allies should agree to a peace conference. In a cable of May 19 House both threatened and cajoled. The discontinuance of submarine warfare, he pointed out, would result in a mounting demand for asserting American rights against the Allies. There was, moreover, a feeling "that the war should end"; and any nation rejecting peace discussions would bring upon itself "heavy responsibility." The United States was ready to join England to free the world "from the shadow of autocracy and the spectre of war," but England "must recognize the conditions under which alone this can become possible and which we are unable to ignore." House attempted to deal with the suspicion that the United States was yielding to German desires. No overtures looking to peace had come from Germany, he said; on the contrary, "the German Ambassador gave me a message from his Government yesterday that German public opinion would not at present tolerate the President as a mediator." In conciliatory vein, House said that it was not the President's idea that a peace conference be called immediately—there would be "ample time to demonstrate whether or not Germany is indeed in a sinking condition and the deadlock can be broken." Finally House emphasized that the matter was one "that will not bear delay."

Writing to Grey on May 23, House spoke of the advantages of a peace of moderation such as American intervention might procure, and in a letter of the twenty-seventh he pointedly reminded Grey that a peace conference would result either in Germany's abandoning her extreme demands or in America's joining the war against her.[10] The appeals were, however, to no avail. Grey no longer was interested.

II

In the midst of the *Sussex* crisis on April 14, Wilson had declined an invitation to speak to the first national assembly of the League to Enforce Peace to be held in Washington May 26 and 27, 1916. Germany's acceptance of Wilson's demands in the *Sussex* case changed his mind. This, it seemed, was the moment to make use of the House-Grey agreement, and accordingly the cable of May 10, seeking Grey's cooperation, was sent. At the same time House arranged a new invitation to the President by the League to Enforce Peace, and this was accepted on May 18.[11]

It was the original intention that the speech of May 27 would both identify the policy of the United States with the league idea and announce the President's purpose of calling a peace conference. To assure favorable reception of the speech by the Allies, Wilson desired his proposal for a league to conform with what had passed between House and Grey. He requested House "to formulate what you would say, in my place, if you were seeking to make the proposal as nearly what you deem Grey and his colleagues to have agreed upon in principle." House's recollection of the conferences in London was, Wilson said, so much more accurate than his that "I would not trust myself to state the proposition without advice from you." [12]

As we have seen, Grey's uncooperative attitude was quickly apparent; moreover, as Wilson observed to House on May 22, the Allies were actually "becoming alarmed" at the possibility of the United States making a move for peace. The upshot was that the President reluctantly modified his speech so as not to do more than hint at a negotiated peace.[13]

In the speech as delivered this hint came in the penultimate paragraph and was followed by a definition of the national interest which constitutes a landmark of American foreign policy:

If it should ever be our privilege to suggest or initiate a movement for peace among the nations now at war, I am sure that the people of the United States would wish their Government to move along these lines: First, such a settlement with regard to their own immediate interests as the belligerents may agree upon. We have nothing material of any kind to ask for ourselves, and are quite aware that we are in no sense or degree parties to the present quarrel. Our interest is only in peace and its future guarantees. Second, an universal association of the nations to maintain the inviolate security of the highway of the seas for the common and unhindered use of all the nations of the world, and to prevent any war begun either contrary to treaty covenants or without warning and full submission of the causes to the opinion of the world—a virtual guarantee of territorial integrity and political independence.

The second point is the crux of Wilson's pronouncement. It was addressed to the problem of American security in the twentieth century as the Monroe Doctrine was addressed to that problem in the nineteenth century—and, singularly enough, like the Monroe Doctrine, it was the product of the interaction of British and American policy.

Wilson's justification for abandoning neutrality toward European politics was both specific and general. The war, he said, was like a great flood which, "spread far and wide to every quarter of the globe, has of necessity engulfed many a fair province of right that lies very near to us. Our own rights as a Nation, the liberties, the privileges, and the property of our people have been profoundly affected." These were the specific reasons adduced by Wilson. But was the United States to revolutionize the whole basis of its political connection with the rest of the world merely in order to insure the unrestrained movement of American property and citizens? The economic dislocations and the human tragedies suffered by the neutral could not be blindly disregarded. Nor would a universal guarantee of territorial integrity and political independence be an excessive price to pay for an undisturbed existence—if indeed such an undertaking by the United States in association with other nations were to be successful in preserving the peace. Yet might it not unnecessarily result in involvement in other peoples' quarrels?

Merely because the neutral's lot was hard, one could

not justify the risks entailed in the broad political commitment which Wilson was proposing. Only if the future portended permanent encroachments of a kind to undermine American security could the new departure be seriously entertained. Wilson did not elaborate the meaning of the current war for our permanent interests. To have done so would have called for speculation regarding future German enmity and British friendship which might have destroyed any prospect of American mediation. It could also have stirred violently partisan reactions in the American public. Wilson's reference to future contingencies was therefore in general terms. "We are participants, whether we would or not, in the life of the world. The interests of all nations are our own also. We are partners with the rest. What affects mankind is inevitably our affair as well as the affair of the nations of Europe and of Asia."

This employment of broad statement not only conformed with the tactical requirements of both international and domestic politics, but it was congenial to Wilson on another score. He desired a basis for American policy in the interests of the international community as a whole. He was convinced that "the peace of the world must henceforth depend upon a new and more wholesome diplomacy. . . . It is clear that nations must in the future be governed by the same high code of honor that we demand of individuals." In speaking thus, Wilson was addressing the United States no less than other nations. "We must . . . admit," he said, "that we have ourselves upon occasion in the past been offenders . . . ; but our conviction is not the less clear, but rather the more clear, on that account." The nations, he continued, "should agree to co-operate in a common cause, and . . . should so act that the guiding principle of that common cause shall be even-handed and impartial justice." Translated into more specific objectives, this meant three things:

First, that every people has a right to choose the sovereignty under which they shall live. Like other nations, we have ourselves no doubt once and again offended against that principle when for a little while controlled by a selfish passion as our franker historians have been honorable enough to admit; but it has become more and more our rule of life and action. Second, that the small states of the world have a right to enjoy the same respect for their sovereignty and for their territorial integrity that great and powerful nations expect and insist upon. And, third, that the world has a right to be free from every disturbance of its peace that had its origin in aggression and disregard of the rights of peoples and nations.

Finally Wilson accorded special emphasis to a point reminiscent of House's observation in August 1914 that the war would have been impossible had the nations been meeting at regular intervals in pursuit of common objectives. The point recalls Grey's belief that Germany's refusal of a conference in 1914 was the last and fatal step leading to war. These views, held by others as well, are mirrored in Wilson's address, although balance of power, and not merely justice, is here visualized as a component of future stability:

One observation on the causes of the present war we are at liberty to make, and to make it may throw some light forward upon the future, as well as backward upon the past. It is plain that this war could have come only as it did, suddenly and out of secret counsels, without warning to the world, without discussion, without any of the deliberate movements of counsel with which it would seem natural to approach so stupendous a contest. It is probable that if it had been foreseen just what would happen, just what alliances would be formed, just what forces arrayed against one another, those who brought the great contest on would have been glad to substitute conference for force. If we ourselves had been afforded some opportunity to apprise the belligerents of the attitude which it would be our duty to take, of the policies and practices against which we would feel bound to use all our moral and economic strength, and in certain circumstances even our physical strength also, our own contribution to the counsel which might have averted the struggle would have been considered worth weighing and regarding.[14]

Not until after Wilson's peace note of the following December did domestic opposition to the President's new policy assume serious proportions. Meanwhile there was not only a notable lack of opposition, but widespread and articulate support. Although the immediate stimulus for Wilson's advocacy of a league of nations came out of the actual diplomacy of the war, the idea was abroad in many minds.[15] Beginning early in the war, a nonpartisan but mainly Republican group of leaders worked out with great thoroughness a new departure for American policy centering about the idea of a league to enforce peace, and in July 1915 an organization of that name was founded for propagating the program.[16] The labors of the League to Enforce Peace provided the climate of opinion which made Wilson's first public league pronouncement politically feasible. There was ample justification for House's contemporary statement to Grey that public opinion would uphold the President in his purpose to insist that the United States should do her part in the maintenance of peace.[17]

It was not at home but abroad that the speech was unfavorably received. Aimed chiefly at Great Britain, it failed except in certain restricted circles to get a sympathetic response. Rather too grandiloquently, Wilson had said of the war: "With its causes and its objects we are not concerned." The British press seized upon this statement as still another indication of Wilson's alleged blindness to the German menace; indeed it was charged that the President was lending himself to the machinations of German diplomacy. Ambassador Page reported that the speech indicated to the British that the President did not understand the war and that "he was speaking only to the gallery filled with peace cranks . . . They are therefore skittish about the President." Grey wrote to House that he "read the speech

in the light of my talks with you and welcomed it."
Nonetheless he complained that Wilson had mentioned
"the security of the highway of the seas . . . without
any definition of what is meant." Grey also regretted
Wilson's dismissal of the causes and objects of the war
as being of no concern to the United States.[18]

Months of hope and effort hence had culminated
in disappointment and anticlimax. There was not the
slightest indication that the British Government would
assist in opening the way to a negotiated peace. House
and Wilson could not fail to be embittered. House on
June 29 told Noel Buxton, a member of Parliament visiting in America, that he found Britain's protestations
of high purpose tiresome. Had the French rather than
the Germans violated Belgium, he declared, Britain
would nonetheless have sided with France and Russia,
for it was "the stress of the situation" which compelled
the British to go in against the Central Powers. "Primarily it was because Germany insisted upon having
a dominant army and a dominant navy, something
Great Britain could not tolerate in safety to herself."
Wilson too was thoroughly exasperated, blaming not
the people of the warring nations but their leaders.
These, he wrote to House, exhibited "a constantly nar-
rowing, instead of a broad and comprehending view
of the situation." They would wake up "some surprising morning" to discover that the rest of the world "has
a positive right to be heard about the peace of the
world." He concluded that it was now "up to us to judge

for ourselves when the time has arrived . . . to make an imperative suggestion"—such a one as "they will have no choice but to heed, because the opinion of the non-official world and the desire of all peoples will be behind it." [19] It was in this mood and with this intention that Wilson six months later, in the last weeks of 1916, launched his independent peace move.

III

In the interval Europe remained occupied with the struggle of arms. Through nearly the whole of 1916 the fighting was maintained at such a pitch of intensity as to invite disbelief that human flesh and spirit could withstand the strain. Hardly had the German attack at Verdun slackened after four months of uninterrupted battle, when on June 1 the British launched their great offensive in the valley of the Somme. There, except for only one intermission in September, battle raged until mid-November. Yet the result, both in the Somme and at Verdun, was stalemate. Only in Eastern Europe, where Rumanian entry into the war on the Allied side resulted by December in German occupation of that land, did the year's fighting bring any significant shift in the battle lines.

In the United States meanwhile the presidential campaign was in progress—in fact, the campaign, as well as the battles, kept Wilson from his mediation move until December 18, 1916. Wilson, however, did not neglect to prepare the ground against the day when

he would make his "imperative suggestion." He set
about focusing American policy on a new objective.
Whereas in the preparedness addresses a few months
before, he had taken maritime rights as the point of
American interest, not in a single address in the period
from May 27, 1916 to the end of the year did he men-
tion freedom of the seas, or the German submarine, or
the British blockade—although in the speech in August
1916 accepting his renomination he defended the differing attitude of the United States toward belligerent
practices at sea on the ground that those resulting in the
loss of life, in contrast to those involving mere property
rights, had to be countered by direct challenge and
immediate resistance. To neutrality he did refer, but
only by way of warning that it was not a practical
course for the future.[20]

The current war was discussed hardly at all in these
addresses of 1916. Wilson was seeking orientation not
in terms of events but ideas. His emphasis, for the time
being, was on ends and not means. The most notable
feature of his speeches was the definition of American
nationalism in terms of democratic ideals, and identification of those ideals with the universal interests of
mankind. This theme he repeated many times, but perhaps his Omaha address on October 5 expresses it in
fullest amplitude.

He there declared that "we have never yet sufficiently
formulated our program for America with regard to the
part she is going to play in the world, and it is impera-

tive that she should formulate it at once. . . . We are holding off," he said, "not because we do not feel concerned, but because when we exert the force of this Nation we want to know what we are exerting it for." He was insistent about this: ". . . we ought to have a touchstone. We want to have a test. We ought to know, whenever we act, what the purpose is, what the ultimate goal is." He continued:

Now the touchstone is this: On our own part absolute singleness of heart and purpose in our allegiance to America, . . . by holding the doctrine that is truly American that the States of America were set up to vindicate the rights of man and not the rights of property or the rights of self-aggrandizement and aggression. . . . When you are asked, "Aren't you willing to fight?" reply, yes, you are waiting for something worth fighting for; you are not looking around for petty quarrels, but you are looking about for that sort of quarrel within whose intricacies are written all the texts of the rights of man, you are looking for some cause which will elevate your spirit, not depress it, some cause in which it seems a glory to shed human blood, if it be necessary, so that all the common compacts of liberty may be sealed with the blood of free men.[21]

There was in this nothing of fear. On the contrary there was exuberance and, indeed, readiness to claim leadership on behalf of a nation which stood for the highest aspirations of mankind. In this same vein Wilson on an earlier occasion drew an idyllic picture, more suggestive of a heavenly vision than of the toilsome history of the human race. Americans, he said, should

rejoice to look forward to the days in which America shall strive to stir the world without irritating it or drawing it on to new antagonisms, when the nations with which we deal shall at last come to see upon what deep foundations of humanity and justice our passion for peace rests, and when all mankind shall look upon our great people with a new sentiment of admiration, friendly rivalry and real affection, as upon a people who, though keen to succeed, seeks always to be at once generous and just and to whom humanity is dearer than profit or selfish power.[22]

Only rarely have individuals succeeded in achieving the position of trust and affection which Wilson in 1916 coveted for the United States; never, unfortunately, has a nation attained it. Wilson was attempting to lead the American people into a new era which required a new attitude and policy toward the world. But there was no use having a program, as he pointed out in his Omaha speech, unless the concerted force of the nation was behind it, and this required "a unification of spirit and purpose in America which no influence can invade." To achieve this he spoke in terms of hope and pride. How, indeed, could a nation with so fortunate and isolated a past have accepted the responsibilities and burdens of the future unless by this path?

Yet the self-gratification which it entailed was not without a price. This was not the failure of these sentiments to sustain the national policy after the war was over—for the arguments of safety and advantage, being less persuasive to American opinion, were not readily available in any case; the price consisted in the exaggerated expectations in the United States as regards international organization in particular and American exertions in international politics in general. These expectations easily survived the isolationist years of 1919–39; indeed, rather than diminishing, they were still further stimulated by a conscience-stricken attitude toward our own irresponsibility. In consequence, when today's circumstances have finally forced leadership upon the American people, the citizens of the United States are inclined to petulance toward those international frustrations and compromises which, in domestic politics, we have without undue cynicism learned to abide.

During the latter half of 1916 Wilson for the most part marked time in his policies toward the European war. Verdun and the Somme made the Allies less than eager to compromise their war aims; the Germans likewise hesitated to compromise, in expectation of military success if not victory; Wilson himself, facing what proved a most difficult and extremely close election, hesitated to move on the diplomatic front. Not until December 18, 1916 did Wilson finally launch his peace move.

In the form of a diplomatic note, it was designed to force the belligerents to state their war aims.[23] On the basis of such statements, made privately to Wilson or declared publicly, it was hoped that negotiations then might get underway. The note to the belligerents was even released to the press. The object of Wilson's move, unlike House's peace diplomacy earlier that year, was to subject the belligerent governments to the pressure of public opinion—their own and that of the world. To this end the note spoke with moving eloquence:

If the contest must continue to proceed towards undefined ends by slow attrition until the one group of belligerents or the other is exhausted; if million after million of human lives must continue to be offered up until on the one side or the other there are no more to offer; if resentments must be kindled that can never cool and despairs engendered from which there can be no recovery, hopes of peace and of the willing concert of free peoples will be rendered vain and idle.

Wilson asserted that each of the belligerents "would be jealous of the formation of any more rival leagues to preserve an uncertain balance of power amidst multiplying suspicions; but each is ready to consider the formation of a league of nations to insure peace and justice throughout the world." In the accomplishment of this great purpose the people and government of the United States, he said, stood "ready, and even eager, to cooperate . . . when the war is over, with every influence and resource at their command." The United States, he added, was not at liberty to suggest the terms on which the war itself should be concluded.

The peace note was itself designed to generate certain pressures. There were also other means of influencing the responses of the belligerents. The economic dependence of the Allies on the United States offered one such means, and Wilson exploited it. The embargo legislation of September 1916 was ready at hand. Another weapon was restriction of American credit. Speaking of America's newly acquired financial power, the President declared on November 4, 1916, that "We can determine to a large extent who is to be financed and who is not to be financed." [24] Later that month the Federal Reserve Board issued a statement which at Wilson's own suggestion had been revised and strengthened. Prompted by the financial straits which had overtaken the Allies, forcing Great Britain and France to seek short-term unsecured loans, the board declared that it did "not regard it in the interest of the country at this time" that member banks "invest in foreign treasury bills of this character." Consternation followed in Allied quarters. Wilson was pleased.[25]

If the Allies would not willingly lend themselves to a negotiated peace, the President was now disposed to force them to negotiate. His objective had not changed since spring, but his tactics had.

Secretary Lansing, still unwilling for Germany to "break even," was doubly alarmed. "Suppose," he wrote Wilson on December 10,

that the unacceptable answer comes from the belligerents whom we could least afford to see defeated on account of our national interest and on account of the future domination of the principles of liberty and democracy in the world—then what? Would we not be forced into an even worse state than that in which we are now? [26]

Colonel House, although still favoring a negotiated peace, likewise advised against such a course as that taken by Wilson. Less confident than the President of the impact of appeals to reason, impressed with the diplomatic weakness arising from American military unpreparedness, House continued to believe that prior Allied approval of American mediation was the only lever that could move events in the desired direction. Moreover, he feared that Germany would seize the peace note as an opportunity to maneuver the Allies into an unfavorable position and would then unleash the submarine in circumstances preventing a vigorous American reaction. Why, House asked, should the United States pull German chestnuts out of the fire? [27]

IV

The situation was most complex. It was well known in Washington that the civilians in the German Government could not much longer hold back the submarine. The *Sussex* pledge was crumbling. Wilson, eager to make a last try for peace before the German challenge fully materialized, believed that there was a good chance to force the belligerents into negotiations. But in any event his position would be stronger all around if a break with Germany were preceded by a peace endeavor—providing that the Allied side did not put itself in the position of obstructing a reasonable peace. Actually this was a serious risk only if Germany were willing to work for a peace of compromise and reconciliation, and in that case Wilson in all probability would have viewed the situation as one not of risk but of opportunity. Germany would then have captured for herself the role in which the President and House had envisioned Great Britain. Such a substitution was not one which Wilson would have willingly sought; by the end of 1916, however, his attitude toward the Allies was no longer as sympathetic as it had been. A great opportunity existed for German policy.

Did the policy actually adopted by Berlin offer to Wilson the opening for which he was looking? After capitulating to Wilson's demands in the *Sussex* case, the German Government expressed from time to time the desire that Wilson employ his good offices to start peace conversations. During the autumn of 1916 these suggestions became more insistent, culminating in October in a message by the Kaiser himself to Ambassador Gerard, at the time in the United States on leave. The burden of the message was that unless peace were soon achieved through diplomacy the German Government would have to exercise the freedom of action that it had reserved in its reply to the *Sussex* note.[28] In the end the German Government did not wait for Wilson, but on December 12 itself sent a peace note.

Bethmann-Hollweg was the main force behind the pressure on Wilson and the German note of December

12. Always pessimistic as to the possibility of a military decision, he believed that German interests could best be served by an early peace. Yet constantly pitted against the military leaders, he was not a free agent. Closely linked with the great debate between military and civilian elements in Germany over the role of the submarine in German strategy was a debate no less vigorous over war aims. Belgium was the focal point of this controversy, for Germany's relation to Belgium was the measure, more than any other single factor, of the extent of future German influence in Europe. By the same token the Belgian question was in the fore of French and, particularly, British war aims. In Western Europe the future of Belgium was the test of the success or failure of the war effort on each side.

Bethmann seemed to favor restoration of Belgium and even the payment of reparations to that country. Nonetheless this personal judgment was hardly discernible in his public utterances which, although always vague, yielded sufficiently to the annexationist point of view to forestall a government crisis over the question of war aims. We have already noted that in his address to the Reichstag on April 5, 1916 he hedged as regards Belgium.[29] It remains to consider how Belgium figured in Germany's interest in a negotiated peace at the end of 1916.

The German Government proceeded to form a program in rather specific terms. Bethmann proposed that guarantees for German security be sought in direct negotiation with King Albert of Belgium. If negotiations were unsuccessful Germany would then annex a strip of territory including Liege, to protect her western industrial area. The Supreme Command, however, speaking through Hindenburg, went further than Bethmann and wished, in addition to annexing Liege, to attach Belgium economically to Germany, secure German ownership of the Belgian railways, and provide for right of military occupation. England, Hindenburg suggested, should pay an indemnity for German evacuation of Belgium, and Germany should acquire the Belgian Congo. Bethmann objected to an indemnity from England on the ground that it would make any negotiation futile; the *quid pro quo* for German withdrawal should, he said, be return of the German colonies and perhaps acquisition of the Congo. But with these exceptions Bethmann acquiesced in the Hindenburg program. The war aims thus arrived at were, in generalized form, approved by the Kaiser in November.[30]

Since there was little in the inner history of the German position that suggested any real possibility for a negotiated peace, we are scarcely surprised at the character of the public statements issuing from Berlin at the time. The German peace note of December 12, though suggesting negotiation, gave no indication of terms and was couched in truculent and arrogant language.[31]

Nor did the German response to Wilson's own appeal of December 18 advance the cause of negotiation. Designed to limit Wilson's role to nothing more than good offices, Berlin's reply of December 26 emphasized direct negotiation with the Allies. Cooperation in the "sublime task" of preventing future wars was pledged "only after" the end of the current war.[32] And not until January 31, 1917, did Germany respond to Wilson's urgent suggestion that terms be confidentially communicated to him. Consisting of the broad statement of war aims arrived at in the preceding November, the message indicated that the terms set forth were those which would have been advanced had the Allies accepted the German offer of December 12.[33] Timed to reach the President along with the simultaneous news of unrestricted submarine warfare, the communication suggested that Germany would respond to any continued efforts by Wilson for peace, if such would "lead to a peace acceptable to Germany."

Wilson's determination to use any opening, from whatever side it came, is clear. There can, of course, be no certainty that success would have been achieved had Germany taken full advantage of the opportunity thus presented. The situation was fraught with complexity, such as the French demand for the return of Alsace-Lorraine. Yet a clear statement by Germany renouncing all designs on Belgium might well have opened a channel. Professor Hans Gatzke in his recent volume, *Germany's Drive to the West,* has suggested that

England might have been willing to break her commitments under the secret treaties of London and make a

separate peace with Germany; or else she could bring sufficient pressure to bear on France, so that the latter could
give up her aims in Alsace-Lorraine; or maybe a clear
German statement would have strengthened the peace-
loving groups within the Allied nations, who in turn might
have forced their governments to negotiate peace with
Germany.[34]

And short of actual peace negotiations, still another effect might have been achieved. A sincere and determined German effort toward peace would have made
Wilson's subsequent break over submarine warfare
much more difficult, if not almost impossible.

The balance of political forces in Germany, particularly the great influence of the Supreme Command,
strongly favored unrestricted submarine warfare rather
than a negotiated peace; elimination of both England
and France as serious rivals in the West was a prospect
too alluring to resist. Not wanting to forego the possibility of maximum gains, the German Government
equivocated on whether anything less would be acceptable, finally adopting a military policy leading to
all or nothing. As we noted elsewhere, on January 9,
1917 the gamble of unrestricted submarine warfare had
been irrevocably taken.

Much political profit accrued to the Allies from the
German policy. It was, of course, unearned inasmuch
as their response to Wilson's endeavors was scarcely
more cooperative than Germany's. Lloyd George, who
in the autumn of 1916 became identified with the pol-

icy of a knockout blow, had on December 5 replaced
Asquith as prime minister; the fiery Welshman was
adamant against a negotiated peace. Nor was the political complexion in France any more favorable to
peace without victory. The Allied reply of January 10,
1917 to Wilson's peace note showed that the Allied
Governments were not in a bargaining mood and would
be satisfied with nothing less than military decision
over the Central Powers. As for any "discussion of
future arrangements destined to insure an enduring
peace," such must await "satisfactory settlement of the
actual conflict." [35]

Wilson still persisted in his purpose. On January 22,
1917 he addressed the Senate on the principles of a
stable peace.[36] "No covenant of co-operative peace that
does not include the peoples of the New World can
suffice," he said, "to keep the future safe against war."
But, he added, no one could join in guaranteeing anything but a just peace. He did not mean that the United
States "would throw any obstacle in the way of any
terms of peace the governments now at war might agree
upon, or seek to upset them when made, whatever they
might be." Thus Wilson seemed to suggest that America, under no compulsion of necessity, would be free
to abstain from political relations with Europe if the
peace were something less than just. Indeed Wilson
spoke in terms of service. The American people "cannot in honor withhold the service to which they are
now about to be challenged. . . . But they owe it to

themselves and to the other nations of the world to state the conditions under which they will feel free to render it." The service was "nothing less than . . . to add their authority and their power to the authority and force of other nations to guarantee peace and justice throughout the world."

"There must be," Wilson said, "not a balance of power, but a community of power." Yet "the organized major force of mankind" which he saw was not the power of victor over vanquished. Rather the war must end in "peace without victory," for "only a peace between equals can last." But what sort of equality did he mean? Was it merely an equality of legal status, or one of bargaining power? The latter seems implied. Wilson beforehand had spoken disapprovingly of any intention on the part of statesmen on either side to "crush their antagonists." Moreover, in proceeding to a new and separate point, he stated that peace must be founded on "an equality of rights" as "between big nations and small, between those that are powerful and those that are weak." As among the major antagonists, then, was not Wilson emphasizing a material rather than legal equality? Did he therefore adequately express the full import of his own proposal for "peace between equals" when he said, "Mankind is looking now for freedom of life, not for equipoises of power"? Did he mean that justice can be so well recognized, so nearly approximated, as to make material elements of political power a matter of indifference? Wilson's language actually suggests that international politics henceforth would be so securely established on legal and moral principle as to render any clash of interests wholly tractable.

Having made his points for peace without victory, and the equality of large and small states, Wilson added other aspects of a stable peace: the right of a people to choose its own sovereignty; the right to a direct outlet to the sea; disarmament. Nor was another, long familiar, point omitted. "The freedom of the seas," Wilson said, "is the *sine qua non* of peace, equality, and co-operation." But freedom of the seas was beginning in Wilson's vocabulary to encompass more than—indeed, something different from—neutral trade and travel in time of war. "No doubt," he continued, "a somewhat radical reconsideration of many of the rules of international practice hitherto thought to be established may be necessary in order to make the seas indeed free and common in practically all circumstances." The problem was "closely connected with the limitation of naval armaments and the cooperation of the navies of the world in keeping the seas at once free and safe."

Wilson hence was touching a very fundamental problem—whether international law should continue as in the past to allow belligerents to compete for supremacy on the seas (reserving a certain modicum of undisturbed use to neutrals), or whether in the interest of the international community it should bar the aggressor from legitimate use of the sea lanes. Wilson doubtless did not fully comprehend the direction in which his thought was moving, for at the conclusion of his address he said that in proposing freedom of the seas he was advocating that which "in international conference after conference representatives of the United States have urged with the eloquence of those who are convinced disciples of liberty."

The incompatibility of traditional freedom of the seas with the collective-security aspect of a league of nations presented a troublesome question with which Wilson had struggled for many months. The difficulty sprang from the fact that, whereas freedom of the seas was geared to the transitory problems of trade in wartime, a league of nations assumed a broad political interest extending into the future. The latter concept of what the national interest required was of an order radically different from the former; stepping from one to the other was not like ascending the rungs of a ladder, but as Wilson was so uncomfortably aware in composing his War Message like abandoning one platform for another.

Freedom of the seas has since disappeared from the lexicon of American diplomacy. The fact that it went unmentioned in the Versailles Treaty was remarked upon by Wilson himself. Addressing an audience in September 1919 he related a "practical joke" on himself:

One of the principles I went to Paris most insisting on was the freedom of the seas. Now, the freedom of the seas means the definition of the right of neutrals to use the seas when other nations are at war, but under the League of Nations there are no neutrals, and, therefore, what I have called the practical joke on myself was that by the very thing that I was advocating it became unnecessary to define freedom of the seas. All nations . . . being comrades and partners in a common cause, we all have an equal right to use the seas.[37]

But we must add most emphatically that freedom of the seas would have dropped out of sight even had it not encountered in the League Covenant a superior legal formula governing use of the seas.

The idea of collective security afforded a policeman's cloak for the emerging political awareness of the United States, but in any event freedom of the seas would have receded along with the historical circumstances which gave it its old prominence. Actually it was no longer possible to act as though our relation to European politics was peripheral, confined to matters of trade. Momentarily in the first World War freedom of the seas, for reasons largely extraneous to its own inner assumptions and purposes, burned with deceptive brilliance, only to suffer an early demise.

The address of January 22, 1917 was indeed a far cry from the preparedness speeches of a year before. From the narrow base of maritime rights Wilson had shifted to broader foundations relating to the settlement of the war itself. Troubled by lack of logical continuity in his policy, Wilson endeavored to use freedom of the seas as a bridge between the two phases. In this he failed for freedom of the seas could not be made to face both ways. If the United States was henceforth to concern itself with the great issues of world politics, neutral rights could no longer be represented as the cynosure of American policy. However, a wholly fortuitous connection between these disparate aspects of Wilson's policy was established, not in Washington but in Berlin. Unrestricted submarine warfare, which swept away every vestige of neutral right on the seas, simultaneously proclaimed the intent of the German Government to dictate a peace on its own terms. Wilson responded with war. Not because vindication of maritime rights seemed to him to justify so extreme a measure; nor because war was a chosen instrument for achieving a league of nations; nor for any other constructive purpose. Germany's new course, whether its consequences be judged from the standpoint of neutral rights or of the future shape of world politics, left no alternative to war. Circumstance took control, reducing policy to futility.

Caught in the tide of events, Wilson on the eve of delivering the War Message to Congress sought the companionship of his friend Frank I. Cobb of the New York *World*. Because of a delay in receiving the presidential summons, Cobb arrived at the White House at one o'clock in the morning of April 2. He found the President assailed with doubts, more "worn down" than Cobb had ever seen him. Wilson's main concern is reminiscent of his earlier response to Lansing's ideo-

logical prodding. The President told Cobb that a declaration of war "would mean that Germany would be
beaten and so badly beaten that there would be a dictated peace, a victorious peace. . . . The President said
that such a basis was what the Allies thought they
wanted, and that they would have their way in the
very thing America had hoped against and struggled
against." [38]

In the interwar years, from 1918 to 1939, popular
opinion in America generally viewed our entry into
the first World War as an isolated episode, unrelated
to the past, unprophetic of the future. Consistent with,
and indeed dictated by, this view were explanations of
involvement which dwelt on the vicissitudes of the law
of neutrality and the exigencies of trade, portraying
thereby a blundering policy yielding opportunistically
to any momentary pressures. Since the second World
War, however, students have felt the need for wider
perspective, and have begun to test Wilson's policy
against broad political considerations. Some recent critics[39] have charged that Wilson saw the war as a struggle between good and evil and sought to crush the
latter preparatory to attainment of perpetual peace.
These new critics, unlike those of interwar years, do
not object that Wilson dropped the traditional American mask of indifference toward European politics.
They contend that he replaced it with one of utopian

mien—that in moving away from the old habits of American diplomacy he went too far. The correct policy for Wilson, they maintain, would have been calculation and restraint aimed at ending the war as soon as possible without catastrophe to either side, thereby preserving a balance in Europe which would least disturb the outside world and contribute most to the future stability and pacification of Europe itself.

These views, cogently and forcefully expressed, have had a most beneficial effect in stimulating reassessment of American diplomacy during the first World War. Yet even by these latter-day standards Wilson's diplomacy did not lack acumen.

Wilson was picking his way amid the confusion of a major turning point in history, and his policy was in constant process of mutation, each phase mingling with later stages. The rules of maritime warfare were the first point of departure. Then mediation became the main objective. Finally, a league of nations, transformed from an inducement to a negotiated peace into a war aim, emerged as the major goal. Mediation had the most to offer, but it is doubtful whether Wilson's failure to achieve a negotiated peace can be attributed wholly or even mainly to factors over which he had control. A consummate diplomacy, backed by strong armament, supported by a united public opinion, ready to make sacrifices for something less than promises of a radically new future, might have enabled the United States to halt the war. But Americans had not yet demonstrated, no less to Europe than to themselves, that they were capable of large and sustained military action overseas. Nothing less than such a prospect could have stayed the belligerents, each of whom felt that only destruction of the enemy could render the future secure, and that only thus could the frightful costs already exacted by the war be justified.

NINE

A New Mold for American Policy

OUR EARLIEST experiences with foreign relations, in the period beginning with the American Revolution, required hard decisions and provided for the nation only a narrow margin of safety. In this respect the diplomacy of the Founding Fathers was not unlike today's. What came to be regarded as the traditional pattern of American policy, however, is of nineteenth-century origin. The announcement of the Monroe Doctrine in 1823 coincided with the beginning of an extraordinary period for the United States, in which the demands of security progressively relaxed. The Doctrine was a carefully considered response to a situation containing some elements of menace; but, oddly enough, the subsequent security of the nation was not attributable to its enforcement. For, as things turned out, there was no need to enforce it. This lack of serious occasion (except for the French intervention in Mexico during the American Civil War) for invoking the Doctrine, rather than the fact of its existence, underlay the unprecedented freedom of action of the United States in the nineteenth century; and this in turn gave rise to the isolationist tradition.

If we look for an explanation of so extraordinary a situation, we will find it in a circumstance not fully appreciated at the time, the character of our relations with Great Britain. Britain was herself a North American power—indeed at the end of the Napoleonic wars the dominant power in the Western Hemisphere. It followed that Great Britain was the main factor in our nineteenth-century situation, and the New World was the testing ground of Anglo-American relations. Fortunately accommodation rather than rivalry emerged as the dominant feature of Anglo-American relations. The achievement of this harmony between the two great English-speaking peoples is a lesson in statesmanship. Yet, because of its very completeness, accommodation exacted a price. In the United States it fostered indifference toward foreign policy which hampered the nation in responding with alert realism to the vastly altered conditions of world politics confronting it in the present century.

The first half of the twentieth century has been a transitional period in American history marking the end of one era and beginning of another. We had on the eve of the new century engaged in a small war of our own choosing. The imperial fruits of the ensuing peace treaty with Spain were regarded with considerable uneasiness. Events, however, soon pushed us into the main stream of international politics quite without regard to our own desires in the matter. Unwilling voyagers, we steered an erratic course. It required a second World War, the postwar pressure of Soviet Communism, and the new weapons of mass destruction to make us begin to exert our full influence in world affairs.

The war of 1914–18 presented the first major challenge to the pattern of our foreign relations as established in the nineteenth century; it also produced a response which even today continues to condition American policy. Already fully fashioned by April 1917, the response consisted of a league of nations with a universal guarantee of territorial integrity and political independence. This was a far cry indeed from adherence to the law of neutrality which in 1914 had been the automatic policy of the United States.

By what path did Woodrow Wilson arrive at the position of 1917, based on assumptions so radically different from those of traditional American policy? Speaking before the Senate in January 1917, Wilson contended that the United States, if it joined other nations in "guaranteeing the permanence of peace," would not break with tradition but actually fulfill "all that we have professed or striven for." He said he was proposing

that the nations should with one accord adopt the doctrine of President Monroe as the doctrine of the world: that no nation should seek to extend its polity over any other nation or people, but that every people should be free to determine its own polity, its own way of development, unhindered, unthreatened, unafraid, the little along with the great and powerful. . . . There is no entangling alliance in a concert of power. When all unite to act in the same sense and with the same purpose all act in the common interest and are free to live their own lives under a common protection.

But we must judge this attempt to relate the new policy to the old a failure, for actually the historical record does not support the suggestion of an unbroken line of development from the Monroe Doctrine to the League of Nations. To be sure the Monroe Doctrine was designed to preserve the territorial integrity and political independence of the nations of the Western Hemisphere, but it had an obverse side: an attitude of aloofness toward Europe which had crystallized into a sort of permanent neutrality toward European politics. Essentially the United States, without full awareness, had in the nineteenth century sought a relationship to Europe not unlike that of neutralization attained by Switzerland. However, less undemanding than Switzerland, we had staked out a vast hemispheric area of primary interest. Moreover, much of the Western Hemisphere was economically underdeveloped and politically unstable, and it could not, therefore, escape the consequences of a major shift in the European balance of power. It was inevitable that with the first disturbance of such a nature the United States would drop its indifference toward European politics. The first World War was that occasion, and American policy responded in the halting, devious way that we have described.

We have seen that neutrality in 1914 was no mere personal preference of Wilson's. Its adoption was determined by history, whose molds are not easily broken and never so by intellectual processes alone. In fact, until the character and course of the war had emerged, it was unclear whether neutrality was the right or wrong policy. But as the war's true nature unfolded, American policy, adapting to the fact of a cataclysmic European and world struggle for power, early became a policy of benevolent neutrality strongly favoring the Allies. Yet, though the spirit of American neutrality departed increasingly from the letter until the discrepancy was wide indeed, Wilson steadfastly refused to acknowledge the divergence. Undoubtedly Wilson entertained a lingering regard for neutrality, the more so as a base from which to seek mediation, but his failure to characterize his policy openly for what it was—in such terms as House, for instance, employed privately —was due above all to a divided and clamorous public opinion, always on the verge of paralyzing disunity. No longer a private citizen in 1914–17, Wilson was the head of a great government, and frankness appeared not a simple virtue and not always expedient.

Seeking the flexibility denied to a policy tied to the tactics of the submarine, Wilson endeavored to de-emphasize the rules of maritime warfare and to take the ultimate political effects of the European struggle as the gauge of American action. It was in consequence of this endeavor that the league of nations became the dominant feature of his policy. The idea had been much abroad in the public mind, but as official policy the league emerged laboriously out of Anglo-American diplomacy, stemming from the efforts of House and Wilson on behalf of a negotiated peace. The initial attempts to mediate studiously avoided any commitment concerning future use of American power. Yet, as one observer expressed it, England was fighting for the nursery; as indeed was Germany also—with the difference that the latter was seeking to overturn the *status quo* which the former was determined to maintain. The war was not a mere quarrel over relative advantage but a struggle in which the future of great nations was at stake. Any attempt to mediate, therefore, had to take into account the dominating passion for security. In keeping with this characteristic of the war, Sir Edward Grey reacted to American proposals for mediation by advancing an idea of future concerted action against aggression. The foreign secretary was looking at the European situation, and saw the league as a device for bringing American power to bear in a Europe no longer capable of controlling itself. In a manner even more direct than that employed by George Canning in 1823, Grey was endeavoring through the New World to redress the balance of the Old.

Wilson's incorporation of the league idea into American policy was in response to Grey's initiative, but the idea did not have the same connotation for both men. Grey's thinking was empirical, in terms of the European problem; Wilson's idealistic, and of universal application. Grey saw the league as an elaboration of the traditional pattern of diplomacy; Wilson saw it as a new and independent force in the world capable of overriding the old animosities and conflicts. To Grey the league was a means of channeling American power; to Wilson it was more the rallying point of world opinion.

Such in any event was the guise in which Wilson eventually depicted the league, though we have noted occasions when the President assessed the problem of American foreign policy in different terms. Not always had he regarded justice as a goal directly accessible through good will and rationality. In the debate with Lansing over the implications for American policy of the ideological aspect of the war, in the candid expression of misgivings to Frank I. Cobb on the eve of the War Message, and concealed in the January 22, 1917 address to the Senate—indeed underlying Wilson's whole policy of peace without victory—was an appreciation of the balance of power point of view: namely, that stability is to be found in an equilibrium of forces no less than in moral excellence.

Recognizing that these points of view are logically incompatible but that neither is exclusive of the other, we must ask why the idealistic element in Wilson's policy was finally so preponderant. To answer that this outcome accorded with Wilson's philosophical and temperamental leanings would not seem to cover the whole ground. Wilson, whether consciously or not, adapted his arguments to the requirements of public opinion, and nostalgic for the nineteenth century, the American nation wished to minimize the very exertion which Sir Edward Grey deemed the essential thing. Unaccustomed to the risk and burden of international responsibility, Americans were above all responsive to expressions of hope, pride, and sentiment. Thus the league was depicted in a fashion reflecting the very isolationism to which it was the supposed antithesis.

Notes

CHAPTER ONE. PRIOR TO 1914: ANGLO-AMERICAN AND GERMAN-
AMERICAN RELATIONS

1. Worthington C. Ford, ed., *The Letters of Henry Adams,*
1892–1918 (2 vols., Boston, Houghton Mifflin, 1938), II, 642.

Apropos of the first Moroccan crisis (1905), Adams wrote
to a friend: "We have got to support France against Germany,
and fortify an Atlantic system beyond attack; for if Germany
breaks down England and France, she becomes the center of a
military world, and we are lost." *Ibid.*, p. 461.

2. See Samuel Flagg Bemis, *A Diplomatic History of the*
United States (New York, Henry Holt, 1936), p. 405.

3. Cf. Robert L. Schuyler, *The Fall of the Old Colonial*
System: A Study of British Free Trade, 1770–1870 (New York,
Oxford University Press, 1945).

4. Cf. Charles P. Stacey, *Canada and the British Army,*
1846–1871 (London, Longmans, Green, 1936). For the withdrawal of the British West Indian naval squadron see Harold
and Margaret Sprout, *The Rise of American Naval Power,*
1776–1918 (Princeton, Princeton University Press, 1939), p.
252.

5. Regarding the World War period Harold and Margaret
Sprout, *Rise of American Naval Power*, p. 363, comment: "While
following a diplomatic course that envisaged our entry into the
war on the side of the Allies as a possible and increasingly
probable eventuality, the Administration persistently declined
to authorize the specific preparations necessary to put the Navy
in readiness for the kind of war then in progress." Admiral
W. S. Sims in testimony before a subcommittee of the Senate
Naval Affairs Committee (66th Cong., 2nd Sess.), published as
Naval Investigation, 1920, pp. 3213, 3216, noted that "the
words 'war' or 'preparedness for war' were practically never
used by the Secretary or his advisers" and that "the Secretary

conscientiously avoided any reference to a possibility of war in his plans and recommendations for the guidance of the Navy Department." Quoted in *Rise of American Naval Power*, p. 353n. For General Bliss' account of Wilson's angry reaction in 1915 to a newspaper suggestion that the General Staff was preparing a plan in the event of a war with Germany, see Frederick Palmer, *Newton D. Baker: America at War* (2 vols., New York, Dodd, Mead, 1931), I, pp. 40–41.

6. "For nearly a century the framers of American naval policy had proceeded on the assumption that commerce raiding and passive coast defense were the Navy's two basic functions in war." Harold and Margaret Sprout, *Toward a New Order of Sea Power: American Policy and the World Scene, 1918–1922* (Princeton, Princeton University Press, 1940), p. 7. For a full account of the evolution of American naval policy in this period see Harold and Margaret Sprout, *Rise of American Naval Power*, chapters XII-XV.

7. For a critique of Mahan's thesis see Harold and Margaret Sprout, *Toward a New Order of Sea Power*, pp. 9–15. For an account of Mahan's impact on the naval policies of the Great Powers see Margaret Sprout, "Mahan: Evangelist of Sea Power," in Edward Mead Earle, ed., *Makers of Modern Strategy: Military Thought from Machiavelli to Hitler* (Princeton, Princeton University Press, 1943), pp. 415–445.

8. Alfred Vagts, "Hopes and Fears of an American-German War, 1870–1915," *Political Science Quarterly*, vol. 54 (1939), 527; the article is concluded in vol. 55 (1940), 53–76.

9. The German ambassador in London, Count Paul von Wolff-Metternich reported in 1908 Sir Edward Grey's comment that "the British Government never includes the fleet of the United States in a calculation of the 'two-Power standard.'" Grey had described a war between the United States and England as "unthinkable." The Kaiser refused to believe this and commented in a marginal annotation: "Very superficial. Such a war could quite well come about—or one with Japan." *Die Grosse Politik der Europäischen Kabinette, 1871–1914* (40 vols., Berlin, 1922–27), XXIV, 44–46; quoted in E. L. Woodward,

Great Britain and the German Navy (Oxford, The Clarendon Press, 1935), p. 169. Only on the premise that Great Britain was subject to serious embarrassment elsewhere than in the North Sea did the German naval policy make sense, and to any inquiry into the validity of this premise the Kaiser closed his mind.

10. Alfred Vagts, "Hopes and Fears of an American-German War," *Political Science Quarterly*, vol. 55, 63n.

CHAPTER TWO. THE SUBMARINE: POINT OF DEPARTURE FOR AMERI-CAN POLICY

1. Gerard to Bryan, February 4, 1915. *Foreign Relations, 1915, Supplement*, p. 94.

2. The first official receipt of the memorandum was from the German Embassy on the eighth. *Ibid.*, pp. 95–97.

3. Bryan to Gerard, February 10, 1915. *Ibid.*, pp. 98–100.

4. Edwin Borchard and William P. Lage, *Neutrality for the United States* (2nd ed., New Haven, Yale University Press, 1940), Appendix A.

5. See Germany's first *Lusitania* note, May 28, 1915. *Foreign Relations, 1915, Supplement*, p. 419. In the case of eight American ships which came in contact with mines, responsibility was undeterminable; five were sunk and three damaged, with a loss of four lives. E. Borchard and W. P. Lage, *Neutrality for the United States*, Appendix A.

6. Up to the end of the war in 1918 Norway suffered the loss of 896 ships—49.3 per cent of its tonnage in 1914—with a loss of lives totaling 2,105. Carnegie Endowment for International Peace, "Economic and Social History of the World War," *Sweden, Norway, Denmark, and Iceland in the World War* (New Haven, Yale University Press, 1930), no. 7, 360. An account of the submarine in Norwegian-German relations may also be found in Paul G. Vigness, *The Neutrality of Norway in the World War* (Stanford, Stanford University Press, 1932). Norway was the heaviest loser among the neutrals. The Dutch

loss in ships to the end of 1916 was 53, and by the end of 1918 134. For Denmark the comparable figures are 85 and 274. For Sweden 88 and 183. P. C. Jessup and others, ed., *Neutrality, Its History, Economics and Law* (4 vols., New York, Columbia University Press, 1935–36), III, Edgar G. Turlington, *The World War Period*, 222, 224, 219.

During the two-month period following the adoption of unrestricted submarine warfare and preceding our entrance into the war, nine American vessels were lost, resulting in sixty-four deaths. E. Borchard and W. P. Lage, *Neutrality for the United States*, Appendix A.

7. E. Borchard and W. P. Lage, *Neutrality for the United States*, Appendix C. This summary does not include cases such as the *Sussex* in which American lives were endangered but not lost. Of the total deaths, 141 were those of passengers and 35 of crewmen. The toll after unrestricted submarine warfare was inaugurated and before the United States declared war was 19 American lives on 6 belligerent and 1 neutral vessel.

8. Lansing to Bryan, April 2, 1915. *Papers Relating to the Foreign Relations of the United States: The Lansing Papers 1914–1920* (2 vols., Washington, U.S. Government Printing Office, 1939–40), I, 365.

9. Lansing to Bryan, April 5, 1915. *Ibid.*, pp. 369–371.

10. *Ibid.*, pp. 373–374. Italics are Lansing's.

11. *Ibid.*, p. 368.

In Lansing's judgment, war between the United States and Germany would have the following consequences:

"Commercial situation would not be changed so far as Germany is concerned, except that German naval forces would have greater right to interrupt trade with Allies.

"The United States could not send an army to Europe, hence no increased military strength to Germany's enemies on land.

"The British Navy being already superior to that of Germany, the addition of the naval force of the United States would have no effect on the situation at sea.

"There might be created a state of civil discord, and possibly of civil strife, in the United States, which would cause this Government to retain for its own use the munitions and supplies now being sent in great quantities to the Allies.

"The interned German vessels would be seized by the United States."

12. Lansing to Bryan, April 2, Wilson to Bryan, April 5, 1915. *Ibid.*, pp. 367, 369.

13. Diary entry, April 5, 1915. Chander P. Anderson Diary and Papers, Library of Congress.

14. Incidental to the Mexican civil war, death and injury had resulted to scores of Americans. Beginning in 1912 and on numerous occasions thereafter the Department of State urged Americans to leave Mexico. Cf. *Foreign Relations, 1915,* p. 837ff.

In a cablegram of May 19, 1915, Gerard reported from Berlin that "Germans of position" refer to the Mexican policy and "cannot see why the American Government should enforce the protection of cargoes of munitions by the presence of American passengers in British vessels who can travel in American ships in perfect safety and without causing complications." *Foreign Relations, 1915, Supplement,* p. 402.

At the time of the controversy between Wilson and Congress over the armed merchantman, the comparison between the President's Mexican and German policies made by his opponents prompted Lansing to make this distinction in a press conference: Since the high seas are common to all nations, "a noncombatant, whether neutral or not, has a right to pass to and fro without having his life endangered." However, land is always under the sovereignty of a nation and the noncombatant "only has the right to pass to and fro with the consent of the authorities." New York *Times,* Feb. 23, 1916.

15. The gist of the memorandum is that "the case does not present a question of national affront, but merely the question of whether a German submarine was acting lawfully or unlawfully in sinking the *Falaba* without taking every precaution to save Thrasher's life. . . . This view of the case reduces it to a pe-

cuniary claim for indemnity involving merely a disputed question of liability." Writing to Bryan on April 6, Wilson acknowledged receipt of the Anderson memorandum and said that he read it with the "closest attention." *Lansing Papers*, I, 372.

16. Anderson MSS.

17. Bryan to Wilson, April 2, 1915. *Lansing Papers*, I, 366.

Bryan queried the President further on April 8: "What claim can this Government rightfully make for unintended loss which ordinary diligence would have avoided?" *Ibid.*, p. 376.

18. Wilson to Bryan, April 3, April 6; Bryan to Wilson, April 7, 1915. *Ibid.*, pp. 368, 373, 375.

19. Lansing wrote to the President April 10: "The significant fact to my mind is that the submarine's commander allowed ten minutes for the crew and passengers to leave the vessel, showing that he did not act on the suspicion that the vessel was armed and might attack him. If he allowed no time for escape, he might enter that plea, but, since he gave *some* time, he should have given sufficient.

"It seems to me that the question of arming British vessels, or Germany's belief that it is being done, disappears from the *Falaba* case." *Ibid.*, p. 377.

20. Wilson to Bryan, April 22, 1915. *Ibid.*, pp. 377–378.

21. Wilson to Bryan, April 28, 1915. *Ibid.*, p. 380.

This letter was in response to one of the twenty-third from Bryan, who feared that such a note as was proposed would "inflame the already hostile feeling against us in Germany, not entirely because of our protest against Germany's action in this case, but in part because of its contrast with our attitude toward the Allies." Bryan proposed as an alternative that Wilson appeal to the nations at war to consider terms of peace; he eloquently pointed out the benefits that would accrue to all concerned from the laying down of arms. In his reply Wilson was at a loss to find a concrete point of departure for such an appeal: "We know their minds and we know their difficulties. They are dependent upon their own public opinion (even Germany) and we know what that opinion is. To insist now would be futile and would probably be offensive. We would lose such influence as we have for peace." *Ibid.,* pp. 378–380.

22. Lansing to Bryan, May 5, 1915. *Ibid.,* pp. 384–385.

Lansing did not adhere to this view for long. Under the impact of the *Lusitania* incident, he advised Bryan that the February 10 note required the American Government to "hold Germany to a strict accountability for the loss of American lives and property within the 'war zone.'" If anything less had been intended, it was the Government's "manifest duty to its own people to have said so, and to have issued a public warning to them to keep them off British ships and to say to them 'If you go, you go at your own peril.'" Lansing to Bryan, May 9, 1915. *Ibid.,* p. 388.

23. Thomas A. Bailey, "The Sinking of the *Lusitania,*" *American Historical Review,* vol. 41 (October 1935), 57.

24. The *Lusitania,* the argument ran, was not "an ordinary unarmed merchant vessel," but rather an auxiliary cruiser "included in the navy list published by British Admiralty," and that she "had guns on board which were mounted under decks and masked." This argument was weak, and the latter allegation of fact wrong. Also false was the charge that the *Lusitania* carried Canadian troops. The charge was true that she carried ammunition (4,200 cases of cartridges for rifles and 1,250 empty shrapnel cases). Moreover, one half of the cargo, in monetary value, consisted of materials for the use of the Allied forces. From an abbreviated copy of the manifest in the New York *Times,* May 8, 1915, quoted in *ibid.,* p. 61. But there was nothing in the traditional rules whereby this would justify the omission of visit and search and of making adequate provision for the safety of passengers and crew. For the arguments see the German note of May 28, 1915. *Foreign Relations, 1915, Supplement,* pp. 419–421.

25. The American Government was first apprised of these British practices in a note from the German Government of February 15, 1915. *Foreign Relations, 1915, Supplement,* pp. 104–105. Gerard commented in a cable from Berlin, July 5, 1915:

"English passenger ships sailing with orders to ram submarines and often armed [cannot] be put quite in the category of altogether peaceful merchantmen." *Ibid.,* p. 461.

26. In the third *Lusitania* note, July 21, 1915, the American position is modified regarding this point: "The events of the past two months have clearly indicated that it is possible and practicable to conduct . . . submarine operations . . . in substantial accord with the accepted practices of regulated warfare. . . . It is manifestly possible, therefore, to lift the whole practice of submarine attack above the criticism which it has aroused." *Ibid.,* p. 481.

27. *Ibid.,* pp. 393–396.

28. The *New York* of the American Line sailed two hours later than the *Lusitania* for the same port, Liverpool. The records of the company show that the *New York* had room for 300 more passengers. The total number of Americans departing on the *Lusitania* was 197. See T. A. Bailey, "Sinking of the *Lusitania*," p. 67. In a cablegram of July 5, 1915, Gerard commented: "When Americans have reasonable opportunity to cross the ocean why should we enter a great war because some American wants to cross on a ship where he can have a private bathroom?" *Foreign Relations, 1915, Supplement,* p. 461.

See also Merle E. Curti, *Bryan and World Peace* (Smith College Studies in History, Northampton, Mass., 1931), XVI, 200–222.

29. Wilson to Lansing, July 13, 1915. *Lansing Papers,* I, 456.

30. Lansing to Wilson, July 14, 1915. *Ibid.,* p. 457.

31. Robert Lansing, *War Memoirs of Robert Lansing* (Indianapolis, Bobbs Merrill Co., 1935), pp. 46–47. Lansing said that he was speaking on his own authority, knowing that Wilson might disavow him.

32. *Foreign Relations, 1915, Supplement,* p. 560.

33. *Ibid.,* pp. 530–531.

34. Enclosure, Lansing to Wilson, November 11, 1915; enclosure, Lansing to Wilson, January 7; Wilson to Lansing, January 10, February 16, 1916. *Lansing Papers,* I, 489–490, 514–

515, 532–533. For the German memorandum see *Foreign Relations, 1916, Supplement*, p. 171.

35. *Foreign Relations, 1916, Supplement*, p. 172.

36. Enclosure, memorandum of German Government on treatment of armed merchantmen, Gerard to Lansing. *Ibid.*, p. 165.

37. Lansing to Wilson, September 12, 1915. *Lansing Papers*, I, 330.

38. Compare *Foreign Relations, 1915, Supplement*, pp. 394 and 437. Italics supplied. The adjective "unarmed" was used in Wilson's original draft of the note of May 13 and was seconded by Bryan. Lansing proposed "unresisting." *Lansing Papers*, I, 396, 399.

39. Lansing to Wilson, September 12, 1915. *Lansing Papers*, I, 331.

40. Wilson to Lansing, September 13, 1915. *Ibid.*, p. 332.
Actually, the case was closed by the gun being removed from the *Waimana* without prejudice to the principle involved. Lansing to Page, October 18, and Collector of Customs at Norfolk to Secretary of the Treasury, September 22, 1915. *Foreign Relations, 1915, Supplement*, pp. 577, 850–851. The *Waimana* carried one 4.7 gun astern, which the British Government contended was defensive armament well within the accepted rule, and which therefore in no way prejudiced the status of the *Waimana* as a merchantman.

41. London *Times*, March 26, 1913, quoted by A. Pearce Higgins, "Armed Merchant Ships," *American Journal of International Law*, vol. 8 (October 1914), 705–722. In this article, which was prepared in July 1914, the author stated: "There are now between 40 and 50 British merchant ships carrying guns for defence and others are in progress of being equipped. It has also been stated that German merchant ships are being similarly armed."

42. *Foreign Relations, 1915, Supplement*, pp. 653–654; and *Foreign Relations, 1916, Supplement*, pp. 191–198. These were confidential instructions captured by the Germans, copies of which were transmitted by the latter to the Department of State.

43. Archibald Hurd, *The Merchant Navy* (3 vols., London, John Murray, 1929), III, 111.

44. *Foreign Relations, 1916, Supplement*, pp. 147–148.

45. Lansing to Wilson, January 17, 1916. *Lansing Papers*, I, 336.

46. Page to Lansing, January 25, 1916. *Foreign Relations, 1916, Supplement*, pp. 151–152.

47. Lansing to Wilson, January 27, 1916. *Lansing Papers*, I, 338.

48. Circular telegram, Lansing to diplomatic officers in European countries, February 16, 1916. *Foreign Relations, 1916, Supplement*, p. 170.

49. For these negotiations see Chapter Seven.

50. Bernstorff assured Lansing that it was not the intention of his government "to revoke the pledges given on September 1 and October 5, 1915," and imparted the information that "the orders issued to the German naval commanders are so formulated that enemy liners may not be destroyed on account of their armament unless such armament is proved." *Foreign Relations, 1916, Supplement*, pp. 181–182.

51. Ray Stannard Baker, *Woodrow Wilson, Life and Letters* (8 vols., Garden City, Doubleday, Doran and Co., 1927–39), VI, 165.

52. *Ibid.*, pp. 167–169. This letter was widely publicized, as was Senator Stone's.

53. New York *Evening Post*, March 8, 1916, quoted in Charles C. Tansill, *America Goes to War* (Boston, Little Brown & Co., 1938), p. 484. For Ray Stannard Baker's account, which is uncritical of Wilson's position, see *Life and Letters*, VI, 154–176.

54. Lansing to Wilson, March 27, 1916. *Lansing Papers*, I, 537–539.

55. Wilson to Lansing, March 30, 1916. *Ibid.*, p. 539.

56. *War Memoirs of Robert Lansing*, p. 136.

57. *Ibid.*, p. 137.

58. Lansing to Wilson, April 12, 15, 1916. *Lansing Papers*,

I, 546–547, 549–550. Lansing also observed: "I do not see that we gain anything strategically by postponing an action which I believe, and I think you agree with me, we will have to take in the end."

59. *Foreign Relations, 1916, Supplement*, p. 234.

The note concluded: "Unless the Imperial Government should now immediately declare and effect an abandonment of its present methods of submarine warfare against passenger and freight-carrying vessels, the Government of the United States can have no choice but to sever diplomatic relations with the German Empire altogether. This action the Government of the United States contemplates with the greatest reluctance but feels constrained to take in behalf of humanity and the rights of neutral nations."

Condemnation of the submarine was stated as follows: "It has become painfully evident to it [the American Government] that the position which it took at the very outset is inevitable, namely, the use of submarines for the destruction of an enemy's commerce is, of necessity, because of the very character of the vessels employed and the very methods of attack which their employment of course involves, utterly incompatible with the principles of humanity, the long-established and incontrovertible rights of neutrals, and the sacred immunities of non-combatants."

For Lansing's comments see *War Memoirs*, p. 139.

60. Diary entries, March 27, 29, 1916. Charles Seymour, ed., *The Intimate Papers of Colonel House* (4 vols., Boston, Houghton Mifflin Co., 1926), II, 226, 228–229.

61. House recorded the following on May 3: "I find the President set in his determination to make Germany recede from her position regarding submarines. He spoke with much feeling concerning Germany's responsibility for this worldwide calamity, and thought those guilty should have personal punishment. . . .

"The last time I was here [in Washington] he was so disinclined to be firm with Germany that I feared he might destroy his influence. I therefore did all I could to make him stand firm.

I evidently overdid it, for I now find him unyielding and belligerent, and not caring as much as he ought to avert war." *Ibid.*,
pp. 239–240.

62. Gerard to Lansing, April 20, 1916. *Foreign Relations,
1916, Supplement*, pp. 239, 241.

63. Gerard to Lansing, May 4, 1916. *Ibid.*, pp. 259–260.

64. Lansing to Gerard, May 8, 1916. *Ibid.*, p. 263.

65. The American Government was notified that the German
Navy would endeavor to stop "all sea traffic with . . . every
available weapon and without further notice" in certain defined
"blockade zones" around Great Britain, France, Italy, and in the
Eastern Mediterranean. There were certain minor mitigations.
Neutral vessels on their way to ports in the blockade zones "will
be spared during a sufficiently long period." Neutral vessels in
ports of the blockade zones on February 1, were to be spared
if they sailed before February 5. The safety of passengers on
"unarmed enemy passenger ships is guaranteed . . . for a sufficiently long period." One American passenger steamer a week
might sail to and one from Falmouth; these were to carry prescribed markings. *Foreign Relations, 1917, Supplement*, pp.
101–102.

66. From November 13 to January 12 there had been eight-
een such instances. Lansing to Wilson, January 15, 1917. Wilson
Papers, Library of Congress.

67. *Foreign Relations, 1916, Supplement*, pp. 313, 319.

68. *Lansing Papers*, I, 575.

69. Quoted in U.S. Senate, *The Special Committee Investigating the Munitions Industry*, 74th Cong., 2nd Sess. (Parts 25–
35 contain the hearings, Washington, Government Printing Office, 1937), Part 28, 8575.

CHAPTER THREE. THE SUBMARINE IN GERMAN POLICY

1. Carnegie Endowment for International Peace, *Official
German Documents Relating to the World War* (2 vols., New
York, Oxford University Press, 1923), II, 1117–1121.

2. *Ibid.*, pp. 1122–1127.

3. *Ibid.*, pp. 1128–1130. Italics are Falkenhayn's.

4. Herbert Henry Asquith was British prime minister from 1908 to 1916, and Sergei Dmitrievich Sazonov was Russian minister of foreign affairs from 1910 to 1917.

5. In fact, the Navy on February 23 had already given explicit orders to this effect. Arno Spindler, *Der Handels-krieg mit U-Booten* (3 vols., Berlin, E. S. Mittler & Sohn, 1934), III, 88–89. It was decided, however, to leave the American Government with the impression that no important modification had been made of the announcement of February 8. Under instructions, Bernstorff told Lansing on February 28 that enemy liners were "not to be destroyed on account of their armament unless such armament is proved."

6. *Official German Documents*, II, 1130–1139.

7. Bethmann-Hollweg to Gottlieb von Jagow, March 5, 1916. *Ibid.*, pp. 1139–1142. Orders issued to submarine commanders provided that: "1. Enemy merchant ships encountered in the war zone are to be immediately destroyed. 2. Enemy merchant ships encountered outside the war zone are to be destroyed only if armed. 3. Enemy passenger steamers, armed or unarmed, must not be attacked without warning whether encountered within or without the war zone." Order of March 13, 1916, MS. German Marine Archives quoted in Charles C. Tansill, *America Goes to War*, p. 491.

8. Spindler, *Der Handels-krieg*, III, 368. As early as January 1, 1916, Tirpitz believed that there were enough submarines on hand to force England to sue for peace within two months. Report of Bethmann-Hollweg, January 4, 1916. *Official German Documents*, II, 1117. But Tirpitz's blind confidence was not shared by others. On March 3, 1916 the Kaiser expressed the opinion to the chancellor that there were "far too few U-boats to overcome Great Britain." Bethmann-Hollweg to von Jagow, March 5, 1916. *Official German Documents*, II, 1140.

9. From the official record of the proceedings, *Official German Documents*, II, 1155–1163.

10. Captain von Bülow to Admiral von Holtzendorff, September 10, 1916. *Ibid.*, pp. 1165–1166.

11. Secretary of Legation von Lersner to the Foreign Office, December 20, 1916. *Ibid.*, p. 1199.

12. Secretary of Legation von Lersner to the Foreign Office, December 22, 1916. *Ibid.*, p. 1200. "After quite a lengthy debate," Lersner reported further, "it seemed that the General would be willing to permit the passage of liners to England." Ludendorff, however, "would certainly demand that they carry no absolute contraband."

13. Secretary of Legation von Lersner to the Foreign Office, December 23, 1916. *Ibid.*, pp. 1201–1202. Hindenburg recalled that at the Pless Conference in August Bethmann-Hollweg had "made the decision on the question of launching of an unrestricted U-boat war depend upon my statement of opinion that from the military standpoint the time had come." Hindenburg added that "this moment will be the end of January."

Bethmann-Hollweg replied on the same day. Despite his protests, the last paragraph of this telegram reveals how much ground he had already lost: "I . . . venture to assume that your Excellency will be in a position at that time to concentrate the necessary troops at both the Dutch and Danish frontiers. On this condition, and to the extent that I find myself able to agree with your Excellency that the advantages of an absolutely ruthless U-boat war are greater than the disadvantages resulting from the United States joining our enemies, I shall be ready to consider the question even of an unrestricted U-boat warfare. There are no objections for preparing for conferences with the Supreme High Command of the Army and the Chief of the Admiralty Staff as soon as our peace move has been brought to a definite conclusion as the result of the answer which the Entente will make." Bethmann-Hollweg to Secretary of Legation von Lersner, December 23, 1916. *Ibid.*, p. 1203.

14. Counselor of Legation Baron von Grünau to the Foreign Office, January 8, 1917. *Ibid.*, pp. 1205, 1320–1321.

Not only was use of the submarine to be unqualified, but there was to be no prior revocation of the promise given the United States on May 4. This omission was urged by the Navy on the ground that Great Britain should not be given an opportunity to prepare for the onslaught. The Navy also felt that if the United States were suddenly confronted with the "absolutely conclusive results" of ruthless submarine warfare it might "confine itself to the use of big words" and might "wait for a little while to see what results the first weeks of the U-boat war will bring." Admiral Holtzendorff to General Ludendorff, December 10, 1916 (copy sent to Foreign Office). *Ibid.*, p. 1183.

15. Bernstorff to the Secretary of State, January 10, 1917. *Foreign Relations, 1917, Supplement 1*, pp. 82–86. There had also been indications that intensified submarine warfare would not stop with the armed merchantman but would include all shipping. One such was a naval intelligence report transmitted by Lansing to Wilson on January 3. *Lansing Papers*, I, 576–579.

16. Gerard to the Secretary of State, January 21, 1917. *Foreign Relations, 1917, Supplement 1*, pp. 91–92.

17. Wilson to Lansing, January 24, 1917. *Lansing Papers*, I, 581.

18. Lansing to Wilson, January 17, 1917. *Ibid.*, p. 580.

19. Wilson to Lansing, January 31, 1917. Italics are Wilson's. Lansing to Wilson, January 31, 1917. *Ibid.*, pp. 581, 582–591. Lansing recommended that "a reasonable maximum limit of armament for defensive purposes under present conditions would it is believed, be the following: four guns of six inches or less caliber, placed anywhere on the ship, with an officer for each gun, and a number of men for each gun equal to the caliber in inches, the officers and men not to be members of the regular military forces detached for temporary duty, but still in the service and pay of the government, though they may be members of the reserve."

20. Professor Tansill's view is that a decision at that time to classify the armed merchantman as a belligerent vessel "would have compelled the disarmament of the British merchant ships and would have led to a friendly understanding between the United States and Germany relative to the conduct of submarine warfare. It would have removed the only serious cause of friction in German-American relations." C. C. Tansill, *America Goes to War*, p. 429.

Edwin Borchard and W. P. Lage, speaking of the American application of the law of neutrality during the period 1914–1917, maintain that "the failure consistently to apply the principles and rules of neutrality . . . served largely to drive the United States into the European war. It was, therefore, not neutrality, or the laws of neutrality, which were at fault, but the unwise human administration of laws, which, properly administered, would adequately have protected the United States against intervention." *Neutrality for the United States,* vi–vii.

21. In speaking to the Reichstag on April 5, Bethmann-Hollweg was seemingly more conciliatory than his military colleagues on the crucial question of Belgium. Nevertheless, he did not see on this occasion a restoration of Belgium to its pre-war status; "things cannot be what they were before. . . . We must create real guarantees that Belgium never shall be a Franco-British vassal." Nor could Germany "sacrifice the oppressed Flemish race, but must assure them sound evolution which . . . is based on their mother tongue and follows their national character." Germany's desire was for "neighbors that do not form coalitions against us, but with whom we can collaborate and who collaborate with us to our mutual advantage." New York *Times,* Apr. 6, 1916.

22. Holtzendorff to Hindenburg, December 22, 1916. *Official German Documents,* II, 1214–1219. The document, entitled "With Regard to the Necessity of an Early Launching of the Unrestricted U-Boat War," to which this letter of transmittal refers, is found on pp. 1219–1277.

23. Under-Secretary of State of the Imperial Chancelery Wahnschaffe to Bethmann-Hollweg, January 9, 1917. *Ibid.,* pp. 1206–1208. The Admiralty had delayed until January 6 sending a copy of its document of December 22 to the civilian officials.

Helfferich spelled out his point about American sacrifices at home as follows: "If the outcome of the war were dependent thereon, I would not consider it at all impossible that the United States would be able to bring about a ten per cent restriction on its normal consumption [of wheat] in favor of England, whereby 1.7 million tons . . . would at once be released to meet an

English shortage of three months. And if a half of this amount were to be sunk on the voyage to England—a percentage far outstripping the possibilities estimated by the Admiralty Staff— such a step would be of invaluable, or perhaps decisive assistance to England."

24. During the crisis over the *Sussex*, Admiral Holtzendorff, in sharp contrast to previously expressed views (to which, however, he soon reverted: cf. memorandum of August 31. *Ibid.*, pp. 1152–1154.) counseled on April 30 that it would be worth while to "attempt to keep America out of the game," and that in order to do so Germany might well forego the "few hundred thousand tons of enemy merchant tonnage which we could in the meantime destroy." If the United States could be brought "to exert effective pressure upon England, to the end that legal trade of neutrals with combatants is resumed, we will thus receive the economic strengthening which will enable us to maintain our favorable military situation for a prolonged time and thus to win the war." Holtzendorff to Admiral von Müller, April 30, 1916, which was shown by the latter to the Kaiser the following day. Spindler commented that the Kaiser accepted this about-face of his responsible naval adviser as a "liberation." Spindler, *Der Handels-krieg*, III, 143–144, 145.

CHAPTER FOUR. THE DEFENSE OF TRADE

1. Ambassador Page to the Secretary of State, March 15, 1915. *Foreign Relations, 1915, Supplement*, pp. 144–145.

2. Secretary of State to Ambassador Page, March 30, 1915. *Ibid.*, p. 152.

3. *Why We Went to War* (New York, Harper and Bros., 1936), pp. 119, 122.

4. U.S. Senate, *Munitions Investigation*, Part 26, 7934. Shipments to the United Kingdom in the latter three-year period totaled $4,485,000,000, an increase of 158 per cent; to France $2,894,000,000, 382 per cent; to Canada $1,557,000,000, 53

per cent; to Russia $930,000,000, 1,157 per cent; and to Italy $815,000,000, 303 per cent.

5. Under this heading are included shells and projectiles (loaded), nitro powder, nitro cellulose, T.N.T., cordite, gun cotton, etc.

6. *Ibid.*, pp. 7786, 7936–7940.

An itemized tabulation of munitions exports in C. C. Tansill, *America Goes to War*, p. 53, comes to a similar figure, $2,187,-948,000.

7. As early as December 4, 1914 Gerard cabled there was "universal, very bitter, and increasing feeling in Germany because of reported sale by Americans of munitions of war . . . to Allies." *Foreign Relations, 1914, Supplement*, p. 578. On February 14, 1915 Gerard reported that the belief in Germany was "that great quantities of munitions are sent from America, thus prolonging the war. . . . I assure you the situation is very tense." *Foreign Relations, 1915, Supplement*, p. 104.

8. *Foreign Relations, 1915, Supplement*, pp. 157–158.

The Secretary of State replied on April 21 that any change in American neutrality statutes during the progress of the war "which would affect unequally the relations of the United States with the nations at war would be an unjustifiable departure from the principle of strict neutrality." *Ibid.*, p. 162. A strong legal argument against this often reiterated position may be found in a memorandum submitted by Charles Cheney Hyde to Secretary Lansing, January 11, 1916. *Munitions Investigations*, pp. 8469–8473.

9. *Munitions Investigation*, Exhibits on pp. 9205–9206. Great Britain owed $1,476,511,000; France $675,315,000; Russia $86,000,000; and Italy $25,000,000.

Tansill in *America Goes to War*, Appendix B, included Canadian loans made for war purposes and arrived at a grand total of $2,263,400,000. He then subtracted municipal loans (made to French and British cities) and gave the total of $2,145,000,000 for war purposes.

10. Secretary of State to J. P. Morgan and Company, August 14, 1914. *Foreign Relations, 1914, Supplement*, p. 580.

11. Bryan to Wilson, August 10, 1914. *Lansing Papers,* I, 131–132.

12. The intimation that the Government would not object was conveyed by Lansing after a conversation with the President on October 23. See Lansing's memorandum of this conversation, *ibid.,* p. 140.

13. *Munitions Investigation,* Exhibit on p. 8708.

Public acknowledgment of the modified loan policy was made in a press release March 31, 1915: With respect to credit arrangements, the Department "has neither approved . . . nor disapproved—it has simply taken no action in the premises and expressed no opinion." *Lansing Papers,* I, 146.

14. In the hearings of the Nye Committee, Senator Bennett Champ Clark persisted, despite the highly circumstantial character of the evidence, in maintaining that Morgan and Company's withdrawal of support for sterling exchange at this time was a carefully devised move to force the Administration to abandon its initial policy toward loans to the belligerents. *Munitions Investigation,* pp. 7853–7871. If this was the company's intention, any added pressure felt in Washington could not be separated from the already exigent necessities of the general commercial situation.

15. McAdoo to Wilson, August 21, 1915. *Ibid.,* pp. 8123–8125.

16. Lansing to Wilson, September 6, 1915. *Lansing Papers,* I, 144–146.

17. Radio address, June 7, 1935, quoted in Charles Seymour, *American Neutrality 1914–17* (New Haven, Yale University Press, 1935), p. 85.

18. *Munitions Investigation,* Exhibits on pp. 8642–8643, 8924–8928.

19. *Munitions Investigation,* pp. 8632–8633, 8622. However, in the case of the British debt to Morgan and Company, which stood at $345,000,000 at the time of American entry into the war, $700,000,000 in securities served as collateral.

The number of private persons possessing Allied bonds, secured and unsecured, was estimated by J. P. Morgan and

Company to be 400,000. New York *Times,* Jan. 7, 1936.

20. See Alice M. Morrissey, *The American Defense of Neutral Rights, 1914–1917* (Cambridge, Mass., Harvard University Press, 1939), pp. 196–197.

21. See Alice M. Morrissey's conclusion in her cogent study of the economic aspects of American policy. *Ibid.,* pp. v, xi, 197.

22. Secretary of Commerce William C. Redfield to Secretary of State, October 23, 1916. *Foreign Relations, 1916, Supplement,* pp. 466–477.

23. The term used by Senator Homer T. Bone of Washington in the foreign policy debates in 1937. He contended that "we ought to cut off trade with belligerent countries in time of war." Senator William E. Borah of Idaho replied that "we found out during the early days of the World War that somebody aside from Du Pont was interested in economic conditions. . . . The farmers of the country, the producers of the country, the miners of the country, were here in Washington, and they were well represented; and they were not hucksters. They were the producers." *Congressional Record* (75th Cong., 1st Sess.), vol. 81, part 2, 1682, and part 3, 2679. In the law of May 27, 1937, Congress did not take the drastic action advocated by Senator Bone; significantly, it went no further than the adoption of a cash-and-carry policy.

24. "So-called" because, instead of sustaining freedom of the seas which constituted a main feature of historical neutrality, it abandoned neutral rights which the United States had previously defended with great vigor. The law of November 4, 1939 prohibited the making of loans to belligerents; required that foreign ships transport goods destined for a belligerent port, title to which goods must have passed to the purchaser before they are carried away; banned American vessels from "combat areas" and American citizens from taking passage on belligerent vessels; forbade the arming of American merchantmen; and invited the President to use his discretion in denying the use of American ports to belligerent submarines and armed merchantmen. This act was essentially the same as that of May 1937 except for the

omission of an embargo on munitions and the addition of the provision concerning combat areas.

25. Secretary of the Navy Frank Knox, testifying before the House Foreign Affairs Committee October 13, 1941 on the resolution to repeal the ban on arming American merchantmen, said that he "readily recognized that those who voted for it [the neutrality legislation] felt that they had very substantial reasons for doing so. First, [they] . . . did not want the United States involved in incidents which might lead to war, and second, they did not want the United States involved in war as a result of the action of private individuals who were keen to make profits out of trading with belligerents. In this particular and in this sense, it may be said with justification that the act has been successful—the United States has not gone to war over incidents, and it has not been dragged nearer to war by any act of private interests or private individuals."

Believing that commercial considerations were irrelevant in the situation confronting the nation, however, Knox said that "we should measure our action" by recognizing that "our true interests and security [lie] in the removal of every restriction and handicap upon our efforts to so influence the outcome of the war as to be sure that the land on the opposite shore of the Atlantic shall remain in the hands and under the control of a friendly power." *Hearings on H. J. Res. 237,* 77th Cong., 1st Sess. (Washington, Government Printing Office, 1941), pp. 7–10.

26. American exports to Germany fell from $341,875,820 in the year ending June 1914 to $28,656,206 in the fiscal year 1915. For the comparable periods in 1916 and 1917 they were $272,981 and $1,049,340 respectively. Suggesting some compensation, however, was the increase in American exports to Norway from $9,063,646 in 1914 to $82,337,804 in 1917. Exports to Sweden also increased in a degree which suggested that Germany benefited. Department of Commerce, *Foreign Commerce and Navigation of the United States for the Year Ending June 30, 1918* (Washington, Government Printing Office, 1919), no. 5, p. 842.

CHAPTER FIVE. THE DEFENSE OF PRINCIPLE

1. Ray Stannard Baker and William E. Dodd, eds., *The Public Papers of Woodrow Wilson* (2 vols., New York, Harper and Bros., 1925–26), I, 157–158.

2. *Ibid.*, pp. 224–226.

3. *Ibid.*, p. 321.

4. Quotation supplied by Ray Stannard Baker and found in Harley Notter, *The Origins of the Foreign Policy of Woodrow Wilson* (Baltimore, Johns Hopkins Press, 1937), p. 98.

5. Address on preparedness before the Interdenominational Meeting at Aeolian Hall, New York, January 27, 1916. *Public Papers*, II, 3–4.

6. *Ibid.*, I, 406–428.

7. See memorandum prepared by the War College Division of the Office of the Chief of Staff, September 11, 1915. *War Department, Annual Reports, 1915* (Washington, Government Printing Office, 1916), I, 116–118. This memorandum appears as appendix C to the Secretary of War's annual report to the President.

8. Address to Congress, December 7, 1915. *Public Papers*, I, 416.

9. Address before the Manhattan Club, New York, November 4, 1915. *Ibid.*, p. 385.

10. Internal evidence places Tumulty's memorandum no later than the first week of December 1915. Wilson MSS., Library of Congress.

11. Diary entry, November 4, 1914. *Intimate Papers of Colonel House*, I, 299.

12. House to Wilson, July 14, 1915. *Ibid.*, II, 19.

13. House to Charles Seymour, April 6, 1926. *Ibid.*, II, pp. 84, 289–290.

14. Address to Railway Business Association, New York, January 27, 1916. *Public Papers*, II, 5. But at St. Louis a few days later he said: "Our security is in the purity of our motives.

The minute we get an impure motive we are going to deserve to be insecure." In saying this, in an extemporaneous speech, he was leading up to the opposite position: "The peace of the world, including America, depends upon the aroused passion of other nations and not upon the motives of the United States." *Ibid.,* p. 111.

15. Wilson was aware of this obstacle from the beginning. In a diary entry November 4, 1914 House recorded that in a discussion of the question of a reserve army Wilson "did not believe that there was any necessity for immediate action; he was afraid it would shock the country." Moreover, Wilson took the view that "even if Germany won, she would not be in a condition seriously to menace our country for many years to come." House combated this idea, stating that "Germany would have a large military force ready to act in furthering the designs which the military party evidently have in mind." *Intimate Papers,* I, 298–299.

16. Note of July 21, 1915. *Foreign Relations, 1915, Supplement,* p. 481.

17. Address of January 31, 1916. *Public Papers,* II, 58, 61.

At Des Moines February 1 Wilson expressed the same thought: "What is America expected to do? She is expected to do nothing less than keep law alive while the rest of the world burns. . . . The only thing, therefore, that keeps America out of danger is that to some degree the understandings, the ancient and honorable understandings, of nations with regard to their relations to one another and to the citizens of one another are to some extent still observed and followed. And whenever there is a departure from them, the United States is called to intervene, to speak its voice of protest." *Ibid.,* p. 75.

18. Address at Topeka, February 2, 1916. *Ibid.,* p. 91.

19. In his addresses to the Railway Business Association, New York, January 27, and at Des Moines, February 1, 1916. *Ibid.,* pp. 8, 82.

20. Wilson to Senator William J. Stone, February 24, 1916. *Ibid.,* p. 123.

21. *Official Report of the Proceedings of the Sixteenth Repub-*

lican National Convention (New York, The Tenny Press, 1916), p. 280.

22. Lansing believed that Bryan might be interested in Root's opinions. Although Lansing subsequently decided against transmitting the report to Bryan, Anderson's diary contains the record of the interview. The entry is dated May 15, 1915. Anderson MSS.

23. Bryan to Wilson, June 5, 1915. Bryan Letter Book, Library of Congress, quoted in Merle E. Curti, *Bryan and World Peace*, p. 212.

24. Address to the National Press Club, May 15, 1916. *Public Papers*, II, 171–172.

In the preceding section of this chapter it has been noted that Wilson's initial position, which was closely similar to Bryan's, underwent an evolution. Referring to his address to Congress of December 1914, in which he had opposed preparedness, Wilson told an audience in New York on January 27, 1916 that "more than a year has gone by since then and I would be ashamed if I had not learned something in fourteen months. The minute I stop changing my mind with the change of all the circumstances of the world, I will be a back number." *Ibid.*, p. 10.

25. "The Forces that Make for Peace," *Report of the Sixteenth Annual Meeting of the Lake Mohonk Conference* (Lake Mohonk Conference on International Arbitration, 1910), p. 172. Quoted in Curti, *Bryan and World Peace*, pp. 138–139.

26. *World Peace, a written debate between William Howard Taft and William Jennings Bryan* (New York, George H. Doran Co., 1917), pp. 139–141.

Bryan cited examples of American success in conquering "with its ideals rather than with its arms." "Within a decade China, the sleeping giant of the Orient, has aroused itself. Breaking off its monarchial fetters, it has declared itself a republic; and, passing over imperial designations, it has honored our nation by giving to its chief executive, the title President. . . . Russia has overthrown its arbitrary government and commenced to build a national authority upon popular consent. Surely the

American people . . . must find great satisfaction in the increasing influence exerted by our example."

27. Lansing complained that Gerard mailed the memorandum instead of cabling it. Lansing to Wilson, February 7, 1915. Wilson MSS.

28. Entry of April 15, 1915. Lansing Diaries, Library of Congress. This, as are most of the "diary" entries, is in the form of a memorandum by Lansing to himself.

29. May 3, 1915. *Ibid.* Lansing was quite emphatic: ". . . at the present time when half the world has gone mad, when great empires are staggering under the sledge-hammer blows of their adversaries, when governments and individuals are laboring under intense excitement, common sense, as well as generous sentiments, demands that a neutral should not insist as to conduct which he knows will not be followed, that nations which are struggling for their lives should not be asked to step aside and let a neutral nation pass, that a neutral should give a proper proportion to his commercial interests in comparing them with the great enterprise of war."

30. May 25, 1915. *Ibid.*

Nearly a year later Lansing expressed similar views orally, which prompted one of his auditors subsequently to write: "I have been somewhat disturbed over a statement which you made to the effect that there might be conditions under which a nation might do things which were in violation of settled principles of international law, provided the doing of those things were essential to self-preservation." Lansing replied: "I do not think you have cause for anxiety as to my attitude. What I said at dinner that night was for private consumption only. I endeavored to lay bare the philosophy of belligerent conduct and to show the position which would result from applying logic to the abstract question of inhumanity in an international war. Don't for a moment conceive that I am guided by such principles, which seem to me contrary to the spirit of modern civilization." Edward N. Smith to Lansing, April 5; Lansing to Smith, April 11, 1916. Lansing Papers, Library of Congress.

31. "Consideration and Outline of Policies, July 11, 1915." *War Memoirs of Robert Lansing*, pp. 19–21. Italics in the original. The concluding quotations are from portions of the memorandum not included in the *Memoirs* and are from the Lansing Diaries.

32. Lansing, *War Memoirs*, pp. 172, 173.

33. These latter quotations, which are not included in the *Memoirs*, are from the original memorandum dated only September 1916 in the Diaries.

34. December 3, 1916. Lansing Diaries.

35. Lansing, *War Memoirs*, p. 172.

36. December 3, 1916. Lansing Diaries.

37. Lansing to Wilson, January 23, 1917. Wilson MSS.

38. Diary entry of February 4, 1917. *War Memoirs*, p. 213. In a note to Wilson on February 2 Lansing set forth "some thoughts on Germany's broken promise and the crime of submarine warfare." There followed a measured denunciation: "Deceived and humiliated it [the American Government] has but one course to pursue and that is to denounce as outlaw the government which has treated it with contempt, has imposed upon its good will, has done to death its citizens, has ignored the most sacred rights, and has presumed . . . that the United States would submit to its arrogance and insults rather than come to an open breach of friendly relations." Lansing to Wilson, February 2, 1917. Wilson MSS.

39. *War Memoirs*, p. 212.

40. David F. Houston, *Eight Years with Wilson's Cabinet, 1913 to 1920* (2 vols., New York, Doubleday, Page & Co., 1926), I, 229.

41. February 4, 1917. Lansing Diaries.

42. Diary entry, February 4, 1917. *War Memoirs*, p. 214. Lansing commented that "his argument did not impress me as very genuine, and I concluded that he was in his usual careful way endeavoring to look at all sides of the question."

43. March 19, 1917. Lansing Diaries. This entry was made at 9:00 A.M. that morning. The war, Lansing added in his hastily written note, might last two or three years, even five, he said,

and he counted also the loss of American lives. But he was confident the results would justify the sacrifice. He was convinced that "we must go through with it. I hope and believe the President will see it in this light."

44. Lansing, *War Memoirs*, p. 233.

45. Lansing to Wilson, March 19, 1917. *Ibid.*, p. 234. Lansing, who felt that the situation urgently demanded an early declaration of war, was reduced to arguing in circles. "I think that these incidents, however, show very plainly that the German Government intends to carry out its announced policy." "With the greatest reluctance," he had come to "the conviction that war is bound to come," and this being the case, the question was "whether or not the greatest good will be accomplished by waiting until some other events have taken place before we enter the conflict." The advantages of immediate participation appeared "to be based largely upon the premise that war is inevitable. Of course if that premise is wrong what I say is open to question." He then added two other premises: that the Allies represent the principle of democracy, and that democracy must succeed "for the welfare of mankind and for the establishment of peace."

46. The following account of the views expressed by Lansing in the Cabinet meeting of March 20, 1917 is based on an entry of that date in the Lansing Diaries.

47. "I must have spoken with vehemence," he added, "because the President asked me to lower my voice so that none in the corridor could hear."

48. April 7, 1917. Lansing Diaries.

49. See, for example, Henry F. Pringle, *Theodore Roosevelt, A Biography* (New York, Harcourt, Brace and Co., 1931), pp. 387–397. Allan Nevins in his *Henry White; Thirty Years of American Diplomacy* (New York, Harper and Bros., 1930) writes approvingly of Roosevelt's role. For a keen and appreciative account of Roosevelt's diplomacy see Lewis Einstein, *Roosevelt: His Mind in Action* (Boston, Houghton Mifflin Co., 1930), pp. 127–147.

50. Quoted in W. D. Puleston, *Mahan: The Life and Work*

of Captain Alfred Thayer Mahan (New Haven, Yale University Press, 1939), pp. 182–183.

51. Letter to Captain William S. Cowles, October 27, 1911. *Letters from Theodore Roosevelt to Anna Roosevelt Cowles* (New York, Charles Scribner's Sons, 1924), p. 296.

52. Hermann Hagedorn, *The Bugle That Woke America* (New York, John Day Co., 1940), pp. 17–18, 65–66.

53. This conversation is recorded by Eckhardstein in his *Die Isolierung Deutschlands,* and is quoted in H. Hagedorn, *Bugle That Woke America,* p. 9. Early in the war Roosevelt spoke similarly to Professor Kuno Meyer, German exchange professor at Harvard, who, endeavoring to impress Roosevelt with the certainty of a German victory, predicted that after taking the channel ports Germany would "make a raid on England and smash the British Empire." Hagedorn, *Bugle That Woke America,* pp. 63–64.

54. Quoted by Hagedorn, *Bugle That Woke America,* p. 17.

55. Vol. 107, pp. 1011–1015, and vol. 108, pp. 169–178 respectively.

56. This passage appeared in the September 23 issue of *Outlook,* p. 173. In Roosevelt's first book on the war, which appeared in January 1915, it was for the most part omitted and in its place appeared the following: "President Wilson has been much applauded by all the professional pacifists because he has announced that our desire for peace must make us secure it for ourselves by a neutrality so strict as to forbid our even whispering a protest against wrong-doing, lest such whispers might cause disturbance to our ease and well-being. We pay the penalty of this action—or, rather, supine inaction—on behalf of peace for ourselves, by forfeiting our right to do anything on behalf of peace for the Belgians in the present. We can maintain our neutrality only by refusal to do anything to aid unoffending weak powers which are dragged into the gulf of bloodshed and misery through no fault of their own." *America and the World War* (New York, Charles Scribner's Sons, 1915), p. 27.

57. Letter in collection of Theodore Roosevelt Papers, Library

of Congress, quoted by Russell Buchanan, "Theodore Roosevelt and American Neutrality, 1914–1917," *American Historical Review,* vol. 43 (1937–38), p. 776.

58. Joseph Bucklin Bishop, *Theodore Roosevelt and His Time* (2 vols., New York, Charles Scribner's Sons, 1920), II, 372.

59. Recorded by J. Medill Patterson in *Roosevelt as We Knew Him,* quoted by H. Hagedorn, *Bugle That Woke America,* pp. 64–65. Concerning Belgium, Roosevelt wrote to a German correspondent, Baron von Stumm: "The commission of such a wrong unsettles the relations between other nations and the nation that has committed the wrong. What is the use of Germany assuring the United States, as it has done, that it never intends to seek territorial aggrandizement in America, when we have before our eyes the fate of Belgium and must know that, if Germany destroyed the British Empire, it would act toward the Panama Canal and toward the western hemisphere generally precisely as it deemed German interests required?" Hagedorn, *Bugle That Woke America,* pp. 54–55.

60. On this same occasion, some three months after the declaration of war, Roosevelt identified the German menace with an explicitness which he had avoided during the neutrality period. Although the nation was at war, "we are not yet awake," Roosevelt said. "We live on a continent. We have trusted to that fact for safety in the past. We do not understand that world conditions have changed and that the ocean and even the air have become highways for military aggression. . . . Unless we beat Germany in Europe, we shall have to fight her deadly ambition on our own coasts and on our own continent." Quoted in H. Hagedorn, *Bugle That Woke America,* p. 142.

Speaking at about the same time, Lansing was expressing similar misgivings as to the public's conception of why the United States was at war. "I sometimes think that there prevail very erroneous impressions as to the reasons why we entered the war, not the immediate reasons, but the deep underlying reasons. . . . Would it be easier or wiser for this country single-handed to resist a German Empire, flushed with victory and with great armies and navies at its command, than to unite with the brave enemies of that Empire in ending now and for all time this menace to our future? . . . The day has gone by when we can measure possibilities by past experiences or when we believe that any physical obstacle is so great or any moral influence is so potent as to cause the German autocracy to abandon its mad purpose of world conquest." William M. Lewis, ed., *The Voices of Our Leaders* (New York, Hinds, Hayden and Eldredge, Inc., 1917), pp. 64–72.

61. "The World War: Its Tragedies and Its Lessons," *Outlook*, vol. 108 (September 23, 1914), p. 177.

62. *America and the World War*, pp. 109–111. In his succeeding book, *Fear God and Take Your Own Part* (New York, George H. Doran Co.), published in February 1916, Roosevelt made these same points in even shriller tones.

63. Roosevelt to Lee, March 16, 1915. Letter in Theodore Roosevelt Papers, Library of Congress, quoted by Russell Buchanan, "Theodore Roosevelt and American Neutrality," p. 790. On pages 786–789 Buchanan related the astonishing story of Roosevelt's self-assumed role as adviser to the British Government on the best propaganda approaches to American opinion.

64. *Fear God and Take Your Own Part*, p. 353.

In an interview after the *Lusitania* disaster, Roosevelt urged that the government take possession of all the interned German ships, including the German warships, and hold them "as a guarantee that ample satisfaction shall be given us. Furthermore it should declare that in view of Germany's murderous offences against the rights of neutrals all commerce with Germany shall be forthwith forbidden and all commerce of every kind permitted and encouraged with France, England, Russia, and the rest of the civilized world." *Ibid.*, p. 355.

CHAPTER SIX. THE EMERGENCE OF THE LEAGUE IDEA

1. Address to the Daughters of the American Revolution, Washington, October 11, 1915. *Public Papers of Woodrow Wilson*, I, 378.

2. Georg Cohn, *Neo-Neutrality*, translated from the Danish by Arthur S. Keller and Einar Jensen (New York, Columbia University Press, 1939), p. 9.

3. *New Republic*, vol. 8 (1916), 151.

4. The article entitled "The United States and Anglo-German Rivalry" appeared originally in *National and English Review* (January 1913), a British publication. In the following month it was reprinted in the American journal, *Living Age*, vol., 18 (February 8, 1913), 323–332. Einstein had at first failed to find a publisher in the United States (cf. Lewis Einstein, *Roosevelt: His Mind in Action*, p. 219). This article, together with a subsequent article entitled "The War and American Policy," was published in a small book early in 1918 entitled *A Prophecy of the War* (New York, Columbia University Press, 1918), for which Theodore Roosevelt wrote a foreword.

5. This article entitled "The War and American Policy" appeared in the *National and English Review* in November 1914. It is incorporated in *A Prophecy of the War*.

6. Diary entries, April 9, August 30, 1914. *Intimate Papers*, I, 246, 275.

7. Diary entry, August 6, 1914; House to Wilson, August 22, September 18, 1914. *Ibid.*, pp. 318, 284–285, 324–325.

8. *Foreign Relations, 1914, Supplement*, p. 42; and House to Wilson, September 18, 1914. *Intimate Papers*, I, 324–325.

9. Diary entries, September 20, 1914, January 25, 1915. *Intimate Papers*, I, 327, 357, 327–328.

10. Ambassador Spring-Rice to Sir Edward Grey. *Ibid.*, pp. 328–329.

11. Diary entries, December 17, 20, 23, 1914. *Ibid.*, pp. 340, 341, 341–342.

12. Diary entry, January 13, 1915. *Ibid.*, p. 352.

13. W. H. Page to Secretary Bryan, January 15, 1915. *Ibid.*, pp. 354–355.

14. Diary entry, January 12, 1915; Gerard to House, January 20, and Gerard to Wilson, January 24, 1915; Grey to Spring-Rice, January 22, 1915. Spring-Rice passed this last communication on to House. *Ibid.*, pp. 340, 345, 355–356, 347–349.

15. Grey to Spring-Rice, December 22, 1914, January 2, 1915. George Macaulay Trevelyan, *Grey of Fallodon* (Boston, Houghton Mifflin Co., 1937), p. 357.

16. House to Wilson, February 9, 1915. *Intimate Papers*, I, 363–364.

17. Diary entry, February 10, 1915. *Ibid.*, pp. 368–369.

18. *Ibid.*

19. Grey to Spring-Rice, June 1915; Grey to Lord Crew, June 14, 1915. Trevelyan, *Grey of Fallodon*, pp. 361, 362.

20. Writing to a friend on September 9, 1915, Grey said that he wanted a "good peace," by which he meant "a peace that will be made of a determination not to have this sort of war again. We cannot get this I fear unless the United States will take a hand in making the peace, and they have missed the opportunities of asserting themselves; or rather their public opinion not having chosen to assert itself by now is likely not to do so at all. Their best men are willing to see the true issues involved, but the bulk of the people do not." *Ibid.*, p. 360.

21. Zimmermann to House, February 4; House to Zimmermann, February 17; and Zimmermann to House, March 2, 1915. *Intimate Papers*, I, 371, 375, 391.

22. House to Wilson, March 20; diary entry, March 24, 1915. *Ibid.*, pp. 402, 403.

23. House to Wilson, March 27, 1915. *Ibid.*, p. 410.

24. Grey to House, April 24, 1915. *Ibid.*, p. 425.

25. Diary entry, May 30, 1915. *Ibid.*, pp. 453–454.

26. Diary entry, August 21; House to Wilson, August 22, 1915. *Intimate Papers*, II, pp. 30–31.

27. Diary entry, October 1915. *Ibid.*, p. 85.

28. House to Page, August 4, 1915. *Ibid.*, pp. 60–62.

29. Thus he recorded in his diary November 17, 1915: "We [the Administration] are beset on all sides, both at home and abroad. . . . The part that gives one faith in the course we are pursuing, is that all the critics differ violently among themselves as to the remedy. I have no doubt that it is the right course and will so prove itself, provided it is not made impossible by the extremists here and abroad. It is all very clear in my mind what

this country should do. The question is, Can the President do it unmolested? The convening of Congress puts a new and disturbing element into this situation. The constant changes in the Cabinets in France and England do likewise. . . . I am glad my philosophy holds me serene. I do the best I can each day and give the best advice to the President of which I am capable, and let it rest at that." *Ibid.*, p. 93.

30. The year 1915 had not witnessed the reversal of Germany's initial successes for which the Allies had hoped. Although Italy had gone to the side of the Allies, her campaign against the Austrians in the Trentino and along the Isonzo was inconclusive. Nor had the Italian intervention relieved the Teutonic pressure on the Russians, who were forced to abandon their earlier gains in Galicia and to surrender Poland, Courland, and parts of Lithuania. Meanwhile the French and British assault on the Dardanelles failed disastrously, and Bulgaria joined the Central Powers. Serbia was overrun. Rumania and Greece had no choice but to remain neutral. In the West, French and British armies, despite frightful expenditure of blood, could not prevail against the strongly entrenched Germans. Only at sea, where German commerce had been swept away, was the war favorable to the Allied cause. But in this theater ruthless submarine warfare, held in check only by American diplomacy, threatened Allied commerce itself. During the fall of 1915 Gerard sent a stream of admonitory messages to House. On October 1 he wrote: "Of course I may be affected by the surroundings, but it seems to me Germany is winning this war." On November 2: "Germany seems to be winning this war, to us here. Efforts to starve her out will not succeed. . . . The military are careless of public opinion of neutrals; they say they are winning and do not need good opinion. I am really afraid of war against us after this war—if Germany wins." On November 16: "The German people are still absolutely, and probably justifiably confident in the results of the war." *Ibid.*, p. 81.

31. This conversation, recorded in House's diary, took place in early October 1915. House had been encouraged to formulate a policy based on this view by what the President had told him

a short time before. "Much to my surprise," House wrote, the President "said he had never been sure that we ought not to take part in the conflict and, if it seemed evident that Germany and her militaristic ideas were to win, the obligation upon us was greater than ever." *Ibid.*, pp. 84–85.

32. Diary entry, October 11, 1915. *Ibid.*, p. 86.

33. Grey to House, August 10, August 26, 1915. *Ibid.*, pp. 87–88, 88–89.

34. Grey to House, September 22, 1915. *Ibid.*, p. 89.

35. House to Grey, October 17, 1915. *Ibid.*, pp. 90–91.

36. In returning the draft to House, the President referred to this and one other change as "unimportant" and "verbal," which "do not alter the sense of it. I do not want to make it inevitable quite, that we should take part to force terms on Germany, because the exact circumstances of such a crisis are impossible to determine. The letter is altogether right. I pray God it may bring results." *Woodrow Wilson, Life and Letters,* VI, 128.

37. Grey to House, November 9, 1915. *Ibid.*, p. 130.

38. Telegram, Wilson to House, November 10; House to Wilson, November 10, 1915. *Ibid.*, pp. 130–131. The letter may also be found in *Intimate Papers,* II, 92.

39. Wilson to House, November 11, 1915. *Life and Letters,* VI, 131. Italics in original.

40. Speaking on the origins and objects of the war, Asquith said publicly on September 25, 1914: "I should like . . . to ask your attention . . . to the end which . . . we ought to keep in view. Forty-four years ago, at the time of the war of 1870, Mr. Gladstone used these words. He said: 'The greatest triumph of our time will be the enthronement of the idea of public right as the governing idea of European politics.' . . . Little progress it seems, has as yet been made towards that good and beneficent change, but it seems to me to be now at this moment as good a definition as we can have of our European policy—the idea of public right. . . . It means first and foremost, the clearing of the ground by the definite repudiation of militarism as the governing factor in the relations of States and

in the future moulding of the European world. It means next that room must be found and kept for the independent existence and the free development of smaller nationalities each with a corporate consciousness of its own. . . . And it means finally, or ought to mean, perhaps by a slow and gradual process, the substitution for force, for the clash of competing ambition, for groupings and alliance and a precarious equipoise, of a real European partnership based on the recognition of equal right, and established and enforced by a common will." *Speeches by the Earl of Oxford and Asquith, K.C.* (New York, George H. Doran Co., 1927), pp. 217–218.

It is interesting to note, however, that it is a European, rather than world-wide, association which is here envisaged.

CHAPTER SEVEN. THE HOUSE-GREY MEMORANDUM

1. Grey to House, July 14, 1915. *Intimate Papers,* II, 55. However, even this estimate proved too sanguine.

2. Grey to House, November 11, 1915. *Life and Letters,* VI, 131–132; *Intimate Papers,* II, 98.

3. Wilson to House, December 24, 1915. *Life and Letters,* VI, 138.

4. *Ibid.,* pp. 139, 146.

Because of an error in transmission, Wilson's cable of the eleventh must have been particularly distressing to House. As it was received, the last sentence read: "This is just." *Life and Letters,* VI, 146n.

5. See above, pp. 40–43.

6. *War Memoirs of Robert Lansing,* pp. 102–103.

A year later (in a diary entry of January 28, 1917) Lansing expressed this same view and concluded that "we must . . . wait patiently until the Germans do something which will arouse general indignation. . . ." He hoped "that those blundering Germans will blunder soon because there is no doubt but that the Allies in the west are having a hard time and Russia is not succeeding in spite of her man power." *Ibid.,* p. 208.

Carrying coals to Newcastle, House on November 28, 1915 "tried to impress upon Lansing the necessity of the United States making it clear to the Allies that we considered their cause our cause, and that we had no intention of permitting a military autocracy to dominate the world, if our strength could prevent it. We [the United States] believed this was a fight between democracy and autocracy and we must stand with democracy." *Intimate Papers*, II, 100–101.

7. House to Wilson, January 13, 16, 1916. *Intimate Papers*, II, 132, 133–134.

With respect to Germany, House added a postscript: "Of course, I do not mean to advise that diplomatic relations should not be immediately broken if the Central Powers sink another passenger ship without warning. If this were not done, it would discredit us everywhere and greatly minimize your influence."

8. Wilson to House, February 13; House to Lansing, February 14, 1916. House MSS., Yale University Library, quoted in Tansill, *America Goes to War*, p. 427.

9. House to Wilson, January 8, 1916. *Life and Letters*, VI, pp. 141–142.

10. House to Wilson, February 3, 1916. *Intimate Papers*, II, 147.

11. Viscount Grey of Fallodon, *Twenty-Five Years* (2 vols., New York, Frederick A. Stokes Co., 1925), II, 134.

12. House to Wilson, January 30, 1916. *Intimate Papers*, II, 145–146.

13. Diary entry, February 2, 1916. *Ibid.*, pp. 157–158.

14. House to Wilson, February 9, 1916. *Ibid.*, pp. 164–165.

15. House to Wilson, February 10, 1916, and diary entry of same date. *Ibid.*, pp. 171–173.

16. Diary entry, February 11, 1916. *Ibid.*, pp. 174–176.

House had mentioned this latter possibility to Grey and Balfour on first arriving in London in January. He had added, however, that the President believed that "in order to justify our existence as a great nation, it would be necessary to bring to bear all our power in behalf of peace and the maintenance of it." Attempting to shake the confidence of Grey and Balfour in ultimate victory, House had also suggested that, after Germany had come to terms with her continental enemies one by one, England would be alone and that her sea power "would not last three months . . . because all nations would protest against the restrictions on trade." Then followed this interesting observation: "They did not think to turn this argument against us, which they might have done, by saying that if such things happened, the democracies of the world would of necessity be compelled to become autocracies for self-preservation. So I let it go as our thought of their danger and of our willingness to contribute to the welfare of civilization, as we understand it." House to Wilson, January 11, 1916. *Ibid.*, pp. 119–121, and Wilson MSS.

17. Lloyd George himself sought this meeting as a sequel to an earlier one in January. On that occasion House had been impressed with Lloyd George's "insistence that the war could only be brought to an end by the President, and that terms could be dictated by him which the belligerents would never agree upon if left to themselves." The Englishman was hopeful that the Allied campaigns of the following summer would tip the balance against Germany and believed that American intervention should be timed for about September 1. Diary entry, January 14, 1916. *Intimate Papers*, II, 128–129.

18. Diary entry, February 14, 1916. *Ibid.*, pp. 179–182.

19. Diary entry, February 15, 1916. *Ibid.*, p. 183. In his *Twenty-Five Years*, II, 124, Grey's attitude is further revealed. The House-Grey memorandum was, he states, "one of the only two papers, private or official, that I deliberately took home with me when I left the Foreign Office." His resignation occurred in December 1916.

20. Diary entries, February 17, 22, 1916. *Intimate Papers*, II, 184. "I feel the responsibility I have taken in this matter," House wrote, "for it is upon my assurance that the agreement will be carried out that they are preparing for this quick and powerful offensive." As a measure of precaution, House asked Grey "to send Lord Reading to the United States in the event I cabled for him, in order that he might go with me to the President and take back direct word of any modification or

amplification of our agreement." Diary entry, February 23, 1916. *Ibid.*, p. 196.

21. *Ibid.*, pp. 201–202.
22. See diary entry, March 6, 1916. *Ibid.*, p. 200.
23. *Ibid.*, p. 202.
24. House to Grey, March 10, 1916. *Ibid.*, p. 220.

CHAPTER EIGHT. WILSON'S EFFORTS TOWARD PEACE

1. In a conversation with Bernstorff on March 12, House expressed the hope that there would be no more submarine outrages, for another such "would precipitate war, and I gave him my reasons for believing that it would be the worst thing not only for Germany but for the Allies as well; that if we became involved, there would be no one to lead them out." In response to Bernstorff's inquiry as to when the United States might intervene, House replied "not until after their Western offensive had been finished and perhaps not until the Allies had made a counter-offensive. He wished to know how long I thought this would take. My opinion was it might be several months. . . . If things can be held as now, I believe that our plan will work out before midsummer and perhaps much sooner." House to Wilson, March 12, 1916. *Intimate Papers*, II, 224–225.

2. House to Wilson, April 3, 1916. *Ibid.*, pp. 229–230.
3. Diary entry, April 6, 1916. *Ibid.*, p. 231.

The casual way in which this decision was reached is worth remarking upon since the manner was entirely typical. House was staying at the White House. "Before the President started his dictation, we held a conference where we met in the hall just outside my room; and it lasted so long that he gave up all thought of his mail and dismissed his stenographer so we might finish." The result was the cable to Grey.

4. Grey to House, March 24, 1916. *Ibid.*, pp. 273–274.
5. Grey to House, April 7, 1916. *Ibid.*, p. 276.
6. House to Grey, May 10, 1916. *Ibid.*, pp. 278–279.

The cable was supplemented by a letter sent by House the

following day. ". . . it would not be a good thing for England," if America got into the war. "It would probably lead to the complete crushing of Germany and Austria; Italy and France would then be more concerned as to the division of the spoils than they would for any far-reaching agreement . . . looking to the maintenance of peace." House believed that the German capitulation in the *Sussex* affair was indicative of a "wearing-down process" which had made Germany "sensible of the power we can wield. . . . it seems certain that at a peace conference she would yield again and again rather than appeal to the sword." British leaders, House said, "will take a great responsibility upon themselves if they hesitate or delay; and in the event of failure because they refuse to act quickly, history will bring a grave indictment against them." House to Grey, May 11, 1916. *Ibid.*, pp. 279–280.

7. Grey to House, May 12, 1916. *Ibid.*, pp. 282–283.

Apparently only in the face of impending defeat and the consequent disintegration of the alliance was Grey prepared to invoke House's plan. Such is the conclusion to be drawn from a memorandum of about the first of December 1916, which Grey prepared in the belief that he would be away from England for a month or longer while leading a mission to Russia and that the parlous state of Allied affairs might make it necessary in his absence that the full Cabinet be informed of the House-Grey agreement. In the actual event, however, the Asquith Government resigned, whereupon Grey put the House-Grey agreement and the covering memorandum in possession of his successor, Arthur Balfour.

"Nothing but the defeat of Germany," Grey asserted, "can make a satisfactory end to this war and secure future peace." In stating her determination to continue the war, Britain must, however, make clear that her object "is not to force, but to support" her Allies. "Increasing mischief," Grey warned, was resulting from German propaganda, which "insinuates that France, Russia, and Belgium could have satisfactory terms of peace now, and that they are continuing the war in the interest of Great Britain to effect the ruin of Germany, which is not necessary for the safety of the Allies, but which alone will satisfy Great Britain." The Allies could not be expected to continue the war "against their will, or beyond their strength." Accordingly, if it should become evident that peace was "inevitable before Germany is defeated, then I would submit that the intervention of President Wilson—(if it is still available in the spirit described)—should be seriously considered." Grey, *Twenty-Five Years*, pp. 130–133.

8. Diary entry, May 13, 1916. *Intimate Papers*, II, 283–284.

9. Wilson to House, May 16, 1916. *Life and Letters*, VI, 212–213.

10. House to Grey, May 19, 23, 27, 1916. *Intimate Papers*, II, 286–287, 287–288.

11. Diary entry, May 9, 1916. *Ibid.*, 294; and *Life and Letters*, VI, 216.

12. Wilson to House, May 18, 1916. *Life and Letters*, VI, 216.

13. Wilson to House, May 22; diary entry, May 24, 1916. *Ibid.*, 219n; *Intimate Papers*, II, 294.

14. Address before the League to Enforce Peace, Washington, May 27, 1916. *Public Papers of Woodrow Wilson*, II, pp. 184, 185–188.

15. Compare for example, point two of Wilson's May 27 statement with the proposition formulated in Grey's letter of September 22, 1915. For the latter, see above, p. 207.

16. See Ruhl J. Bartlett, *The League to Enforce Peace* (Chapel Hill, University of North Carolina Press, 1944). This is the definitive account of the origins and activities of The League to Enforce Peace.

17. House to Grey, May 11, 1916. *Intimate Papers*, II, 280. The only important dissent at the time came from the Secretary of State. House in a letter of May 21 admonished Wilson to seek Lansing's advice: "He might be useful and he would surely be offended if he did not know of this important step." *Ibid.*, p. 297. It is doubtful, however, whether Lansing saw a draft of the speech. Nonetheless, writing from a sick bed May 25, he addressed himself to the program of The League to

Enforce Peace, taking issue with the idea of coercion by physical force on a universal basis. He did not believe it was wise "to limit our independence of action, a sovereign right, to the will of other powers beyond this hemisphere." He was prepared, however, to organize the international application of force on a regional basis—which, he pointed out, would not endanger the Monroe Doctrine. If a universal organization were to be formed, he would limit its sanctioning authority to economic measures. *Lansing Papers,* I, 16–18.

18. Page to House, May, 30, 1916; Grey to House, n.d. *Intimate Papers,* II, 301–302, 302–303.

19. Diary entry, June 29; Wilson to House, June 22, 1916. *Ibid.,* pp. 265–266; *Life and Letters,* VI, 226–227.

20. Address at Shadow Lawn, New Jersey, September 2; and address at Cincinnati, October 26, 1916. Public Papers, II, 282, 287; 381–382.

21. Address at Omaha, October 5, 1916. *Ibid.,* pp. 346–348.

22. Speech accepting renomination, September 2, 1916. *Ibid.,* p. 291.

23. *Foreign Relations, 1916, Supplement,* pp. 98–99.

24. Speech at Shadow Lawn, November 4, 1916. *Public Papers,* II, 391.

25. *Munitions Investigations,* Part 28, p. 8735; *Life and Letters,* VI, 378.

Bernstorff informed Berlin in a cable of December 1, 1916 that "the warning of the Federal Reserve Bank with regard to the unsecured obligations of foreign Powers is the first indication that this Government proposes to exert pressure on our enemies in the cause of peace." *Official German Documents,* II, 997.

26. Lansing to Wilson, December 10, 1916. *War Memoirs,* p. 180.

27. Diary entry, November 14, 1916. *Intimate Papers,* pp. 390–392. See also pp. 388–389.

28. *Ibid.,* p. 184; *Life and Letters,* VI, 361–362; *Official German Documents,* II, 987.

29. See above, page 292, n. 21.

Bethmann's position in a conference with the military at Pless, August 31, 1916, seemed to indicate his attitude toward Belgium. A telegram to Bernstorff followed on September 2: "Would peace mediation by Wilson be possible and successful if we were to guarantee Belgium's unconditional restoration? Otherwise the unrestricted U-boat war will have to be carried out in dead earnest." *Official German Documents*, II, 983, quoted in Hans W. Gatzke, *Germany's Drive to the West* (Baltimore, Johns Hopkins Press, 1950), pp. 139–140. See also Bethmann's statement to the papal nuncio on June 26, 1917 that Belgium should be given back her complete independence, a statement which Gatzke accepted at full value. *Germany's Drive to the West*, p. 183.

30. For the relevant documents see *Official German Documents*, II, 1059–1064.

Speaking to Prince von Bülow in the autumn of 1916, the Kaiser said: "Albert shall keep his Belgium, since he too is King by Divine Right. . . . Though, of course, I imagine our future relationship as rather that of the Egyptian Khedive to the King of England." Prince von Bülow, *Memoirs* (3 vols., London, 1932), III, 281–282, quoted in H. W. Gatzke, *Germany's Drive to the West*, p. 144.

31. *Foreign Relations, 1916, Supplement*, p. 94.

32. *Ibid.*, p. 118. See also Zimmermann to Lersner, Secretary of Legation at German Headquarters, December 24; Zimmermann to Count Wedel, German Ambassador at Vienna, December 25, 1916. *Official German Documents*, II, 1087–1088.

33. Wilson's suggestion was strongly seconded by Bernstorff in a cable to Bethmann-Hollweg, December 29, 1916. *Official German Documents*, II, 1010–1011. See also Bernstorff to House, January 31, 1917. *Intimate Papers*, II, 431–433.

34. *Germany's Drive to the West*, p. 289. Gatzke continued: "Considering these various possibilities, a clear German statement on Belgium would have been decidely worth trying. Not to have made it remains a grave blunder of German foreign policy during the World War."

35. *Foreign Relations, 1917, Supplement 1*, pp. 6–8.

36. *Public Papers,* II, 407–414.

37. Address at San Diego. *Ibid.,* p. 294.

38. John W. Heaton, comp., *Cobb of "The World"* (New York, E. P. Dutton and Co., 1924), pp. 268–270.

39. George F. Kennan, *American Diplomacy, 1900–1950* (Chicago, University of Chicago Press, 1951), Chapter IV, "World War I"; and Hans J. Morgenthau, *In Defense of the National Interest* (New York, Alfred A. Knopf, 1951), pp. 28–33.

Index

Adams, Henry, 1
Algeciras Conference, 151, 152, 182, 194
Anderson, Chandler P.: views on *Falaba* case, 24–25; interviews Elihu Root, 122
Angell, Norman, 173–180
Anglo-American relations, 3–11. *See also* Great Britain
Anglo-Chinese War, 9
Arabia, 56
Arabic, 33
Armed merchantmen: question of, considered in *Falaba* case, 27–28; and *Lusitania* case, 30, 37–38; position of British Admiralty, 30; German declaration of Feb. 8, 1916, 36; earliest American position, 37–38; and Hague Conference, 39; British countermeasures, 39–40; Lansing's views, 40–43; attitude of Congress, 44; McLemore and Gore resolutions, 44–45, 47; Bethmann-Hollweg's views, 68–69; Wilson doubts soundness of his position on, 75–79
Asquith, Herbert, 223, 225

Balance of power viewpoint, 4, 5, 16–17; Wilson appreciates,

144; influence on Theodore Roosevelt, 151–154; Belgium's relation to, 161; historic role in American foreign relations, 181, 186; House's views, 188, 190; Wilson's views, 260–261, 264–265, 274–275; Western Hemisphere in relation to, 271–273; views of Grey and Canning, 273
Balfour, Arthur, 223
Belgium: retention by Germany demanded, 65; central issue of war in the West, 16, 177, 191, 192, 197, 198; Theodore Roosevelt on, 155–160, 164–165; Bethmann-Hollweg on, 255–256; German Government policy debated, 255–256
Bethmann-Hollweg, Theobald von: opposes unrestricted submarine warfare, 66–69; capitulates to military, 72, 74, 83; and German war aims, 79; views on Belgium, 255–256
Blockade, British, 86
Bryan, William Jennings: views on *Falaba* case, 26–27; position in *Lusitania* case, 32–33; bans loans to belligerents, 91–92; summary of views on *Falaba* and *Lusitania* cases,

321